A CHRISTIAN HANDBOOK TO THE PSALMS

R. E. O. WHITE

THE PATERNOSTER PRESS
WILLIAM B. EERDMANS PUBLISHING COMPANY

The majority of the biblical quotations in this book are from the Revised
Standard Version of the Bible, copyrighted 1946, 1952, © 1971, 1973.

Scripture quotations designated NEB are from the New English Bible.
Copyright © The Delegates of the Oxford University Press and the Syndics
of the Cambridge University Press 1961, 1970. Reprinted by permission.

CONTENTS

TO GWYNETH

*in conversation with whom, at breakfast-
time prayers, many of these insights
took shape*

INTRODUCTION*

Hymns possess for Christian hearts a fascination all their own. In a single service of worship we often borrow the thought and poetry of several wholly unknown individuals, all from widely separated centuries and varied circumstances, from different denominations of the church, but each expressing something of Christian faith and experience which we thus make our own.

Older hymnbooks offer little help in visualizing the author and his or her situation; even names and dates are omitted. We are left to wonder and imagine—if we think at all about the source of the words we use: to notice old-fashioned words or spellings, quaint expressions, phrases that suggest a Puritan or Catholic or "early Church" background, or perhaps a line that betrays a woman writer.

Occasionally we may discover a hymnbook that bears marginal notes by some previous owner who, loving hymns, jotted down scraps of information, sermon illustrations, or traditional lore concerning particular hymns: "written after trying to commit suicide from Westminster Bridge"; "written after a fierce thunderstorm in a forest had awakened terror"; "a wonderfully martial hymn from a woman bedridden for many years"; "written in a very short time during the intense pain of a broken engagement due to the onset of blindness." Sometimes such marginal notes record tunes found to be suitable or popular for particular hymns. Some of these historical notes may be true, some partly true, and some pure invention, but all seek to add interest and power to the hymns we use to worship God.

The Book of Psalms is exactly such a wide collection of anonymous poems, many fitted out with traditional marginal notes at their head concerning authors and circumstances. And exactly the same close attention and caution will yield similar fascination for the modern reader, and similar spiritual enrichment.

Perhaps few, even among those of us who love hymns, pay much attention to the poetic structure and form of Christian praise,

---

*This introduction includes notes applicable to many of the psalms, here collected together to avoid repetition in the text.

1

unless we are pulled up short by a line having a syllable too many that trips the tune, or we stumble over a rhyme:

> And how the Master,
>   Ready and *kind*,
> Chided the billows,
>   And hushed the *wind*.

> Teach me some melodious *sonnet*
>   Sung by flaming tongues above;
> Praise the mount — I'm fixed *upon it* —
>   Mount of Thy redeeming love.

Sometimes we admire the ingenuity that produces alternate "feminine" line-endings: "holiness" - "lowliness," "fearfulness" - "tearfulness," "carefulness" - "prayerfulness," "slenderness" - "tenderness"; we wonder just how long the poet could keep that up! Or we enjoy the lovely internal rhyming of the third lines in Palgrave's hymn:

> Thou say'st, "Take up thy cross,
>   O man, and follow Me":
> The night is *black*, the feet are *slack*,
>   Yet would we follow Thee.

> Dim tracts of time divide
>   Those golden days from me;
> Thy voice comes *strange* o'er years of *change*,
>   How can I follow thee?

Hymn-singing becomes immensely more meaningful if we learn to question and to notice everything we sing, such as the deliberate alternating of majesty and meekness, victory and suffering in the separate "verses" of the full version of "Ride on, Ride on, in Majesty." We should speak, though, of separate *stanzas* of a poem to avoid confusion with scriptural verses.

In newer hymnbooks, when authors and dates are provided, we may be puzzled by the addition of "altered" (or "alt."). This is the confession of the selection committee that it has thought fit to change what the poet wrote to accord with modern taste or with congregational circumstances.

Precisely the same questions (including suggested tunes to be used) arise in connection with "the hymnbook of the second temple," our biblical Psalter. Attention to them makes each psalm come alive and speak more clearly to our own hearts.

I. WHY A CHRISTIAN HANDBOOK TO THE PSALMS?

I (i) A Christian handbook is valuable first of all because the hymnbook of Israel has become part of the Christian heritage. The earliest Jewish Christians, worshiping in temple and synagogue, used the Jewish psalms to express their own praise and prayer. In private devotion, too, they doubtless followed the familiar pious pattern of "the psalm for the day."

By the second century, as Tertullian noted, the psalms had been taken over from the synagogue by Christians "in all parts of the world." Evidence abounds that in both Eastern and Western churches the psalms "punctuated" lessons and prayers in most worship services. Even the new, distinctively Christian services of baptism and the Lord's Supper borrowed expressions from the same source. "As a hart longs for flowing streams, so longs my soul for thee, O God..." (Ps. 42) prompted the decorative motif of many elaborate baptistries. "O taste and see that the Lord is good" and "I will take the cup of salvation and call upon the name of the Lord" (Pss. 34 and 116) found their way into the liturgy of the Eucharist.

Late in the fourth century, Chrysostom declared,

'If we keep vigil in the church, David comes first, last and midst. If, early in the morning, we seek for the melody of hymns, first, last and midst is David again. If we are occupied with the funeral solemnities of the departed, if virgins sit at home and spin, David is first, last and midst. In the monasteries, amongst those holy choirs of angelic armies, David is first, last and midst. In the convents of virgins, where are bands of them that imitate Mary; in the deserts, where are men crucified to this world and having their conversations with God, first, midst and last is David.'

Later patterns of Christian worship ensured that the whole Psalter was recited each week, while candidates for ordination had to know the book by heart. In a fourteenth-century "prymer" of private devotion popular in various forms, the Hebrew psalms occupied a significant place. Indeed, the most widely and persistently used of all Christian devotional books, *The Imitation of Christ* by Thomas à Kempis, quotes the psalms more often than the Gospels.

I (ii) Nor is this Christian borrowing from another religion at all surprising. The Hebrew psalms hold up a mirror to religious experience, to reflect with astonishing fullness and frankness its many moods. Exultation and doubt, pain, persecution and sorrow, passion and aspiration, fortitude, bitterness and despair, complaint, gratitude, and heartfelt praise—all find equally candid expression. The utter sincerity, the wide range, and the deep humanity of the psalms make them the voice of Everyman exploring the religious dimension of life.

The variety of circumstance and occasion covered by the psalms is truly amazing. Sickness and restoration, distress and the fear of death are frequently mentioned. So are joy in nature and the moral instructiveness of history. Guilt-laden confession prompts some psalms; so do homesickness, nostalgia, and social and religious protest.

The great religious festivals called forth poems of praise, prayers, and commemoration. National exile and war, local storms, widespread fear and depression, individual and national deliverance, adversity, injustice, and occasions of rejoicing — all moved poets to verse. A number of psalms are simply victory songs. Royal coronations and weddings, pilgrimages, harvests good or bad, family life, the miracle of birth and the gift of children, poverty, wealth, loneliness — every aspect of human life is referred to except humor (but note Ps. 78:65, 66, NEB), courtship, and (with slight reservations) sexual experience (but note Ps. 45:11, NEB). Even elementary education in good behavior, in ethical ideals, and in the nation's origin and story provides material for easily memorable poetry.

And all, literally *all*, is related to God — whether in national penitence, devotion, and thanksgiving, or in personal faith, repentance, avowal, prayer, and hope.

I (iii) No one who knows the Psalter will question the depth and reality of the religious experience it enshrines. Psalm 23 is among the world's finest monuments to confidence in God; Psalm 51 has never been equaled as an expression of penitence; Psalm 73 pours into eloquent language all the struggle of a sincere soul beset by doubt and disappointment. Psalm 103, Psalm 16, Psalm 139, Psalm 91 — the "gems" are numerous; and they are gems just because they focus and irradiate what religious souls have discovered, through countless generations, to be the truth about God and about man's relation to him.

It is of the utmost significance that Christianity has thus inherited and assimilated a book of devotion that testifies to a religious experience antedating the Christian revelation by centuries. Inevitably, Christians have read the psalms with Christian eyes since the coming of Jesus. Though the experience behind the psalms is genuine, and valid for others, it is obviously pre-Christian, neither complete, faultless, nor final. Christians must test even songs so rich and stimulating by the spirit of their Master.

Often they marvel that pre-Christian saints should have discerned truth so clearly, understood God so well. Sometimes they rejoice that what others glimpsed "as in a glass, darkly," Jesus has made so plain. Only occasionally are Christian readers aware that in its passionate and very human sincerity the Psalter gives expression to feelings about which Jesus might well say, "You have heard that it was said by them of old time... but I say unto you...."

Because of this twofold attitude of gratitude and caution toward the psalms, it is especially important to notice how frequently, and in what connections, the New Testament writers quote, allude to, and echo these Hebrew songs. I draw attention to no less than 201 clear "echoes" and a further 273 more distant allusions (indicated by "cf.") in the Christian Testament.

I (iv) If one were still to ask why produce a specifically Christian handbook to an essentially Jewish treasury of religious poetry, we may further reply that, like all hymnbooks, that of Judaism is deeply involved with the history, worship, language, beliefs, and ideals of its own time and milieu.

Many learned volumes explore and debate the background and precise meaning of each poem, its authorship, historical setting, ritual use, and much besides. All this investigation is valuable, and seriously argued theories deserve respect, lest by simple ignorance the original meaning of these great poems becomes distorted, their purpose obscured.

Yet in seeking the timeless religious "message" of the psalms, a somewhat different approach is justified, provided it does not deliberately contradict or despise the opinions, the "conclusions," and even the theories of devoted scholars. It is possible, with due respect, to accept from their work only what is religiously helpful, to leave the arguments to others and seek the spiritual enrichment of the psalms without siding with any of the various "schools" of interpretation or becoming lost among conflicting opinions.

Thus we shall not pursue the many, often fascinating discussions stimulated by the psalms; on the other hand, we shall try not to ignore the canons of sound, historical Bible-study. For the general basis of this handbook I have chosen a translation from Hebrew made by many representative scholars of different "schools," revised after widespread acceptance and use, one which aims to be loyal to a corrected text and to combine the best of the old translation with accuracy and modern speech-patterns — the Revised Standard Version. But I refer constantly to the freer translation offered by the New English Bible, also representative of different points of view, and often arbitrating between earlier versions.

But as the innumerable modern translations and the footnotes to the RSV and the NEB abundantly demonstrate, Hebrew words can carry many meanings, and Hebrew grammar and tenses can offer several variant constructions, especially in poetry. Hebrew is a childlike, flexible, imaginative language; a wholly literal translation would usually be clumsy, and sometimes unintelligible. In addition, the original Hebrew text is sometimes unclear, and ancient translations into Greek and Syriac often differ.

Where alternative translations of individual words and phrases or (rarely) some possible emendation of the text have to be considered, it is not simply because "scholars always disagree," but because the original meaning does remain uncertain, and honest students must humbly acknowledge the fact. No heavy documentation is used, because to indicate the "sources" and "authorities" for every opinion expressed would make for extremely tedious reading, and defeat our devotional purpose.

By far the great majority of translations here cited, usually in quotation marks, are from the RSV or the NEB and their margins, and rarely from the Revised Version of 1881 and the Authorized King James Version (AV/KJV). Quotation marks also indicate either (i) literal translations of the Hebrew, for each of which weighty evidence could be given; or (ii) a free paraphrase of the original in modern speech, to exhibit the fuller meaning condensed in poetic lines.

In no instance is some alternative translation suggested or considered merely because it sounds attractive, or yields "a nice meaning." Faithfulness to the text, where known, and observance of the strict rules of sound translation constitute the first requirement of devotion to the word of God.

Though we shall remember that the Psalter was Judaist in origin, thought, form, and language, yet we shall expect to find in it a very great deal that is timeless and universal, as heart speaks to heart across the centuries, and as by this means God continues to speak to all generations.

II. RECURRENT THEMES

Despite their great variety, the Hebrew psalms necessarily reflect a common background of history and faith. Certain dominant questions, attitudes, and assumptions therefore recur, and it is useful to gather main themes together in order to refer back to them in the discussion of individual psalms. The general preoccupation with praise, prayer, confession, thanksgiving, and religious perplexities is obvious; only a little less obvious is the concentration on the following.

II (i) *Complaint*. A great deal is heard of hardship, personal and social conflict, sickness, affliction, distress, poverty, and the fear of death. Much is said of ill treatment at men's hands, of oppression, slander, and injustice.

Suffering, struggle, and sin lend a somber color to the religious life as described in numerous psalms. It would be an exaggeration to say that such poems are morbidly obsessed with the harder facts of life, but it must be acknowledged that whole passages approach tedium with their reiterated lamentation and questioning:

I cry with my voice to the Lord...
I pour out my complaint before him,
    I tell my trouble before him....
In the day of my trouble I seek the Lord;
    in the night my hand is stretched out without wearying;
    my soul refuses to be comforted.
I think of God, and I moan....
I eat ashes like bread,
    and mingle tears with my drink,
because of thy indignation and anger;
    for thou hast taken me up and thrown me away.
Hear my voice, O God, in my complaint....

(Pss. 142:1, 2; 77:2, 3; 102:9, 10; 64:1)

7

In one important respect this is typical of the Jewish religious outlook, as the books of Job, Ecclesiastes, and Jeremiah sufficiently confirm. That outlook is intensely realistic, determined by a frank, unsentimental assessment of life as too often nasty, brutish, and short; and the Jew is ready to say so, even in pious contexts.

So psalmist after psalmist pours out his complaint to God, with no thought of irreverence. Complaint descends occasionally toward self-pity and despair (e.g., Ps. 53); now and again it rises to energetic protest (Ps. 44); sometimes it demands "Lord, why?..." and "Lord, how long?..."

This realism is the antithesis of wishful thinking. It rejects the pious pretense that for the godly all inevitably goes well. It is no small part of the universal appeal of the Psalter that its confidence and hope are maintained often in the teeth of circumstances. For the psalmists, religious faith is neither a denial of life's hardship and evil nor an escape from reality, but a way of handling life as it is. Easier, oversimplified answers are offered, too: Psalm 37 urges that the spiritual privileges of the godly outweigh all adversity (which is true, but explains nothing); Psalm 91 declares that tragedy never "comes nigh" the righteous, but then corrects itself. The prevailing impression is of an honest, open-eyed confrontation of life's facts. Through Jesus that Jewish realism entered deeply into Christianity.

II (ii) *Deliverance and Vindication.* The plea of these Hebrew poets is less often for sympathy or comfort than for deliverance and *vindication* (Pss. 26:1; 43:1; 54:1; and many other passages). The psalmists protest indignantly at the apparent triumph of falsehood and ungodliness, of injustice and oppression in God's world. Those wielding power in society without conscience or scruple, the faithless within Israel, the pagan influences and oppression introduced by foreign occupation, the slanderers of the righteous, those who plot to trip up the unwary innocent—all rouse fierce poetic anger to demand divine intervention.

The good are constantly beset by "enemies." Sometimes there simmers below the surface of the poetry the later conflict between those who were ready to compromise with the occupying powers, to "liberalize" Jewish ways and ensure their own security and advancement, and those on the other hand who clung tenaciously to everything orthodox, distinctively Jewish, and strictly "lawful." This bitter struggle between "liberal" and "conservative" factions arose soon after the return from exile (Ezra 9:1–4; 10:1–2; Neh. 13:4–5, 10–11; see Isa. 57:20; 58:9; Mal. 2:14–16); it was greatly intensified by Greek attempts to "Hellenize" Jewry (1 Macc. 1:11–15; 2:42, 43), and settled into the Sadducee-Pharisee conflict of the New Testa-

ment. "It is time for the Lord to act, for thy law has been broken..."
(Ps. 119:126) expresses the theme of numerous psalms (cf. Pss. 10;
35:24; 27:64; and further, the discussions of Pss. 140 and 149).

Righteous indignation is sometimes confused with outraged
patriotism (Pss. 44, 60, 83); sometimes with self-justifying self-
righteousness (Pss. 18:20–21; 26; 52); and sometimes with desire for
personal vengeance (Pss. 35, 83, 109, 137, etc.). All the personal
enemies of the godly tend to be seen as enemies of God! But deep
within this confusion lies the earnest heart's cry for the clear vindication of the morality of the world, the longing to see right triumph
over wrong.

We hear the brave affirmation that God does reign, that he will
surely overcome his foes (Pss. 96:10–13; 97; etc.), that he is amused
at men's resistance and will hold his enemies in derision (Pss. 2:4;
37:13; 59:8). We hear too the oft-repeated cry that the wicked shall
be caught in their own snares; the psalmists do not gloat over the
present insecurity and final doom of the ungodly except as evidence
of the triumph of right in a moral world (Pss. 7:15–16; 35:8; 57:6;
141:10).

But still more often we hear a very human impatience implying
that the mills of God grind too slowly. Again and again, with great
daring, the poets suggest that God slumbers:

> Rouse thyself! Why sleepest thou, O Lord?
> Awake!   (Ps. 44:23)

"Awake, Lord!" and "Arise, Lord!" occur very often: the insistent
plea is found in Psalms 3:7; 7:6; 9:12; 12:5; 35:23 ("Bestir thyself");
44:26; 59:4,5; 68:1; 76:9; 78:65 ("Then the Lord awoke as from
sleep, like a strong man shouting because of wine"); 83:1 ("O God,
do not keep silence; do not hold thy peace or be still, O God"); and
102:13. These passages and many more show how eagerly these poets
longed to see God "get moving" in the world.

Similar is the plea that God will "show himself" (Ps. 94:1–3;
cf. Pss. 109, 140), will no longer "stand afar off," "hiding" himself
(Ps. 10:1), but will "make haste" (Ps. 38:22; 40:13; 70:1,5; 71:12;
141:1). These protesters against the state of things even beg that God
will take his hands out of his pockets and *do* something about his
world (Ps. 74:11; cf. Ps. 9:12 in the NEB: "Set thy hand to the task").
"How long?" they demand impatiently (Pss. 6:3; 13:1,2; 35:17; etc.);
"How long, O Lord? Wilt thou hide thyself for ever?" (Ps. 89:46). In
another mood, but facing the same problem of apparent divine
inactivity—even indifference—these troubled souls urge, "Wait!"—
"I wait for the Lord!" (Pss. 130:5; 37:9; etc.).

It is just possible that in a few of these poems some vague idea survives that God himself still struggles with ancient chaos and the monstrous evil that originally opposed creation, an idea deriving (it may be) from Babylonian creation-myths (see Pss. 74:13–15; 89:9–14; 104:6–9). But these are few, and mysterious, hints only; the Hebrew psalmists scarcely question that (in words that in 1940 helped to shape history) "all will turn out right at the end of the day; and we trust that all will turn out yet more right at the end of all the days."

II (iii) *Worship*. One of the most illuminating lines of study has concerned the use of the psalms in the later liturgy of the temple and in the synagogue worship. The heading of Psalm 92, "A Song for the Sabbath," reminds us that Jewish tradition also associated Psalm 24 with the first day of the Jewish week, Psalm 48 with the second, Psalm 82 with the third, Psalm 94 with the fourth, Psalm 81 with the fifth, and Psalm 93 with the sixth. Other traditional "titles" now attached to the psalms, like "To the choirmaster" (Ps. 4, etc.; see below), "A Song at the Dedication of the Temple" (Ps. 30), and "A Psalm for the thank offering" (Ps. 100), are plainly liturgical instructions concerning use on ritual occasions. So is "A Psalm...for the memorial offering" (Pss. 38, 70), recalling the "meal offering" of Leviticus 2:2,9, and suggesting song during the burning of incense.

It can scarcely be doubted, in view of their structure, that Psalm 24:7–10; Psalm 100; and Psalm 118:19–27 have to do with solemn ceremonial processions which figured in Jewish worship:

> Thy solemn processions are seen, O God,
>   the processions of my God, my King, into the sanctuary —
> the singers in front, the minstrels last,
>   between them maidens playing timbrels.   (Ps. 68:24–25)

This suggests that other psalms also may well have been "processional'—for example, Psalm 47:5, 8 and Psalm 98:6. Moreover, Psalm 24:7–10 is plainly *antiphonal*, as is Psalm 136, whether priests and people, priests and choir, or sections of the choir provided the alternate voices in song or choral speech (see Ezra 3:11).

Another traditional psalm-title, "for instruction" (Ps. 60), has been thought to mean (from its root word) "to be taught by heart," and so recited (cf. Deut. 31:19; 2 Sam. 1:17,18) — in spite of the reference to "the choirmaster." Certainly religious education had a prominent place in Jewish worship, both law and history being diligently taught from generation to generation. This may illumine the very didactic poems, like Psalms 105, 106, and other "historical rehearsals"; the continuous repetition of the creed (covering both history and beliefs) in Christian worship is a close parallel.

Psalm 117 looks very much like a brief liturgical "blessing" resembling the Christian "doxology," while Psalm 134 has very much the nature of "Vespers" as the congregation disperses for the night, leaving the night watch to guard the shrine. Psalm 132 mentions the holy Ark of God within the sanctuary; Psalms 149 and 150 refer to sacred dancing; Psalm 141 refers to incense and Psalm 116 to a "cup of salvation."

More debatable are the "Songs of Ascents" (Pss. 120–134). This traditional title probably describes songs sung during the pilgrimage to Jerusalem for the great festivals. This seems more likely than the explanation that the title means "for singing on [certain] temple steps," or is a reference to a supposed "step-like" literary structure or to "going up" from Babylon to Jerusalem. At any rate it is very hard to resist the impression that Psalm 121 refers to the beginning of the pilgrimage to Jerusalem, and Psalm 122 to its end. (See the opening paragraph of the discussion of Ps. 120.)

The "Great Hallel" (meaning "praise") is Psalm 136; later, Psalms 146–150 were called "Hallel," but *the* "Hallel Group" (called the "Egyptian" Hallel from Ps. 114:1) was Psalms 113–118. These psalms were later sung on eighteen special days during the Jewish year. At one time the group was recited as a single composition, the congregation responding with "Hallelujah" after each half-verse. Psalm 135 had a prominent place in the Passover, Psalm 29 in the Jewish Pentecost, and Psalm 76 in the Feast of Tabernacles.

Psalm 51 is for the most part an intensely personal expression of penitence, rooted surely in an individual's experience of sin and remorse. Yet in verses 18 and 19 a national catastrophe, the destruction of Jerusalem, is referred to, while the restoration of sacrificial worship, in strange contradiction of the whole spirit of the psalm (contrast v. 19 with vv. 16, 17), is named as the desired evidence of divine forgiveness. Evidently an originally individual confession has passed into wider use as a congregational act, fitting for some such occasion as the Day of Atonement or during national disaster.

It is frequently difficult to decide what prompted the poet's words, whether the need, conflict, and distress expressed are individual or national or both (see Ps. 130, for example). The answer is "both," not in the implausible sense that "the poet personalizes the nation and speaks in the first person on its behalf," but in the sense that words originally personal have been borrowed for general use. William Cowper, Frances Ridley Havergal, and George Matheson wrote out of immediate private tragedy verses that have become vehicles of faith and surrender for thousands. A large and varied congregation finds no incongruity in singing with deep sincerity, "O love that wilt not let *me* go...."

Thus in eight discernible respects these poems are related to Jewish ritual worship and festal occasions. We must therefore seek the meaning of each poem not only for the writer but for those who later used it in worship. Each poem thus has two dates, that of composition and that of adaptation and use, and so two backgrounds influencing its content. In a few instances this liturgical setting is almost certainly the clue to the psalm's present ambiguities, the poem providing the script for dramatic and dialogue-structured rituals (e.g., Pss. 68, 81). The Psalter is here more "service-book" than hymnbook.

II (iv) *Enthronement*. "Enthronement" ("royal") psalms provide one much-debated example of the use of psalms in public worship: these make much of royalty in general and of the kingship of God in particular (Pss. 2, 18, 93, 97, etc.). In theory Israel's kings were divinely appointed (1 Sam. 12:13; 2 Sam. 12:7–8); their coronation or marriage was a religious occasion (Pss. 2, 72, 45; see 1 Kgs. 1:34); and special functions in worship belonged to them, as David established the Ark, and Solomon dedicated the temple. Monarchy was thus representative: God was the true, abiding, and only king, at first of Israel and later of the world. Several psalms refer to the earthly king as enjoying this favored relation to God ("son," Pss. 2:7; 89:20–27; cf. 2 Sam. 7:14).

It has been suggested that this "theocratic" idea found expression, probably quite early, in annual ceremonies associated with the autumnal New Year festivities and the Feast of Tabernacles, ceremonies in which the re-enthronement of God over Israel was dramatically symbolized. And it has been conjectured that certain psalms had a prominent place in such rituals.

There is nothing improbable about such rituals of re-enactment — rituals as means of teaching or making present again to the minds of worshipers ("re-present-ing") great religious ideas. The Feast of the Passover in Judaism and the Lord's Supper in Christianity both re-enact the past and point to the future while proclaiming in the present a great truth concerning God. A re-enthronement-of-God ritual at the opening of each Jewish year as part of the general religious festivities does not really need the Egyptian and Assyrian "parallels" to explain it.

That God *is* the enthroned king of Israel and the world is mentioned in the psalms eighteen times; the crucial proclamation, "the Lord is King" (literal Hebrew, or "is become king"), occurs in Psalms 47:7, 8; 93:1; 96:10; 97:1; and 99:1 (the RSV has "the Lord reigns"; the NEB varies with "God is king"). This proclamation-form, together with shouting, the blowing of the ram's horn, processions, and the association with the creation story of God's victory over the forces of chaos (Pss. 47:7,8; 98:8; 65:9; 104:12–13; 74:12–13; 68:24–25), suggests that these psalms may well have figured in such "God-enthronement" ceremonies.

This, if true, is very significant. It reflects the influence of the prophets on the psalmists. It firmly underlines the idea that for God so to reign on earth ensured righteousness and holiness among men —which is good news to the godly, a warning to evildoers. It points forward unmistakably to the final divine judgment, when the eternal king will vindicate and avenge his people. And it becomes the foundation on which is later erected a "messianic" interpretation of several of the poems.

As it was natural for the accession of a new king to kindle hopes for a more just order of society (Ps. 72), so it was inevitable that disappointment in earthly "princes" should cause men to look to the divine king, and to his coming representative, as the source of social righteousness and a new order. This again illustrates change of function: poems originally written while Israel had kings and nourished high expectations of good to be accomplished through their reigns came to be transferred and adapted to forward-looking worship in the years when Israel no longer had its own king but looked for the Messiah.

In this way the "royal" or "enthronement" psalms came to possess special value for Christian thought and apologetics, while the central hope of these psalms—for a world fulfilling the divine will—became the text upon which Jesus proclaimed his gospel of the kingdom of God.

II (v) *God and Nature.* The Psalter is the Bible's window upon the world of living Nature. It is true that other biblical writers are aware of Nature's wonders; Amos the countryside prophet observes natural events acutely, and like other prophets uses the scenes and ways of Nature to illustrate and embellish his message. But even his writings, like most of scripture, are much more concerned with history, society, people and their relationships, and moral and theological truth than with the woods and fields, the sky, the hills and sea, the weather, and the endless variety of *life* that forms the theater in which man struts and performs. The Psalter, however, often looks at the surrounding world in its own right and draws attention to it for its own value.

The poets' observation of natural events is remarkably accurate, comprehensive, and wide-ranging. The teeming world of living things—plants and creatures of land, sea, and air—and their names, ways, qualities, and differences are mirrored here as they are in few other places in ancient literature. The changing moods of Nature, the moving seasons — seedtime, rains, "thirst," harvest, "renewal of the earth" — the miracle of day and night, and the coursing sun and stars are all faithfully described. Storm, flood, hurricane, the sullen or ferocious sea, with its dolphins and "monsters," the frightening earthquake, the crackling thunder and startling lightning, the murderous hail and hot, wearying, shriveling simoom from the Eastern desert — all find a place in the psalmists' landscape. Palestine comes alive as a land of beauty and peace, of power and turbulence, of variety, and above all of movement and life.

Here Nature is ever God's handiwork: his voice is in the thunder, his energy is behind the wind, his thought is in the beauty, his power is within the storm, his wrath sends the tempest, his generous gifts — or grievous judgments — are seen at harvest time. Sometimes spiritual truth is illustrated by the soaring mountains, the mysterious sea; sometimes man's place in Nature, and the wonder of man's own natural processes of birth and breathing, of living and dying are the subject. Even so, Nature is not "humanized" or "spiritualized," nor is she made to speak rememberable things.

There is no Nature mysticism in the psalms, as though man could himself ascend through Nature to Nature's God or find in Nature "the garment of the eternal Soul." He may see and hear in Nature the activity, the Word, of the God he has met in tradition, history, worship, the Covenant, and the Law, but he does not discover God by theorizing about natural processes. Nor does he overhear in Nature "the still, sad music of humanity" or feel "a spirit that impels all things," otherwise unknown and undefined.

In Nature, God is active, revealed, at work, but always and essentially different from Nature, prior to it, above it, always a *person*, always transcendent, glorious. In the ancient world Israel alone kept healthily clear of Nature worship.

And in consequence, except for Baalist lapses into fertility rites, Israel kept clear — certainly in the psalms — of sexual imagery and "transference." The nation's poets, like its prophets, saw the dangers of "conforming to Nature" as though there were nothing above it. Naturism, as evidenced by Israel's neighbors and later by the Greeks and Romans, always descends to most unnatural perversions. The psalmists seem never tempted that way.

That is why the love of Nature expressed in the Psalter is so much nearer to that of Saint Francis than of Pan, and the Old Testament's imaginative use of Nature so much cleaner, saner, and happier than that of the Nature religions of antiquity. The Hebrew poets deserve this measureless compliment: that they helped to teach Jesus, and ourselves, that the world about us is our Father's world, given to us to be our home, our delight, and a constant reminder of himself.

II (vi) *Wisdom.* A few psalms betray the influence of a "fraternity" or "school of thought" in Judaism that tended to make less of tradition, law, ritual, and worship than of "good living and high thinking" as the essence of religion. One meets this outlook especially in the books of Job, Proverbs, Ecclesiastes, and the Wisdom of Sirach: since the God who made us rules on high, it is simple common sense to "Remember thy Creator," find out what he wants, and do it. Experience itself teaches that evil living brings evil consequences. Reverence for God, "the fear of the Lord," is therefore the beginning (and the end) of wise living. Thus the "wisdom school" would bring religion down from the peak to the plain, out from the shrine into the marketplace.

The beginnings of this tendency were popularly traced to Solomon's reign; later, a deeper religious insight modified its "humanitarian" and "utilitarian" tone. To speak of psalms having the style of the wisdom literature (e.g., Pss. 1, 32) may mean little more than "this is expressed in the way that, later, wisdom writers came to say things—it reminds us of Proverbs." But occasionally the teaching itself (e.g., Pss. 37, 111) seems nearer to the outlook of the wisdom school than to more traditional Judaism.

III. A GOLDEN TREASURY
OF
RELIGIOUS POETRY

III (i) As we shall see, the Psalter is essentially a miniature library comprising five slim volumes of Hebrew poetry. It is easy to forget this, even when reading modern versions that print poetry distinctively.

In translation we miss much of poetry's play of fancy, the lilt of well-sounding words, the light poetic touch, the numerous Hebrew puns, and, because of its technicalities, almost all that should be said about the clever use of different rhythms — lyrical, lamenting, didactic, martial, and the rest. Moreover, the tide of *poetic* inspiration does not flow with equal fullness through every psalm: a few are labored, pedestrian, almost prosy.

Yet the Psalter *is* poetry, brimming with memorable lines, beautiful expressions, skillful comparisons, bold similes, and poignant prayers. The sheer beauty of most of these poems is, like their message, a gift of God; it is not to be undervalued, even if we ourselves are "not given to spouting poetry."

Poetry is the language in which heart and mind speak together, and so it is especially suitable for religious expression. Even an elementary knowledge of how Hebrew poets wrote greatly stimulates appreciation of their meaning and their power, evident in these lines from Psalm 103:

> The Lord is merciful and gracious,
>   slow to anger and abounding in steadfast love.
> He will not always chide,
>   nor will he keep his anger for ever.
> He does not deal with us according to our sins,
>   nor requite us according to our iniquities.

For as the heavens are high above the earth,
  so great is his steadfast love toward those who fear him;
as far as the east is from the west,
  so far does he remove our transgressions from us.
As a father pities his children,
  so the Lord pities those who fear him.
For he knows our frame,
  he remembers that we are dust.   (vv. 8–14)

That is not only infinitely worth saying, it is exquisitely said.

Passages so printed should warn us to be exceptionally alert. Poetry changes the *subject* as abruptly as does the dictionary (e.g., Ps. 23), and often, without warning, changes the *speaker*, too. One can never appreciate a poem by rushing through it or by looking for logical argument and coherent discussion. Often the connection between one sentence and the next lies in feeling, in associated thoughts, in distant echoes and allusions, in imaginative links. Since God has given us his word, in part, in this poetic form, we should at least take a little care to understand it.

III (ii) Sometimes a poem's beauty is achieved by perfectly chosen words, sometimes by excellence of metaphor—God is a rock, a fortress, a strong shield, a high tower, a shepherd, an intimate friend, a kindler of candles, one highly amused, a mothering hen. The list of vivid pictures for describing God alone is almost endless.

The eastern sun is seen as a rich bridegroom coming from under the wedding canopy, attired in the glorious finery of marriage; the studious man is an evergreen tree; the evil beset the godly as poachers cast their nets in darkness; the broken, defeated man is like a smashed earthen pot. There are scattered through the psalms hundreds of such figures of speech, arresting, perceptive metaphors, each deliberately chosen, polished, and fitted into its place, and each rewarding reflection — not to be missed by dull minds reading carelessly. An extended gloss of "horn" illustrates the richness of this language:

The *"horn"*: the meaning of most metaphors is clear, but "the horn of salvation," of strength or pride, is naturally more familiar to herdsmen than to city-dwellers. Like a man's "right hand" or "outstretched arm," like a horse's "stamping hooves" or "tossing mane," so the ox's strong horns become a symbol of strength, virility, defiance, and victory. The horn may be worn (as on Norse helmets), blown in challenge, tossed in pride, increased by growth ("springing"), made strong for combat (1 Kgs. 22:11), and the leader, the king, the warrior so becomes "the horn" of his people. To raise or exalt the horn is thus to bestow dignity, power, or victory.

Sometimes a poem's beauty lies in powerful description: a storm at sea, the teeming life of hill and valley, woodland and field, the gale tearing through the forest, the unending interest of Jerusalem for the occasional visitor—all are as dramatically depicted as Job's famous war-horse (Job 39:19–25). Occasionally a poet daringly addresses the sea, the mountains, and the earth as living beings. At other times he allows emotion to dominate his language entirely, as in a dirge, a deluge of self-pity, a tearful complaint, a censorious outburst, a resentful protest. In such freedom of self-expression and sincerity of feeling, beauty and eloquence are born.

Modern translations have restored the most familiar mark of poetry: the printing of each complete thought as a separate line. Variations in line length are by no means haphazard; they follow strict poetic rules fully understood only by those competent in Hebrew.

A second familiar mark of poetry, the regular rhythm or beat of stressed syllables, is harder to convey from one language to another, though Psalm 100 comes very near to the original pulse of words. The reader of English must simply accept on trust the assurance of experts that often the beat of stresses, the assonance of vowels, the grinding of harsh consonants, the hissing of sibilants, and the snap of clipped syllables, all almost untranslatable, add enormously to the total effect of spoken Hebrew poetry. Warnings shudder, praise trips gaily, mourning sobs, confession trembles, prayer pleads, anger splutters—so flexible, resonant, and expressive is the Hebrew tongue.

III (iii) For all this, perhaps the most familiar mark of poetry —the use of rhyming sounds to end lines and half-lines—is not found in Hebrew poetry. Hebrew poets were in fact much cleverer than most jingling rhymesters: where moderns rhyme *sounds* by repeating syllables with slight variation ("Jack and *Jill* went up the *hill*"), Hebrew singers rhymed *thoughts*, repeating their ideas in slightly varied expressions, as Psalm 51 illustrates:

Have mercy on me, O God, according to thy steadfast love;
    according to thy abundant mercy blot out my transgressions.
Wash me thoroughly from my iniquity,
    and cleanse me from my sin.
For I know my transgressions,
    and my sin is ever before me....

Purge me with hyssop, and I shall be clean;
   wash me, and I shall be whiter than snow....
Hide thy face from my sins,
   and blot out all my iniquities.
Create in me a clean heart, O God,
   and put a new and right spirit within me.
Cast me not away from thy presence,
   and take not thy holy Spirit from me....   (vv. 1–11)

Similar in pattern is Psalm 132:

"I will not enter my house,
   or get into my bed;
I will not give sleep to my eyes
   or slumber to my eyelids,
until I find a place for the Lord,
   a dwelling place for the Mighty One of Jacob."   (vv. 3–5)

A trebled rhyming of thoughts goes like this:

Blessed is the man
who walks not in the counsel of the wicked,
nor stands in the way of sinners,
   nor sits in the seat of scoffers....
He is like a tree planted by streams of water,
that yields its fruit in its season,
   and its leaf does not wither.
In all that he does, he prospers.   (Ps. 1:1,3)

A six-line thought-rhyme runs as follows:

The law of the Lord is perfect, reviving the soul;
the testimony of the Lord is sure, making wise the simple;
the precepts of the Lord are right, rejoicing the heart;
the commandment of the Lord is pure, enlightening the eyes;
the fear of the Lord is clean, enduring for ever;
the ordinances of the Lord are true, and righteous altogether.
                             (Ps. 19:7–9)

Then it moves into a four-line rhyming cadence:

More to be desired are they than gold,
   even much fine gold;
sweeter also than honey
   and drippings of the honeycomb.   (v. 10)

    This fascinating device can be most cleverly varied; for example, the second thought may echo the first *in reverse*, as it does in some of the Proverbs:

A wise son makes a glad father,
> but a foolish son is a sorrow to his mother.   (10:1)

For a righteous man falls seven times, and rises again;
> but the wicked are overthrown by calamity.   (24:16)

He who conceals his transgressions will not prosper,
> but he who confesses and forsakes them will obtain mercy.
>
> (28:13)

Again, a "stair effect" is possible, the thought "rising" in its echo:

> For lo, thy enemies, O Lord,
>> for lo, thy enemies shall perish;
>> all evildoers shall be scattered.   (Ps. 92:9)

> Ascribe to the Lord, O heavenly beings,
>> ascribe to the Lord glory and strength.
> Ascribe to the Lord the glory of his name....   (Ps. 29:1–2)

The climax and surprise is "worship the Lord in holy array."

Probably the best example of this "stair parallelism" is not from the Psalter but from Jesus. First the thought ascends:

> "Ask, and it will be given you;
> seek, and you will find;
> knock, and it will be opened to you."   (Matt. 7:7)

Then the thought descends:

> "For every one who asks receives,
> and he who seeks finds,
> and to him who knocks it will be opened."   (Matt. 7:8)

An inverted rhyming of ideas occurs in Psalm 30:

(A) To thee, O Lord, I cried; and to the Lord I made supplication:
(B) "What profit is there in my death, if I go down to the Pit?
(B) Will the dust praise thee? Will it tell of thy faithfulness?
(A) Hear, O Lord, and be gracious to me! O Lord, be thou my
> helper!"   (vv. 8–10)

Different again is Psalm 27:

> (A1) The Lord is my light and my salvation;
> (B1)   whom shall I fear?
> (A2) The Lord is the stronghold of my life;
> (B2)   of whom shall I be afraid?   (v. 1)

Here (A2) echoes (A1), but with effective variation, and (B2) echoes (B1) very closely.

In Psalm 40:11–17, after nine regular couplets in which each second line "answers" its first with soothing repetition, the tenth couplet begins, "Thou art my help and my deliverer. . . ." We expect a similarly smooth closing line, such as "Thou art my God and king," but we read instead a startling, urgent summons: "Do not tarry, O my God!"

To watch for such subtleties of construction, decoration, and emphasis greatly enhances one's appreciation of Hebrew poetic skill. Clearly, such repetition-with-variety lends remarkable force to the poet's meaning. The device also assists sometimes in translation, the second thought helping to suggest what the first really meant. But this device of parallel thoughts was even more useful as an aid to memory in a nonliterate age. Most of the examples given, once clearly grasped, tend to echo in the mind of their own accord.

III (iv) We may usefully notice here certain other poetic features that occur frequently in the psalms:

(a) The psalmist often makes use of the refrain. Psalms 107 ("Let them thank the Lord..." in vv. 8, 15, 21, 31), 57 ("Be exalted, O God..." in vv. 5, 11), and 42 and 43 ("Why are you cast down, O my soul?..." in vv. 5, 11, 5) are obvious examples. Psalm 8 begins and ends with its refrain, "O Lord, our Lord, how majestic..." (vv. 1, 9).

(b) The psalmist also employs *acrostics*, ingenious poems in which successive lines begin with successive letters of the Hebrew alphabet, or several lines together begin with the same letter followed by similar groups using successive letters. C. S. Lewis likened such exercises in ingenuity to verbal "embroidery," built up stitch by stitch through long hours of quiet meditation and disciplined craftsmanship. The English sonnet, with its strict rules, demonstrates similar word-skills.

In such artificial constructions the reader will look not for eloquence, argument, analysis, or logical coherence, but instead for detailed, isolated observations suggested by the initial letter required by the alphabetic sequence. The observations or reflections, however, often pursue a common theme.

(c) It is part of a poet's "license" to make use of archaic, unfamiliar, even invented words and oddly shaped sentences where these serve his purpose. A glance through a hymnbook offers many modern examples that we would find strange in everyday conversation: "inly," "Bethlem," "Christly," "illuming," "viewless" (meaning invisible), "peculiar honours," "terrestrial," "supernal," "till moon*s* shall *wax*...." One popular verse ends, "...till Heaven's tomorrow / Dawn on us of homes long expected possessed." Hebrew poets exercised the same license with considerable freedom, and it causes problems.

Words and constructions that are used rarely or only once are very difficult to translate, because only frequent usage reveals what the precise meaning was. Add to this difficulty the centuries of hand-copying, with reed pens on fragile papyrus, by scribes who sometimes did not recognize these rare words and made guesses at them, and who added their own mistakes also (as the manuscripts show), and we begin to see the translator's immense task. That is why footnotes refer us to other versions—Greek ("Grk," Septuagint, or "LXX," all meaning the ancient Greek translation made by "Seventy"), Latin ("Lat" or "Vulgate," a translation made by Jerome), Syriac, and others. Or the translators may offer two or three very different meanings as possible translations of a puzzling passage, and let us choose. Sometimes the footnotes simply declare the Hebrew text "uncertain," "unintelligible"; occasionally they even offer emendations ("Cn" or "Correction").

It is irritating to be asked to surrender a familiar and well-loved verse at the behest of some unknown "scholar" or manuscript "witness." But our knowledge of ancient Hebrew is not perfect, the original text is occasionally obscure or "corrupted" by changes, and in handling God's word honesty is essential. We must not cling to what is familiar simply because "that is how we have always read it," pretending there are no difficulties. But neither must we forget that guesses are only guesses—ours or other people's: they prove nothing. All guesses and speculation as to what a poet "might" have said are better avoided, except where to mention them might suggest *possible* ways out of otherwise insoluble difficulties.

It would be a great loss to grow impatient with the poetic parts of scripture or to imagine they are "too difficult" for "ordinary readers." After all, the poets of religious experience primarily want to set faith singing. It would be a kind of sacrilege to study the psalms looking for doctrine, history, philosophy, ethics, and liturgy, and never once burst into song or lift the heart in thanksgiving, confession, praise, or prayer. Music is given to all generations, but the typical songs of a secular society are either of complaint or of make-believe. Only the heart in tune with God can truly "break forth into singing"—and must do so.

Bewailing the joylessness of modern life, G. K. Chesterton tells of passing "a little tin building of some religious sort, which was shaken with shouting, as a trumpet is torn with its own tongue. *They* were singing, anyhow; and I had for an instant a fancy I had often had before: that with us the super-human is the only place where you can find the human. Human nature is hunted, and has fled into sanctuary."

One feels like that within the Book of Psalms. And there, in sanctuary, the heart must sing.

IV. THOSE HEADINGS AND CLOSURES

IV (i) The headings or "titles" prefixed to many psalms should remind us that we are reading not dead "literature" but songs beloved by living people. Unfortunately, these headings are not original. The ancient Greek translation differs widely here from the Hebrew; the authenticity of these phrases is very doubtful; the words used are sometimes too rare to be translatable, and the phrases themselves are occasionally unintelligible. For such reasons the New English Bible omits them altogether.

Nothing therefore can safely be argued from these headings about the circumstances behind a particular poem. Some appear to relate to the poem's use, some to accompanying tunes, some to sources from which the poems have been collected, as follows:

"According to Alamoth": intended for (boy) sopranos, for viola, or unknown.

"According to Do Not Destroy": indicates some familiar tune, possibly the vintage-harvest (grape-treading) song quoted in Isaiah 65:8.

"According to Muthlabben," "Mahalath," and probably "Mahalath Leanoth" are untranslatable; the last *could* mean "for antiphonal singing."

"According to Shushan" or "Shushan Eduth" (form and translation uncertain): possibly "Lily" (anemone?), "Lily of the testimony" — thought to indicate well-known tunes.

"According to The Dove on Far-off Terebinths": probably indicates a familiar tune.

"According to The Hind of the Dawn": again, probably indicates a well-known tune.

"According to The Sheminith": intended for lower-octave instruments (cello or double bass). But some contend that ancient Eastern music did not use an eight-tone scale and that the meaning is unknown.

"For stringed instruments (neginoth)": almost certainly means to be accompanied by lyre, harp, etc.

"For wind instruments": possibly means sung to the accompaniment of flutes, pipes, trumpets, etc., or (differently translated) to the well-known tune "The Inheritances."

"To the choirmaster," "Chief Musician," or "Precentor" (occurs 55 times): belongs to, or is intended for, a collection of psalms used by some conductor of the temple choir.

"To the Gittith": intended to be sung to a well-known vintage song ("Gath" means "winepress"); less probably, to be sung to the tune or instrument associated with the town of Gath in Philistia.

"Psalm" means strictly a lyric to be sung to stringed instruments.

"Song" has a broader meaning; it translates an old word for any poem, sacred or secular. But note that some of our "psalms" carry both headings, "psalm" and "song."

"A Song of Lovely Things": possibly describes the theme; otherwise probably a tune title.

IV (ii) Other words in the traditional psalm-headings that appear to have musical intention include the following:

Higgaion (untranslated in the RSV; occurring with *Selah* in Ps. 9:16): probably means "with solemn sound" ("sounding chords of the harp," Ps. 92:3, NEB).

"Maskil," understood as meditation, instruction, scarcely fits the following psalm's contents; possibly indicates some "well instructed" (that is, "skillful," "complicated") structure or accompaniment.

"Miktam": has suggested meanings of "golden," "hidden," or "covering" (or "expiating") sin; others take this as a musical instruction.

Selah (occurs 71 times): probably directs instrumentalists to play louder during an interlude in the singing; just possibly it directs the congregation to respond to the choir.

Shiggaion: may direct attention to an irregular meter.

Obviously, these tentative explanations, each involved in much learned disagreement, make it necessary to use great caution in deducing anything at all about a psalm's meaning and purpose. Those familiar with the many strange words that adorn printed music—*diminuendo, largo, allegro ma non troppo,* and the like—and with the various technical terms for different types of poetry — sonnet, lyric, elegy, epic, and the like — will not be surprised that parallel terms in ancient Hebrew are now so obscure.

IV (iii) Even greater caution is necessary in understanding psalm headings which seem to name the authors. The Greek Old Testament ascribes "to David" twelve more psalms than the Hebrew version, including Psalm 137, though David was never in Babylon; and it ascribes others to Jeremiah, Haggai, and Zechariah. In addition, the same Hebrew preposition carries the three meanings "to," "for," and "of." Further, the same psalms are headed "to/for/of David" *and* "to/for/of the choirmaster" (e.g., Pss. 109, 139); "to/for/ of the choirmaster" *and* "to/for/of the Sons of Korah" (Pss. 75, 84); and Psalm 88 has "to/for/of the Sons of Korah/the choirmaster/ Heman the Ezrahite."

Eleven psalms are described as "to/for/of the Sons of Korah," twelve as "to/for/of Asaph"; Psalm 90 bears Moses' name; Psalms 72 and 127 bear Solomon's; Psalm 89 has Ethan's name; Psalm 39 has Jeduthun's (but cf. "According to Jeduthun" of Pss. 62 and 77, suggesting a tune name or a style of singing). As we saw, fifty-five are "to/for/of" an unnamed choirmaster. How are we to understand all this?

According to 1 Chronicles 15:16–24, certain Levites were appointed "as the singers who should play loudly on musical instruments"—namely, Heman, Asaph, and Ethan, who were charged to "sound bronze cymbals." With them were certain "brethren of the second order"; "Chenaniah, leader of the Levites in music, should direct the music, for he understood it." 1 Chronicles 16:37–42 adds the name of Jeduthun to the appointed singers.

1 Chronicles 25 mentions 288 trained singers, "all who were skilful," evidently taking duty in turn by lot, "small and great, teacher and pupil alike." The Chronicler evidently intends us to think of formally appointed "guilds" or choirs of trained singers, bearing these group names, leading the temple worship in his day (cf. also 2 Chr. 29:25–30; Ezra 3:10).

Unless "to/for/of the Sons of Korah" indicates poetry written by a whole family, it seems obvious that this group of psalms also (like those "to Asaph," "to the choirmaster," and perhaps "to Jeduthun") represents a *collection* of sacred songs, either used by or in the style associated with one of these guilds of temple singers, or with the reigning choirmaster at the time. Psalms bearing double ascription would be found in more than one collection.

Seventy-three psalms are headed "to/for/of David," though it is difficult to explain some late Aramaic expressions, references to the temple (e.g. Ps. 65:4), and similar allusions to later historical situations (e.g., Ps. 137) that occur in some of them. But, as we have seen, collectors of poetry frequently edit or adapt what they borrow to suit their own purpose and time (recall Ps. 51 and contrast vv. 16, 19).

It seems probable, therefore, that while a number of psalms were written by David (e.g., Ps. 3; cf. 2 Chr. 29:30; 2 Sam. 1:17–27; Amos 6:5), some of his poems may have been edited for later congregational use; yet others not necessarily written by David have come down to us as items in a collection bearing his name — one of them explicitly assigned to Solomon (Ps. 72; note v. 20). This is in no way unusual: the famous collection of Christian hymns known worldwide as "Sankey's 1200 Hymns and Sacred Solos" actually contains less than twelve hymns by Sankey himself.

IV (iv) The great uncertainty surrounding all these psalm headings applies also to the ten which recall incidents in the life of David, and to similar modern conjectures which try to relate individual psalms to events or periods in Hebrew history. No such guesses must be allowed to control interpretation; only a poem's content can decide its meaning.

It may be helpful sometimes to suggest that a well-known incident *illustrates* the situation with which a psalm deals. Hezekiah's story fittingly illustrates Psalm 46, for instance. Some of the psalm headings have the air of earnest attempts to "locate" hymns in "the Davidic Collection" at appropriate points in David's life, either plausibly (Ps. 18) or most improbably (Ps. 34). But always such attempts are late, conjectural, and traditional. It must be remembered, too, that no illustration or coincidence is ever an argument for origin or a proof of date.

The uncertainty about authorship and occasion matters less than it might appear. We do not greatly trouble ourselves about the date and background of our own hymns if their words suit our purpose. Praise, prayer, confession, and trust are related more closely to the inner life of the pious believer and to the worship of a congregation than to external events in the life of the hymn-writer. Where the setting-in-life of any psalm is reasonably clear, we shall be grateful, but neither traditional headings nor ingenious guesses may be permitted to mislead us.

IV (v) The arrangement of the Psalter in five "books" has been known in the church since the second century, and among Jews much earlier. Jewish tradition likens the five books of praise to the "five books of Moses' law."

Doxologies mark the close of each "slim volume" (the end of

Pss. 41, 72, 89, and 106, repeating that at 41), while Psalm 150 is itself a doxology closing both the fifth book and the whole anthology. Certain literary features, especially the preference in different "books" for "Yahweh" or "Elohim" as God's name, correspond very roughly with the present divisions. So do the duplications that occur and which are otherwise inexplicable: Psalm 14 in Book I is equivalent to Psalm 53 in Book II; Psalm 40:13–17 equal to Psalm 70; Psalm 57:7–11 equal to Psalm 108:1–5; and Psalm 60:5–12 equal to Psalm 108:6–13. The closure of "the prayers of David" in Psalm 72:20 marked only the end of some "Davidic Collection," since further "prayers of David" are added in later collections (now, e.g., in Pss. 86, 142).

Just when our present Psalter took its final shape is, like so much else, learnedly debated. Conclusions vary from around 350 B.C. down to (the *very* latest) 100 B.C. The psalms, therefore, distill some 800 years of religious thought, experience, and worship, and deserve all reverence if for that reason alone.

BOOK I
PSALMS 1–41

1 THE EVERGREEN SOUL

This poem contrasts two lifestyles. The perpetual flourishing and fruitfulness of the godly is a matter of mental climate and continual refreshment. The soul's environment is self-chosen; the godly avoid the contagion of wickedness, the company of sinners, the atmosphere of mockery. The unfailing springs of the soul rise from habitual meditation upon God's revealed will for men and his ways with them. The godly, therefore, are "happy."

In contrast, the ungodly resemble chaff driven before external pressures. Theirs is a dry husk of life, without nourishment or value, weightless, dispensable. Choice of company is no longer theirs; they cannot stand up for themselves in the society of the good. Their manner of life ends inevitably in futility.

This antithesis is the whole point of the psalm; nothing is said of the duty of the godly to befriend and save the wicked. In some ancient copies this poem (inspired by Jer. 17:5–8?) forms an unnumbered "prologue" to the Psalter (or to Book I; see the Introduction IV [v]). This supports the view that "law" ("torah," v. 2) means God's will revealed in nature, history, conscience, experience, and worship, as it does throughout the Psalter, and does not refer to the later Jewish legal system.

A poetic homily is thus provided for the preface, one that defines the issues confronting human choice — God's will, or the pressures of the age; a fruitful life, or mere futility.

New Testament echoes: cf. Matthew 3:12; 2 Timothy 2:19.

2 GOD IS AMUSED

This is a "royal" psalm; see the Introduction, II (iv).

A new king faces at his coronation (v. 6) the revolt of neighboring peoples and "kings of the earth" hitherto under Jewish rule (vv. 1–3). No recorded coronation confronted precisely this situation: those of David, Solomon, and Rehoboam varied from it in details. Perhaps "poetic license" has overdrawn the circumstances.

The new king (through his court-poet?) voices a most courageous defiance. He is totally confident that God appointed him and will uphold him. One so sure of divine vindication can afford to be magnanimous: he pleads for wisdom on the part of his enemies — better to take refuge under God's unswerving purpose than to oppose it and risk his anger.

The poet's language and his expectations are somewhat militaristic (vv. 5, 9), but the style is terse, vivid, dramatic with sudden changes of speaker, reaching the utmost art of Hebrew poetry, according to T. K. Cheyne. The vision of God sitting far above the raging pride and ambition of men, amused at their antics, is one of the great pictures of the Old Testament (cf. Ps. 37:13), as the declaration that the divine purpose is invincible is one of its great truths.

The preservation of the poem shows that its truth and feeling served later needs, as kingship in Israel first disappointed the people and then disappeared, and the hopes once centered upon David's dynasty were transferred to an ideal king still to come "of David's line." Then the courage and confidence which the poem expresses came to focus the nation's reaction to harder, humiliating times, and to nourish the "messianic hope" of a yet more powerful, and even more peaceable, "king of kings."

From this it was a short step for Christians to apply the poem to Jesus (aided by the indefensible translation of v. 11 as "kiss the Son..."), and to appoint it a psalm for Easter Day—Christ's coronation—when God laughed again.

New Testament echoes: Luke 3:22 (some texts); Acts 4:25–27; 13:33; Hebrews 1:5; 5:5; Revelation 2:26,27; 12:5; 19:15.

3   UNDISTURBED REST

For headings, see the Introduction, IV (iii), IV (iv); for Selah, see IV (ii); for theme, vindication, see II (ii).

The traditional association of this poem with Absalom's rebellion against David (2 Sam. 15–18) has in its favor the echoes of surprising numbers, the mockery of his trust in God, and especial danger by night (2 Sam. 15:12,13; 16:8; 17:1). The assurance of God's favor and the effect of imminent dangers upon "God's people" (v. 8) imply *some* royal occasion behind the psalm.

Such a background (or any like it) makes the poem a superb affirmation of trust. Beset by foes and dangers, the author can yet lie down calmly, sleep soundly, awake with confident thoughts of God, and face the new day refreshed in body and spirit. He offers thanksgiving at sunrise for the shield of faith.

The threefold *Selah* and a change of meter at verse 7 show the brief poem has four stanzas: verses 1–2 describe the situation; verses 3–4 recall how often God has answered whenever "I cry aloud," the assurance born of experience; verses 5–6 state the resulting confidence that brings undisturbed rest; verses 7–8 call upon God, too, to awake to the new day, in the certainty that God has already determined the ultimate victory that will vindicate the psalmist's cause. Not only his own welfare but his people's welfare will so be secure.

Experience has taught the psalmist (a) that God *shields* those who call upon him, not promising there shall be no adversaries but foiling all missiles of slander, scorn, mockery, and aggression, and so enabling the soul to rest *within* all emergencies; and (b) that human estimates of the outcome of conflict are wholly unreliable: verse 8 answers the taunt of verse 2 directly (using the same Hebrew word). These two assurances recur through most of the "vindication" psalms.

New Testament echoes: cf. Revelation 7:10; 19:1.

4 GOOD COUNSEL FOR BAD TIMES

For headings, see the Introduction, IV (i), IV (iii); for Selah, see IV (ii). This is one of the most difficult psalms to understand. Amid numerous uncertainties of translation and text (see the Introduction, III [iv] [c]), comparatively clear clues to its meaning are these:

(i) "Vanity" (literal Hebrew) and "lies" (v. 2) are terms the prophets use frequently in their description of idols (Isa. 41:24, 29; 44:9, 10, 20; Jer. 10:14, 15; Amos 2:4; Hab. 2:18–19; Jonah 2:8; cf. Ps. 31:6). The temptation to worship the fertility gods of the settled land instead of Yahweh, God of the nomadic herdsmen, lay precisely in ensuring from them the grain and wine they could provide (v. 7; see Hos. 2:8). This suggests how God's "honor" was suffering "shame" (v. 2)—by rejection, in favor of idolatry.

(ii) In time of want, after a poor harvest, the people have become resentful that the Lord has not blessed them; many cry "O that we might see some good" (RSV) — "be prosperous again!" (NEB). But "the light of thy presence has fled from us, O Lord" (complaint, not prayer, as the NEB has it). Thus they turn again to the nature gods. The poet seems to acknowledge that the people have some grounds for being "perturbed" ("angry," Greek version), but he advises that they shall not let that lead them into sin (v. 4). Better that they should "lie abed resentful" (NEB) if they must, mulling over their bitter thoughts to themselves (v. 11), rather than indulge in spoken blasphemies (cf. Ps. 73:15).

(iii) Instead, let them maintain the proper public rites, offering the due sacrifices—a steadying discipline in hard days. Above all, let them continue to trust in the Lord (v. 5), who holds sacred the godly (or, "who has shown me his marvelous love"). He surely hears those who call upon him (v. 3).

(iv) This good counsel for bad times is set within, and supported by, a fine personal testimony. The poet himself has known "straitened" circumstances (the literal meaning of "distress"), but was "given room," led into abundance (v. 1). What is more, God's joy in the heart surpasses all grain and wine (v. 7). So, instead of taking resentment to his bed as the idolaters do, the poet lies down and sleeps in divine security.

This is a splendidly *satisfied* assurance, proof against the allurements of materialistic religion.

New Testament echoes: Ephesians 4:26; cf. 2 Timothy 2:19.

5 DISTRACTED DEVOTIONS

For headings, see the Introduction, IV (i), IV (iii); for theme, vindication, see II (ii).

The psalmist appears to be of two minds. On the one hand, he offers his morning prayer with sincere mind ("my inmost thoughts," NEB) and eager request ("my cry"), standing within the temple (v. 7), "setting out" before God the morning sacrifice (so the NEB has it, emphasizing a technical term — *possibly* "setting in order" his prayer). That it is a morning devotion is doubly emphasized. We might guess this from the poet's renewed desire for God's presence (v. 7), his "watching" for a sign from God (v. 3), and his prayer that God will lead him in the right way, that the way might be made clear to him, and "easy" ("straight") ahead of him through the day (v. 8; cf. Isa. 40:3, 4 for the prepared "way"). Thus the poet would begin the day with God (v. 3), in God's house (v. 7), and be led onward by God until nightfall.

On the other hand, his mind is troubled, especially concerning enemies, boastful and arrogant, deceitful, flattering people whose words have nothing behind them, like inscriptions on tombs (v. 9, NEB). His description of evil-minded men is full and many-sided, his prayer against them somewhat fierce. He notes particularly that such will not be seeking God's presence on this morning, as he is doing, for such are never "guests" within God's house (v. 4, NEB; cf. Ps. 15). The way in which the psalmist's thoughts revert to these enemies, interrupting his devotions, makes it easy to imagine that the day ahead may bring some encounter with them. He is glad to think God is against them; he asks for guidance lest he be misled or waylaid by them (vv. 8, 9), and prays that God will deal with them (v. 10).

Returning to his devotions, the poet links himself (very wisely) with all who seek the Lord, for his experience is not much different from that of many. He concentrates on the *delight* of those who love God's name and on the *defense* they find in God, their refuge and their shield.

It may seem surprising that a poem on disturbed devotions should be preserved, and shared, in the Hebrew hymnbook, until we remember how easily our own thoughts wander when we are "too worried to pray." Later congregations could so often sympathize with this psalmist when their foes were more numerous than their friends. And so may we.

New Testament echoes: Luke 11:44; Romans 3:13.

6 PROSTRATION RECOLLECTED IN TRANQUILLITY

For headings, see the Introduction, IV (I), IV (iii).

Whether or not the closing verses anticipate restoration or are a later addition recording it, it is obvious the poet has lived to remember his encounter with God in sickness. He describes vividly, as if still suffering, seven dreadful symptoms; he recalls the long nights of weeping, the weariness of pain, the surges of desire that all should end: "O Lord—how long?" Yet the thought of death redoubles grief, for in Sheol, the land of shadows and negation, there is no praise, no sense of God (v. 5).

Moreover, his deepest fear is that God is angry (cf. Jer. 10:24), and will not return (vv. 1, 4). To add bitterness to all else, his enemies take the opportunity his weakness presents to add to his suffering—

possibly, as with Job's friends, by accusing him of great sin. Prostrate and afraid, the poet reaches out only to the faithful "steadfast love" of God, using no other argument. And he recovers, his prayers are heard, and his foes will be frustrated.

Despite Christian use of the poem as a "penitential psalm," the whole tone is clearly pre-Christian. Those who hear and watch Jesus cannot share the common Jewish assumption that great suffering argues great sin. Those who learn of him cannot think of God as judging in anger but only as chastening in love. And to followers of the risen Christ, the future is not negation and shadows but life fulfilled in God. We admire this sufferer's tenacity, and thank God for a yet richer faith.

New Testament echoes: Matthew 7:23; Luke 13:27; John 12:27; cf. Hebrews 12:5–6.

7 INNOCENCE ACCUSED

For headings, see the Introduction, IV (i), IV (iii), IV (iv); "Cush" is not known; for Selah, *see IV (ii); for theme, vindication, see II (ii).*

The solemn oath of innocence (vv. 3–5) and the earnest appeal to God as judge of all peoples to take his throne of judgment as Most High God (vv. 7–8, 10, NEB) so vividly recall the requirements of the law concerning false accusation (Exod. 22:8–11) and the description of the temple as the divine court for settlement of such disputes (1 Kgs. 8:31) that the coincidences can scarcely be accidental. Did the poet himself experience such a trial, and did his poignant record of it and of his feelings pass later into use in the actual trial ceremonies?

There are few more bitter experiences than to be falsely accused. To agree to accept judgment if proved guilty and to appeal to divine upholding require nobility of mind and great integrity. The picture of God seated upon the throne of justice above all peoples is most impressive; so is the account of God weighing minds and hearts, throwing his shield around the innocent (vv. 9, 10), maintaining his righteous indignation evenly—not in spasmodic moods—and sharpening his sword, stringing his bow, and gathering his sudden and silent arrows against the wicked who will not repent (vv. 12–13).

Yet in the course of divine justice on earth, it is not in dramatic crises only that God's judgments are seen. The wicked find that the evil they conceive gives birth to monstrous things; the man who digs a hunting pit for others falls into it himself sooner or later; he who throws stones finds one descending on his own head (vv. 14–16). Evil ever has within it the seeds of its own punishment; such is God's justice.

That God so protects the innocent and punishes the evildoer merits all thankfulness and praise (v. 17). Upon it rests the moral order of the world.

New Testament echoes: James 1:15; Revelation 2:23.

8 GOD'S GREATNESS — AND MAN'S

For headings, see the Introduction, IV (i), IV (iii); for theme, God and Nature, see II (v).

This poem is a superb outburst of wondering worship, prompted by the scale and order of God's work in heaven above and earth beneath. From infants at the breast to the distant stars, all bespeaks God's majesty, and—if the suggested tune, The Gittith, be truly a song for the grape harvest—God's abundant goodness, too. So the exquisite poem opens and closes with God, in adoring refrain.

Yet within that frame is set with equal emphasis the greatness of man, a mere infant in the universe (v. 2) but contributing to God's praise. He is insignificant beside the vastness of the worlds, yet made in God's likeness, "but a little lower than divinity" (paraphrase of the Hebrew, Gen. 1:26, 27; "gods" here may mean angelic beings, as "godlike" — so the Greek version has it — or, with the plural of majesty, "Elohim"—God himself). Man again is the object of God's thought ("mindful") and care, being "visited" by God, not here in chastening (as Job quotes these words, Job 7:17–18) but with gladdening gifts. Moreover, man in Nature has been crowned with glory and set at his creation over all orders of fellow creatures, domestic and "of the field" (that is, wild).

The mention of babes is obscure. The RSV follows the Greek version in making them chant praise, rather than "ordain strength," "establish a bulwark" (Hebrew; the RV, 1881 ed.; and others), or "rebuke the mighty" (NEB conjecture). The underlying thought *could* extend the contrasts already made to include that between the helpless human infant and the mighty foe of the creator — chaos, the perpetual enemy of the divine order (see the Introduction, II [iv]), against whom the praise and testimony of babes have strength.

So the perennial question "What is man?" finds a poetic answer in Nature and the creation story, and in man's place in God's heart. "What a piece of work is man!..." — midway between nothing and deity, abject and august, dust divinely cared for. This is the finest answer ever given until Pilate pointed to Jesus and said, "Behold the man!" In psalm and gospel alike, man finds greatness only within his proper frame, God's majestic purposes. Deny God, and man dwindles to degradation, as modern secular humanism has discovered.

New Testament echoes: Matthew 21:16; 15:27; Ephesians 1:22; Hebrews 2:6–8; cf. I Corinthians 1:27.

9 "JUSTICE IS DONE!"

For headings, see the Introduction, IV (i), IV (iii); on acrostics, see III (iv) (b); for Higgaion, Selah, see IV (ii); for theme, vindication, see II (ii).

Psalms 9 and 10 are often united (as in some ancient Hebrew manuscripts and Greek and Latin versions), mainly because the acrostic form uncompleted in Psalm 9 is pursued in Psalm 10, except in verses 3–11. Certain similarities of language suggest the same author, although differences of thought indicate different circumstances and dates: for example, in Psalm 9 the enemies are "the nations," but in Psalm 10 they are evil men within Israel. Yet Psalm 10:16–17 does appear to return to the theme of Psalm 9. The original relationship of the two psalms is thus inexplicable, but for practical use that matters little.

Despite the artificial alphabetic arrangement, the thought of Psalm 9 is generally coherent. A noble burst of praise is kindled by a recent notable victory over surrounding pagan nations: their retreat, stumbling, fall, and complete overthrow are rehearsed (vv. 1–6). But this is, after all, only the unchanging justice of the God who at all times sits enthroned as judge of the whole earth. Therefore all may find shelter in his just and equitable rule (vv. 7–10). All praise is due to him who thus avenges oppression and does not forget the afflicted and defenseless (vv. 11, 12; "poor," "meek," or "afflicted"—the text is uncertain).

Verses 13–14 apparently interpose a prayer, just possibly for a final battle still to be joined. The poet recalls what God has done in saving him from death, and promises to testify to God's goodness in the open squares of the city. Others think that the assertion that God *has* acted—"Justice is done" (v. 16, NEB)—alternates with prayer so that it may *continue* to be done in every situation where men oppress; so that the meek shall not always be overlooked in the world, nor the presumptuous man be allowed to forget he is but human. Let God ever arise; let justice ever be done!

The Christian may say "Amen," remembering that in God's justice, unlike man's, there is always mercy.

New Testament echo: Acts 17:31.

10 "THE EVIL THAT MEN DO..."

See the opening comments on Psalm 9; recall especially the comments on theme, vindication, in the Introduction, II (ii).

The opening questions perfectly express the poet's deep misgiving and that of good men in every generation. Then follows, in twenty-two swift strokes, a portrait of the wickedness rampant in society and apparently unrestrained by God. The description is remarkable both for its completeness and for its clear analysis of character in an "unpsychological" age. Behind evil deeds lie reprehensible desires, the pride of self-will, an inner moral atheism which denies God's existence in order to assert that no god sees, remembers, or cares— the sinner's wishful thinking.

Greed always for *more;* inability even to understand divine principles, so earthbound are his thoughts; overconfidence that nothing can touch or threaten him, and arrogant disdain of all opposition, while out of the abundance of such a heart his mouth speaks curses, deceit, bullying words, and malice—all this reinforces the evildoer's unscrupulous cleverness (v. 5).

Especially despicable is the sinner's habit of attacking only the weak and defenseless: raiding the unwalled villages open to plunder; lying in wait for the unprotected traveler on lonely roads; pouncing on the unwary as a beast of prey on its helpless victim; snatching at men (for slaves) like a poacher by night; choosing the poor who have no champions, the weak who have no defense against brute force. Evil is ever devious, underhanded, and cowardly; these verses sound like a police report on the state of society.

And yet God has not said a word: to this appalling state of things God seems to have no answer. Why does he stand at a distance, inactive, not interfering? The closing verses resume the thought (concerning victory over the "nations") and the acrostic structure of Psalm 9. Whoever first put the broken poems together seems to plead that God will no longer merely stand within the shadows, keeping watch, but as he has cleansed the land of pagan intruders so now he will cleanse Israelite society of pagan ways. He would have God search out the evildoers until none are left, taking into his own hands the problems of wrongdoing and oppression as he once did (v. 14).

So may the judge enthroned over all once again "show his hand," bringing justice to the orphan and the downtrodden, "that fear may never drive men from their homes again" (v. 18, NEB).

New Testament echo: Romans 3:14.

11 ESCAPISM

For headings, see the Introduction, IV (i), IV (iii); for theme, vindication, see II (ii).

The opening affirmation is the poet's courageous reply to those who counsel flight to safer mountain areas in order to escape the dangers that threaten the good in evil days. Such was David's situation in Saul's court (1 Sam. 18; note 1 Sam. 26:20 for the psalmist's metaphor), or that of the "conservative" righteous defending the "foundations" of society (v. 3) against the newer ideas and more lax ways of later times, when the temple (v. 4) was standing.

The punctuation of verses 2–3 is also uncertain. The attacks of the "wicked" are urged as reasons for flight (RSV, NEB); the helplessness of the good, if religious foundations are destroyed, may be an added reason (RSV), or part of the reply (NEB). It is possible, too, that when the poet asked, "Why do you say flee?" the advisors answered, "It is dangerous to stay...and what can you do if you do stay?" (v. 3) — to which the poet answered, "The Lord will see to that!" (v. 4, paraphrase).

Nevertheless, the poet's meaning is clear. Nothing is gained by escapism. The only security in any evil generation is in the eternal God, who sees all, tests men, hates violence, and loves good deeds. A recent eruption may possibly have recalled the story of Sodom; its lesson, that the unrighteous are themselves in peril, is dramatically recalled (v. 6). Let the righteous stand their ground, for only what God loves shall last, and those who defend it enjoy his favor (v. 7).

New Testament echoes: Matthew 5:34; 1 Peter 3:12; cf. Matthew 23:22.

12 MAN'S WORDS — AND GOD'S

For headings, see the Introduction, IV (i), IV (iii).

"Help, Lord," this psalm begins. So degenerate are the days that godly, faithful men (or loyalty and good faith in themselves, NEB) are hard to find. In a largely nonliterary society, documents like receipts, wills, and agreements are useless; a man's spoken word in promise, testimony, accusation, and oath is all-important, and integrity the basis of social order and justice. The poor, the defenseless, and the uneducated are extremely vulnerable to falsehood in marriage, market, court, employment, and social relationships. Hence the emphasis placed in scripture on simple truthfulness; there seems no need to suggest a party in society were seeking to change the traditional "word of the Lord" in favor of new ideas.

The prayer (vv. 1–4; "double heart" means "duplicity") is answered by the poet in God's name, and this "oracle" awakens grateful response (vv. 6, 7). There is little difference in the Hebrew for "refined silver pouring [from the base of the crucible] onto the ground," and the Hebrew for "silver refined [in a crucible], gold seven times purified" (NEB); the idea, that God's words are genuine, pure metal, is clear. The unexpected ending may be reversed (v. 8, then v. 7); may be understood as verse 7 *although* verse 8; or verse 8 may be taken as a scribe's marginal remark — it certainly seems an anticlimax.

It is a mark of the prevalence in our society of deliberate misstatements in commerce, advertising, publicity, and propaganda that we should regard the psalmist's intense regard for literal truthfulness as somewhat eccentric. But Jesus said, "Let what you say be simply 'Yes' or 'No'; anything more than that comes from evil." It is quite a startling exercise to return just for one day to a "Quaker-like" precision of speech, meaning exactly what we say.

New Testament echoes: cf. Matthew 5:37; Ephesians 4:25.

13 THE DARK NIGHT OF THE SOUL

For headings, see the Introduction, IV (i), IV (iii).

This most poignant cry out of spiritual darkness affords no hint of the original circumstances — and is made universal thereby — but it does analyze acutely the elements of such desolation. A sense of being forsaken, of the hiding of God's face in divine disfavor, of inward anguish (v. 2, a more probable reading than "inward counsels"), and of unbroken sorrow; the vaunting hostility that takes pleasure in his suffering; the underlying fear that he might die without blessing (the only hint of any sickness) — all these comprise a harrowing experience of desolation. Many saints have known it; there came a time when the nation of Israel as a whole shared in it. Hence the preservation of this disconsolate lament in the nation's hymnbook; with us, it might still find a place in some such section as "Patience under Affliction."

But the deep intimacy with God which made possible such uninhibited prayer (reminding us vividly of Jeremiah) does sustain the troubled soul through all. In verses 5 and 6, *memory* and *mercy* triumph over mood, shine through the gloom and point one to the skies.

The Christian has little to add to such resolute trust except still greater reason for clinging to faith, not feelings, and to the love that nothing shall separate us from.

New Testament echoes: cf. Romans 8:35–36; 2 Corinthians 1:3–4, 8–9.

14 WHAT FOOLS MEN ARE!

For headings, see the Introduction, IV (i), IV (iii).
This psalm occurs also in Book II (Psalm 53) in a slightly different version. In both copies there are difficulties of translation in verse 5 (see the Introduction, III [iv] [c]).

It is evidently a godless time, though the poet is concerned mainly with the practical *folly* of atheism. It is to him an age of fools who refuse to see that when God is denied, goodness dies—*folly* (in the conduct of life, v. 2), *filth* (what the RV has for "corruption," vv. 1, 3; the NEB has "vile," "depraved," echoing Gen. 6), and *futility* (producing nothing good, vv. 1, 3) are the moral and social consequences when any generation persuades itself ("says in its heart") that it can live without God and has not God to reckon with. "Wisdom" in Israel had ever a more moral than intellectual nuance; it meant a practical mastery of the art of living known only to the godly.

The crowning act of folly is to "feast upon" the righteous poor, for they are especially "God's people" in Israel (vv. 4–6). To "confound the plans of the poor" (RSV) and "the resistance of their victim was too much for them" are two of many attempts to repair verse 5—recall the Introduction, III (iv) (c). The most probable reading would understand the Hebrew differently: "In the anguish of the poor you shall meet your downfall." That, at any rate, is the point the poet emphasizes. Where the "fools" were readiest to ignore God in ruthlessly ill-treating the helpless, there they are most sure to confront God and come off the worst. Man may sometimes slight God with impunity, but it is utter stupidity to touch God's own!

The only hope for a foolish, trivializing, God-forsaking age is religious revival, for only God can bring men to their senses. (Verse 7 uses "turn again the captivity of" in the generalized, late sense of "restore"; cf. Job 42:10. It could well be a liturgical addition, appropriate when the poet's private protest came to be used in public worship.)

New Testament echo: Romans 3:10–12.

15 PORTRAIT OF A WORSHIPER

For heading, see the Introduction, IV (iii).

Every people has its ideal "hero": the Roman soldier, the Greek sage, the Indian mystic, the English sportsman, the Norse warrior, the American businessman. The Hebrew ideal is the man welcomed into God's presence (v. 1); the psalm's emphasis is upon ethics, but the inquiry concerns who is worthy to be a guest in God's house. Ritual requirements, question and answer at the sanctuary door, a procession singing as it enters, pilgrims camped about the shrine — these are simply *not* mentioned, though worship is presupposed, and afterward an "abiding" in God's presence. The sole issue is, Whom will God entertain?

The welcome worshiper is *a good man*, known by his walk, talk, work, and attitude toward others; he is blameless and sincere, a doer of right and a man of integrity. He is *a good neighbor*, good to know, never causing harm to his acquaintance (less personal than "friend") or repeating any tale that denigrates his neighbor. And he is *a good citizen*, showing scorn for those who undermine morality in society, but always supporting and honoring the godly. His promise is his bond, though it turn out badly for himself. He will never take advantage of the poor man's predicament by lending money and charging interest. (Such "usury" was always condemned in Israel; industrial investment was, of course, unknown.) Nor will the good citizen ever be open to bribery, perverting justice to benefit the rich for his own gain. (Usury and bribery were new and pressing temptations in Israel's increasingly urban, commercialized lifestyle.)

Such integrity, honesty, and loyalty will be acceptable to God and secure among men: "he...shall never be moved," whatever the storm.

So far as it goes, the portrait illustrates the great strength of Judaism, the close connection of religion and morality. Yet it is a portrait in pencil, lacking color, of a somewhat pedestrian goodness, mainly negative. Would one turn easily to such a man in serious trouble or shame? The Christian would wish to add warmth, kindliness, compassion, and love, with something also of enthusiasm, and certainly joy.

New Testament echoes: Matthew 5:23–24; cf. Matthew 7:24–25.

16 ''I AM WELL CONTENT''

For heading, see the Introduction, IV (ii), IV (iii).

In joyous and grateful acknowledgment of the happiness of the godly life, the poet asks only that his present state shall continue: "Preserve me, O God"; "indeed I am well content" (v. 1, RSV; v. 6, NEB). With not the faintest regret he reaffirms *his choice of the Lord* in seven different ways, including his delight in like-minded "saints" (this line is very difficult to translate, as the NEB shows; see the Introduction, III [iv] [c]); *the happy contrast* with idolaters, whose very different choice brings only increasing sorrows; and *a (superstitious?) resolve* not even to mention the names of other gods (vv. 1–4).

This reiterated choice rests upon his strong testimony to what the Lord means to him, as his chief "good" (v. 1; "my felicity," NEB). The Lord is his "chosen portion" and "cup"—his feast. The Lord enlarges ("enhances," "makes spacious") his allotted share in life; the measuring lines marking out his appointed place have fallen very pleasantly. He is well content with his heritage in life. All are metaphors from Joshua's division of the promised land among the Israelite tribes (Josh. 13–21).

Constituent parts of this "heritage" are the divine counsel, especially when in quiet reflection and communion at night God instructs his inner thought; having the Lord always before him to follow, beside him to lean upon and converse with; and undisturbed peace (vv. 7, 8). Thus heart, soul, and body enjoy glad security in divine care (v. 9; the Greek version's "dwell in hope" is misleading here).

The poet requests, and is assured, that his security will be preserved. God will not abandon him to the realm of shades, the ultimate "pit," but preserve him in life, as one wholly dedicated to God. In sum, his choice of the Lord has been entirely profitable; to the end God will show him the clear *path* that enriches life, grant him for company the divine *presence* that ensures joy, and assure him of the *pleasures* ("raptures") *in* God's right hand that are permanent, timeless.

Christians read with heartfelt assent this testimony to the richness of life given up to God. Across the centuries one soul in love with God speaks to all who share that gladness. But Christian hindsight could not help but read into the poem yet greater assurances, giving "holy one" capital letters and seeing "not abandon me to Sheol" (NEB) as pointing to resurrection *from* death, a path to life *at* God's right hand. Thus the ancient testimony provided one of the strong "proof texts" of the gospel from Pentecost onward.

Nor was this deeper, exciting insight misguided: the ultimate argument for immortality, as Jesus showed, is that God will not abandon at the end those who have lived with him (Luke 20:37–38). That is how the apostles understood and extended the words of the ancient poet; they had ample warrant, in the teaching and resurrection of Jesus, to carry hope further than the Jewish poet dared. So Christians read with gratitude, and utter a still more fervent "Amen."

New Testament echoes: Acts 2:25–31; 13:34–37; cf. Matthew 7:14; Luke 10:42 ("chosen portion").

17 THE CASE FOR THE DEFENSE

For headings, see the Introduction, IV (iii); for theme, vindication, see II (ii).

Verses 1–7 have a distinctly forensic flavor. The just cause; the plea for vindication ("justice," NEB); the appeal to "the right" ("equity," literal Hebrew); previous cross-examination in the quiet night when self-doubt and misgiving often arise; the repeated plea for a hearing (vv. 1, 6); the fivefold protestation "not guilty"; the request for a verdict ("Let judgement in my cause issue from thy lips," v. 2, NEB); and the final submission to the court, "My plea is just" (NEB) —all vividly recall the High Court of heaven, complete with Prosecutor ("Accuser," "the Satan"), in Job 1:6–12; 2:1–6. It is possible, too, that the difficult phrase "by thy hand, O Lord" (v. 14) refers to the judge's wordless but decisive gesture.

The poet's picture is clear: a soul appears before God to plead for fair judgment, declaring his innocence, arguing from previous investigation and a good record, asking for clemency and protection. In verses 7 and 8 "the apple of the eye" is an English expression for the eye's pupil, as something diligently guarded; the Hebrew phrase is "little man," supposedly meaning the tiny reflection in the pupil of someone very close. The bird and fledgling figure (v. 8) is equally beautiful. In asserting his innocence, the poet duly acknowledges God's "words" (v. 4) and his "steadfast love" (v. 7); his righteousness is "of God" (v. 1; so the Greek version has it).

Verses 9–14 are full of conflict. Deadly enemies—ruthless,

proud, plundering, cunning, and violent as the young lion—waylay the appellant; he pleads divine arbitration between himself and his foes. In the description of these enemies lies the second argument of his case, a counter-accusation of unrestrained cruelty, with a demand for a frightful sentence against them. Verse 14 is very difficult (see the Introduction, III [iv] [c]); the NEB has "make an end of them; thrust them out of this world in the prime of their life, gorged as they are with thy good things, blest with many sons and leaving their children wealth in plenty." (The RSV offers a most beneficent imprecation! To make verse 14 a prayer rewrites it.)

The litigant is sure of divine vindication and of being "satisfied" with the sight ("vision"?) of God (recall Moses' similar desire in Exod. 33:20; cf. Num. 12:8). Some take verse 15 as a prayer. "When I awake" can scarcely mean "in the morning" or "when this trouble is past"; the Greek version and Jewish commentaries suggest "when thy glory appears." Christians inevitably read into the words a reference to waking from death.

The assertion of one's genuine integrity is not self-righteousness but something that approaches it, and it requires great caution. He who pleads divine justice must ever come into court with very clean hands. Moreover, the plea *against* the enemy (and his children!) is plainly pre-Christian. To ask God's verdict to be in our favor is one thing; better to leave God's verdict upon others to his merciful judgment.

New Testament echoes: James 5:5; cf. Matthew 23:27; Luke 16:25; 1 John 3:2.

18 "I CALLED.... HE CAME..."

For headings, see the Introduction, IV (i), IV (iii), IV (iv).
A dozen memorable phrases adorn this impassioned psalm, but what occasioned it? The tradition preserved in the heading is supported by 2 Samuel 22, where this psalm forms a pious appendix to a long summary of David's many deliverances; verses 3, 17, 34, 37–45, and 50 are consonant with this. Verse 28 echoes 2 Samuel 21:17 (cf. 1 Kgs. 11:36); verse 20 *may* recall David's escape from Keilah's "gates and bars" (1 Sam. 23:6–7) or his victory at Jerusalem (2 Sam. 5:6–8); verses 37–48 might similarly be paralleled by episodes of David's military career.

Several words and ideas in the psalm are said to be "ancient": verses 15–16 recall the Red Sea, the eruption of Sinai, and Joshua

10:10–14; the "simplistic" account of God's ways in verses 25–26 is held to be early and naive (contrast Ps. 103:10–11); "Eloah" (v. 32) is an old name for God. For all these reasons, this ringing triumph-song is as likely to be by David as any other in the Psalter. Certainly God frequently "delivered" David out of "straits" into "spacious places" (vv. 19, 36, literal Hebrew).

On the other hand, we find the song in the hymnbook of a later age. The distinction of God's "ways," "ordinances," and "statutes," the notion of "cherubim" (winged creatures guarding God's throne), and the legalistic tone of verses 20–24 have suggested a postexilic atmosphere; verses 43–45 sound like a later idealization of David's empire. A late "sacramental" use of an ancient poem is quite possible —a later (Davidic) king testifying to divine deliverance in a dramatic temple-service possibly including baptism (v. 16), re-enacting a great victory, and celebrating God's creative triumph over his primordial foes (see the Introduction, II [iv]).

The magnificent description of a "theophany" (vv. 7–19) would deliberately utilize older words, phrases, and metaphors associated with the storms, eruptions, and earthquakes surrounding God's previous "comings" at his servant-king's request. That such a liturgical use of the psalm is conceivable shows that it "belongs" to more than one age, and testifies to its eloquence and value.

The titles ascribed in tribute to the God whom the psalmist "loves" are combative but defensive, except for "horn of safety" (see the Introduction, III [ii]). During warfare the poet has encountered death at close quarters, the entangling "cords" of mortal dread, the overwhelming "floods" of weakness, the net and snares of death the hunter (vv. 4, 5). But God came in a mighty convulsion of Nature (vv. 7–16), delivering the poet from death and enemies at once (vv. 17–19).

God did so because he "delighted" in the psalmist, rewarding his integrity and faithfulness, as God ever does (vv. 19–30). The gracious benefits given are beautifully described: God's "coming down" to him has lifted him up (vv. 9, 31–36); the resulting victory has been complete (vv. 37–45). Again the poet acknowledges eloquently the goodness of God (vv. 46–49), and later congregations join gladly in the victory thanksgiving (v. 50).

Christians today find it difficult to enter into the religious militarism that rejoices so fiercely in total victory. Some of the self-applauding phrases (vv. 20–24, with strange repetition) strike a Christian ear as self-righteous, though the alternating pride and gratitude are very "human." Magnificent though the storm-girt "descent" of God undoubtedly is, Christians have learned to marvel less at eruptions than at incarnation. Nevertheless, there runs through the psalm a testimony and a love for God that every reader must admire.

New Testament echo: Romans 15:9.

19 A SUNLIT SABBATH

For headings, see the Introduction, IV (i), IV (iii); for theme, God and Nature, see II (v).

The abrupt change at verse 7, with the absence of God's name "Yahweh" from verses 1–6 and the sevenfold emphasis upon it in verses 7–10, strongly suggests two psalms conjoined. To call verses 1–6 a hymn to the sun-god, borrowed and dutifully corrected by verses 7–10, is less plausible.

Nature herself becomes lyrical in verses 1–6: the *beauty* of the heavens, the stretch ("firmament") of the sky, and the blazing Mediterranean sun bear wordless testimony to the "manifest excellence" of God. The sun's "tent" in the sea (not "in them") is where he rests beyond the western horizon; in the NEB it becomes a Hebrew wedding-canopy. A happy bridegroom in radiant robes, an athlete prepared to stride the heavens with untiring energy reveals to all "under the sun" the glory of its creator.

But there is another light, the inner illumination of the revealed will of God. His stated law, his attested ways, his detailed precepts, his statutory commandments, the inward "fear of the Lord" which guides behavior, God's judgments or decisions accumulating in human experience—these constitute neither yoke nor burden but restored strength, reliable instruction, enlightenment, joy, steadfastness, truth, and right. They are invaluable and they are sweet, offering necessary warning and great reward.

Nevertheless, to know the revealed will of God is not all joy. The divine word becomes a mirror in which we see ourselves, discovering wanderings of desire, missings of the way, unwitting and unintended sins. Who can truly know himself except under the light of truth? (see Jer. 17:9). And sometimes such sinfulness "boils over" (v. 13, literally; not "proud oppressors") in wanton, daring wickedness. The poet asks to be kept from being misled and being overmastered, and so from "great transgression." Sinlessness may be beyond him, but he would that thought, word, and life may be acceptable to God, his rock and his redeemer.

The attempt to find detailed parallels between what is said of the sun and what is said of the word of God is unconvincing. But so beautifully complementary are the two "halves" (or psalms) now that some speak of "genius," while others deny there ever were two poems. The light without and the light within do combine to speak God's glory and move the heart to prayer. As Kant said, "The starry heavens above" and "the moral law within" stir the mind to "ever-increasing wonder and awe."

So would both Jew and Christian feel, each making his way on some glorious "Lord's Day" morning, to sit under the illuminating word and find sweetness, reward, and inward purity.

New Testament echoes: Romans 6:12, 14; 10:18; cf. Romans 1:19, 20; James 1:23, 24.

20 INTO BATTLE...

For headings, see the Introduction, IV (i), IV (iii); for Selah, see IV (ii). Despite its having the appearance of a greeting card (vv. 1–5), this psalm belongs to the very ancient ritual of preparation for battle (cf. 1 Sam. 7:8–9 with 13:9–12); thus it is a companion to Psalm 21.

Some king of Judah (v. 2) seeks in the temple by sacrifice and prayer the blessing of God in coming conflict. A priest (or poet), welcoming him, recites verses 1–3 ("God of *Jacob*" recalls long-past divine providence toward Israel). *Selah* may indicate a musical pause while the sacrifice is offered, and the priest resumes with verses 4–5. The king responds, declaring his faith in the name of God alone, the name in which he will fight (v. 6 with, probably, vv. 7, 8). The "now" seems to indicate that the sacrifice has been accepted — perhaps signified by the priest. (Horses and chariots were alien to nomadic shepherds, and much feared; see Deut. 17:16; Isa. 31:1. "Trust," "boast," or "are strong" has to be supplied; the Hebrew is very brief.) The people respond in chorus, "God save the king" (so the Greek and Latin versions clarify the Hebrew), adding "answer us when we call," meaning "now" or "at the height of battle."

Doubtless the appeal for divine help in human conflicts is often presumptuously made, without warrant. Yet Christians have believed that God is arbiter in all human affairs, and that his will is final. Such a conviction sustains, but also humbles, all who contend for what they devoutly think is right.

New Testament echo: cf. 1 Timothy 2:1, 2.

21 ...AFTER BATTLE

For headings, see the Introduction, IV (i), IV (iii); for Selah, see IV (ii); for "royal" psalms, see II (iv).

Seven echoes of Psalm 20 are here discernible in phrasing, meter, and outline. Some recent success, answering that royal prayer, seems to inspire verses 1–6; the NEB has "well may he exult in thy victory" (v. 1). The "setting of the crown" and the prolonging of life (vv. 3, 4) thus appear to be the result of victory more probably than an allusion to the king's birthday or coronation, or a general assurance of "blessing."

Set in the Psalter as a companion, therefore, to Psalm 20, this poem could fittingly be used in thanksgiving for any military success. It is not clear whether verses 8–12 assure the king that his victory *will be* consolidated, that all enmity will be rooted out (so the RSV has it), or that this *has* happened already (NEB). The threat even to children of enemies is characteristic of "tribal" thought (cf. Josh. 6:21). It remains true that both king (v. 6) and people (v. 13) delight more in God than in victory itself, such success being evidence of divine favor ("presence," "countenance").

So exalted a view of monarchy, and of God's blessing upon it, and such promise of wide sovereignty (vv. 8, 10) led naturally to later Jewish interpretation of this psalm as a prophecy of the Messiah. If the New Testament contains no clear echoes of this poem, Christian usage has gladly followed the Jewish hint and made it a psalm for Ascension Day, "spiritualizing" its more militaristic phrases.

22 THE SOB AND THE SONG

For headings, see the Introduction, IV (i), IV (iii).

The sob is heartrending (vv. 1–21). Despair at the silence, and absence, of God arises from previous intimacy with him ("my God"); the sufferer cannot believe that despite his "shrieking" (a loud shriek of intense pain—literal Hebrew) God has forsaken him. For, as long experience shows, God has ever deserved to be "enthroned on the praises of Israel."

Yet the sufferer is treated with contempt — like "a worm" — socially outcast, mocked for his faith; his enemies know he "rolled" (literal Hebrew) his burden on the Lord, and wait to see if God acknowledges his "servant." In truth the sufferer has depended on God from birth (vv. 9–11); now brutal "bullies" (Bashan was famous for breeding strong oxen) continually beset him, and his exhausted body feels already laid in the all-pervading dust of Sheol. Scavenger dogs (1 Kgs. 21:24) already gather; mummifiers already bind (probably not "pierce") his hands and feet, and divide his garments among them (like brigands?—v. 16). Even yet he pleads for rescue (in v. 20,

KJV/AV, "my only one," "darling," means "my dear life").

The sob seems to fade in a last gasp of despair, but the Hebrew (RSV margin) breaks off suddenly; the last pitiable plea ends with a cry of immeasurable relief: *Thou hast answered me.* God has broken silence! Ancient and most modern versions find this too dramatic, and amend it to "[Save] my afflicted soul...." Nevertheless, the tone does suddenly, totally, and inexplicably change at verse 22 to four-fold praise and limitless hope.

The song (vv. 22–31) has as its main theme praise, glorifying God, testifying to God's response to the sufferer's cry. It is addressed first to a "congregation" at worship, when the sufferer publicly fulfills his vows of thanksgiving with "votive" meal, sacrifice, and benediction (vv. 22–26; cf. Lev. 7:15–16). Unlike men, God does not despise or blame the afflicted. In this thanksgiving the poor shall be fed, the seeker shall find (vv. 24, 26).

The news of such divine compassion passes to the ends of the earth (vv. 27–29). Finally, generations unborn shall hear of the Lord's deliverance. The NEB takes verse 29 as a question: "How can those buried in the earth do him homage...those who go down to the grave bow before him? But I shall live for his sake...." Others find here an unusual hint of future life. Most probably the poet contrasts man's mortality ("cannot keep his soul alive") with the endless coming generations. All shall hear what God has "finished" (v. 31; cf. John 19:30).

To an astonishing extent the story of the death of Jesus could be told in phrases from this psalm; not only was Jesus (in all probability) himself reciting it upon the cross (Matt. 27:46), but thirteen reasonable parallels between psalm and story can be counted. Inevitably, therefore, the story of Jesus' death *was* preserved in this readily available language.

Nor is the correspondence between psalm and later history any mere coincidence. In the closing verses worldwide consequences follow from the suffering described; the only other passage in the Old Testament even approaching this is Isaiah's portrait of the suffering Servant of the Lord (Isa. 52:11–53), in which Jesus found the principle and program of his own ministry, just as (since he quoted it) he found in the psalm a graphic description of his ministry's cost.

It was Jesus, therefore, who found in the Old Testament the profound truth of fruitful, suffering service and gave it embodiment in his own life and death. Psalm 22 and Isaiah 53 converge in his mind, intersect upon his cross. It has been suggested that Isaiah had Jeremiah's character and experience in mind; certainly someone like Jeremiah *could* have written this psalm.

The poem found its way into the nation's hymnbook as the perfect expression of Israel's later faith, that out of all her own suffering in later years, this nation — the Servant of the Lord (Isa. 49:3, etc.) — would yet bring redemption and divine rule to all nations (Ps. 22:27–28). As we know, in the end not the whole nation nor even a "remnant" of the nation but One only fulfilled the task of suffering Servant, to redeem the world through death. That is why Isaiah 53 illumined his experience and Psalm 22 comforted his soul in death.

New Testament echoes: Matthew 27:35, 39, 43, 46; Mark 15:24, 29, 34; Luke 23:34, 35; John 19:23, 24, 28; Hebrews 2:12; cf. John 19:30, 37; 20:25; Philippians 2:10; 2 Timothy 4:17.

23 A TRIPTYCH

For heading, see the Introduction, IV (iii).

One man's exquisite testimony proclaims God to be three things. The first is *a faithful shepherd,* whose provision, protection, and refreshment relieve all anxieties and ensure enduring peace. "Restores my soul" suggests returning a wanderer to the flock, but the word "restores" strictly means "revives." The shepherd figure, central to Israel's nomadic background, necessarily colored her political thought ("shepherd-kings") and her religious hope (Ezek. 34). Very rarely have trust, thought, and perfectly chosen words been so perfectly combined.

God is, second, *a reliable guide.* Expressions like "paths of righteousness," "valley of the shadow of death," "staff" (the word implies "to lean upon"), "fear no evil," and "comfort" ("sympathize," "console") — scarcely appropriate to sheep! — reveal the change of metaphor. Another important figure in a land of few roads, no maps, and numerous dangers, where every journey was an adventure, was the experienced and *trustworthy* guide, who for the sake of his own reputation ("name") would see the traveler safely on his way. The good guide accompanies him ("with me") to the end, armed to defend ("club," literal Hebrew — an iron-tipped club for defense), knowing the right paths, and encouraging ("comforting") the weary. Thus guidance, safety, companionship, and direction are theirs who take God for their guide; the darkest valley has for them no fears ("shadow of death" most probably means simply "intense gloom").

And God is, third, *a loving host.* The spread table, the anointing after a hot journey (cf. Luke 7:46; Ps. 45:7), the brimming cup, the house ("palace," "mansions of a king," literal Hebrew) — all reveal another change of metaphor. The godly are God's guests in this life ("in the presence of my enemies"), feasting at God's table, satisfied, enjoying God. Goodness and mercy "follow" throughout life (probably, as Moffatt's translation has it, "wait upon me"), and this divine entertainment is lifelong ("for length of days," parallel to "all the days of my life," though it is hard to exclude the projection of such hospitality and fellowship into the future).

Psalm 23 is so individual in tone, so warm in expression that there seems no need to suppose a "representative king" speaks for "Israel personified." It is easy to find occasion for each figure in the testimony in the varied life of David — his shepherd's calling, his outlaw years in the wilderness, his being sustained through want by Ziba and Abigail, his restoration after sin to great blessing. But then the psalm has spoken for thousands who never composed a poem in their lives! The author's name is—Everyman.

Christians thankfully endorse all that the psalmist says, glad to hear Jesus echo the psalm's central thoughts and make more clear and certain its final hint of everlasting welcome.

New Testament echoes: John 10:1–16; 1 Peter 2:25; Revelation 7:16, 17; cf. Matthew 8:11; 22:1–14; 26:31; Luke 14:15.

24 FOR THE WORKING WEEK

For heading, see the Introduction, IV (iii); for "enthronement," see II (iv); for Selah, see IV (ii).

The dialogue concerning admission to the hill of the Lord and the challenge at the gates makes clear that this is not a composition of three isolated fragments (as some think) but a series of moves in a solemn ritual procession. The notes struck — God's creation, kingship, and glory, his might and victories—are notes appropriate to the New Year festivities and the Feast of Tabernacles, perhaps including the "re-enthronement" of God.

The one incongruous detail is the *admission* of God (vv. 7, 9); this seems to imply either that "God" (perhaps symbolized by the Ark of the Covenant) has "gone forth" to battle (cf. 1 Sam. 4:3–4), and now returns victorious; or, for purposes of the "re-enthronement" ritual, that God was regarded as having been "theoretically" absent. Alternatively, it is conceivable that a fragment of ritual first composed for the original installation of the Ark at Jerusalem (1 Chron. 15) has been carefully preserved in the ceremonies for which the hymn is later used. The "catechism" of verses 3–5 is so preserved in variant form in Psalm 15. The reference to "ancient" gates of the shrine, though, betrays a date long after David.

The ringing assertion that God created and owns all things, found in the opening chorus of the whole ceremony, may owe something (in v. 2) to the ancient idea of God's creative conflict with chaos and the abyss (see the Introduction, II [ii], II [iv]; Gen. 1:6–9; Exod. 20:4). As the incoming procession inquires about the conditions of acceptance (v. 3), the priests (or the Levite choir) reply with simple ethical demands. "Lifting up the soul to what is false" may include idolatry and superstitious gestures as well as "empty ambition"; verse 6 may be the pilgrims' reply; "such is the generation" (or "the life story"; possibly "the company," meaning "the procession") of the people of "Israel/Jacob" (so the Hebrew has it; this is amended by the Greek and Syriac versions).

The challenge to the "gate" (v. 7) is answered by a question from the priestly "keepers of the threshold." To the splendid confidence of the reply (or password) in verse 8 (which again may echo the story of the creator's victory over chaos and evil), there is no answer but to admit the worshipers to the festival.

The conditions of welcome into God's presence and the reminder of his power as "Lord of armies" apply no less to Christian worship than to temple or later synagogue services. At one time the psalm was used on the first day of each working week; verses 4–5 form a fitting "creed for business," tenets to control the handling of things that God has made if we are again to seek God's presence on the next Lord's Day. It is good, too, to be reminded that the whole earth, with its products and its people, is the Lord's — and *not* Satan's.

New Testament echoes: 1 Corinthians 10:26; 2 Peter 3:5; cf. Matthew 5:8.

25 "LORD, LEAD ME"

For heading, see the Introduction, IV (iii); for acrostics, see III (iv) (b).
An acrostic of prayers, used as an aid to memory, resembles a "mental rosary," the separate thoughts strung like beads upon the Hebrew alphabet. Acrostics often lack coherence, but here the approach, the mood, and the dominant outlook hold the poem together.

The approach is devotional, lifting the soul (v. 1) and the eyes (v. 15) to God, waiting upon him (vv. 3, 5, 21), trusting and taking refuge in him (vv. 2, 20). This is the language of personal religion, and not merely because "I," "me," and "my" occur thirty-three times. Verse 22 is probably a later close (it is impersonal and outside the alphabetic pattern), adapting an individual poem to congregational use; if *this* poem was not originally individual and private, then Hebrew poetry could not express personal devotion.

Other marks of intense piety are here: emphasis upon humility (v. 9), a sense of aloneness (v. 16), and oppression, need, and opposition (vv. 17–19) — feelings that usually, though not necessarily, accompany great earnestness. The poet feels vulnerable, in need of shelter (v. 20).

This is not surprising, for he has sinned greatly (vv. 7, 11, 18) and stands in fear still of being "put to shame" (vv. 2, 3). Yet knowing of old the steadfast love and enduring mercy of God (v. 6), he clings to all he understands of God's goodness, uprightness, and faithfulness (vv. 7, 8, 10), of his salvation (v. 5), his dependable name (v. 11), and his graciousness (v. 16) — but above all he clings to that steadfast, unflinching, covenanted love (mentioned five times).

The poet envies those who steadfastly live in the fear of the Lord, instructed always in the way they should go, themselves continuing in prosperity and seeing their children inherit security. *They* live in the Lord's counsels ("friendship," RSV) and enjoy his unbroken covenant. But that has not been his own experience: his feet are entangled (v. 15), and he asks, movingly, that God will "remember thy mercy.... Remember not the sins of my youth... remember me..." (vv. 6, 7).

The psalmist can affirm not success or sinlessness but sincerity: he looks toward God (v. 15); he can plead integrity and uprightness of purpose (v. 21). Above all, he pleads to be taught God's ways, instructed in the truth and practice of godliness by him who is willing to instruct even "sinners in the way" and who "leads the humble in what is right" (vv. 8, 9). Including references to his "feet," his "transgressing" (trespassing), the thought of guidance in the Lord's way occurs eleven times.

Such is the portrait we piece together from fragments scattered at the dictates of the alphabet: an earnest, humble soul, very conscious of past sins and present frailty, aware of how little he knows of the ways of God but holding on to God's lovingkindness, pleading to be forgiven and taught and held fast.

Every Christian knows that such a soul understands well the ABC's of the spiritual life.

New Testament echoes: Romans 10:11; cf. John 7:17.

26 SELF-DEDICATION, OR SELF-RIGHTEOUSNESS?

For heading, see the Introduction, IV (iii); for theme, vindication, see II (ii).

This is a curiously ambiguous poem. Those who sympathize with it draw attention to the acknowledgment of God's help (vv. 1, 3) as mitigating any impression of self-satisfaction. They suppose the author to be the king, facing some crisis and asking to be vindicated for his faithfulness—asking perhaps by means of an appointed ritual of washing and procession.

Or he is a priest in the temple (vv. 6–8; this takes the hand-washing literally, with procession and devotion to God's house as priestly duties). In that case it is supposed he is protesting his orthodoxy and faithfulness to the old ways against influential leaders who, for power or bribes, compromise with "liberalizing" tendencies which have been introduced by alien rulers. His feet are firmly planted on the "level ground" of loyalty to God's truth (v. 12). The vehemence of his protestations of innocence and of his denunciation of opponents (vv. 4, 5, 9, 10) arises from the sharp conflict between rival "sects" in postexilic Judaism (see the Introduction, II [ii]).

Those who find it difficult to sympathize with the "self-congratulation" of the poem emphasize the twelve (or so) firm claims to divine approval, the "daring" challenge to God to search his very "kidneys" ("reins," meaning "emotions" — literal Hebrew) and "heart" (will) for any unfaithfulness. They reject any supposed crisis or conflict, and point out that no truly pious soul ever claims to "live my life without reproach" (vv. 1 and 11, NEB), totally separate from all contact with sinners, and to be standing secure on level ground, never likely to slip. In this case the acknowledgment of divine help is taken to be quite formal, a sop to religious susceptibilities, like the Pharisee's prayer in Jesus' parable: "*I thank God* I am not as other men" (Luke 18:9–14).

For Christian readers the ambiguity is perhaps the real point. So hard is it to draw the line between commitment and complacency, between self-conscious dedication and self-righteousness. So wide a gulf separates Peter's "Lord, thou knowest that I love thee" from the Pharisee's "I thank God I am not like this publican...." Yet Peter's confession, too, made in public, sounds very often like the Pharisee's, and the Christian Pharisee so often thinks that he is only following Peter's example.

God keep my feet firmly on the ground—on level ground.

New Testament echo: cf. Matthew 27:24.

27 MOUNTAINTOP AND VALLEY

For heading, see the Introduction, IV (iii).

Neither "poetic" alternation of mood nor a supposed pattern of thanksgiving before prayer really accounts for the sudden change (v. 7) in this psalm from gladness to anxiety, from sunshine to shade. It is said that the meter also changes, though the text in verses 7–14 is too uncertain to prove this. The opening words of verse 7 form the *opening* words of other psalms (55, 61, 64). Still clearer is the total change of content in the second section; the sole link—the mention of slander in verses 2 and 12—disappears when verse 2 is correctly translated (as the Hebrew, the RSV margin, and the NEB have it): "evildoers assail me...to eat up my flesh."

The first section exults in God, whose light, salvation, and "stronghold" have dispelled all fear. The enemies are thwarted; henceforth the psalmist can face anything (v. 3). One thing only remains to be desired: to return to the shrine and there dwell in peace, beholding the Lord's loveliness, inquiring about his will (a splendid definition of worship). There God will protect the poet from all enmity, as a powerful sheikh shelters those whom his desert tent entertains, set high beyond the reach of hostility as on some unscalable rock (v. 5).

Then the warrior-poet will give thanks in proper fashion, with sacrifices, shouts of joy, and melodious praise. Unless we must take "temple" (v. 4) literally, all this brings David vividly to mind.

The second section begins with a loud cry, pleads that God will not hide his face or turn the author away in anger or forsake him. He asks God to lead him in an open place where enemies cannot lie in wait, and not abandon him to their violence. Whether God (RSV) or the poet's own heart (NEB) prompts him to seek God's face, he seems unsure of welcome.

Yet faith holds on (v. 14). Although father and mother have forsaken him (RSV), or might do so (NEB), yet the Lord will be faithful and take him into care. He believes that sooner or later he will see the goodness of God in this life; thus he communes within himself, concluding that he has nothing else to do, having prayed, but to be strong, take courage, and wait for God. Such fortitude alone will see him through a bad time.

How these two sections (two psalms?) came to be united is impossible to say. The testimony that emerges is that sometimes one may exult in the marvelous deliverances of God, giving oneself in joyful gratitude to the service of his house; at other times one can only hold on, unhappily but tenaciously, and wait for God to change things. And that *either* situation is a genuine experience of the help God gives.

New Testament echoes: cf. Luke 2:37; John 8:12; 12:35–36.

28 ROYAL INTERCESSION

For heading, see the Introduction, IV (iii); for "royal" psalms, see II (iv).
Apart from the familiar plea that evil shall not be allowed to triumph, three impressions tease the mind after reading this poem: the comparisons with those who go down ("are dragged," NEB) to the pit of Sheol (vv. 1, 3); the somewhat sudden, oblique reference to "God's anointed"; and the prayer "be thou their shepherd."

The "anointed one" praying for the people is presumably the king, possibly David. Assuming that verses 8 and 9 are not a later adaptation of the poem for public worship, this is evidently a royal and representative prayer, which may explain the somewhat formal request to be heard, gesturing toward the holy of holies (vv. 1–2).

Some think that the repeated request to be spared death betrays widespread pestilence which has already claimed many lives. This seems more probable than impending battle, since prevalent wickedness is held to be the cause. The king therefore prays against those who so bring judgment upon the people. Their wickedness includes active pursuit of evil ends, smooth, deceitful speech, and indifference toward God's acts and handiwork (vv. 3–5). The royal poet prays not for vengeance but for justice, for a due reward matching their deeds, and for a "breaking down" of the wicked groups in society.

The king anticipates, gratefully though again a little formally, an answer to his prayer (vv. 6, 7), testifying that God is his own strength, shield, trust, and joy. ("With my song," v. 7, RSV, slightly amends the Hebrew, as does "with my whole body," NEB; the latter may indicate a gesture of complete prostration, appropriate after deliverance of the body from the Pit.) The king adds that for the people, too, God is strength, refuge, and salvation, their true shepherd who will bear them (cf. Isa. 40:11) *for ever.*

Prayer offered against the moral deterioration and the physical danger of society at large is typical of Jewish social responsibility. Too often Christians are content to withdraw from public affairs, to keep themselves "separate" and "set a good example," all too rarely praying for the *world,* as the New Testament advises (1 Tim. 2:1–4).

New Testament echoes: see references for Psalm 23; also 1 Timothy 2:8; 2 Timothy 4:14; cf. Revelation 18:6.

29 GOD WITHIN THE STORM

For heading, see the Introduction, IV (iii); for theme, God and Nature, see II (v).

A mighty storm has swept Palestine, rising over the Mediterranean to the west and echoing across raging waters, sweeping eastward to Lebanon and Hermon ("Sirion"), whose massive heights divert it southward along the face of the east-Jordan plateau, and swinging south and west again across the open moorland of Kadesh, "shaking the wilderness." It has left a trail of damage, forked lightning (v. 5) splitting the great cedars, the very mountains trembling, hills and vales deluged with floodwater. And one devout heart thrilled and exulted at the sight *and sense* of God's majesty and power.

The God who "spoke" Nature into existence still speaks with immeasurable might through Nature; the poet calls first heaven and then earth (probably, v. 2) to worship before such majesty and to acknowledge such great glory.

The "sons of gods" (v. 1, Hebrew) are probably those who "shout for joy" at creation (Job 38:7), angelic beings rather than "gods" (NEB). "Holy array" (festal garments) suggests human worshipers, though the lovely phrase "the beauty of holiness" is almost restored in the NEB's "splendour of holiness." Translation falters in verse 9: if oak trees ever "whirl," then the RSV's "whirling oaks" makes a good parallel with "bare forests," but so does the NEB's "makes the hinds calve" (prematurely, from terror) with "brings kids early to birth."

The picture of God enthroned above the surging floods, "holding the winds in his fists, the waters in the hollow of his palms" (which echoes Prov. 30:4 and Isa. 40:12; see the NEB), scarcely needs Noah's flood to explain it, but it may have mythological overtones for a people who could see in every raging storm a re-enactment of the ancient struggle between chaos and order.

For the rest, this magnificent storm-scape, "the psalm of the seven peals" ("thunders"; in Hebrew, "voices"), whispers, whistles, and thunders to its sublime close like Beethoven's *Pastoral Symphony,* in a quiet and refreshed temple of Nature — heavens and earth together — wherein all speaks "glory" (v. 9). With an exquisite dying fall, the cadence comes to rest on "May the Lord bless his people with peace."

Remarkably, no fear, no superstitious terror, is felt amid this violent tempest (contrast Jonah 1:4–6). The psalmist hears only God's voice within the gale, sees only God enthroned above the flood, and thinks of all that energy, that power and majesty, available as *strength* for the people of God (v. 11).

Why do we imagine God is only in the peace, and never in the storm?

New Testament echo: cf. John 12:27–30.

30 BEAUTY FOR ASHES

For headings, see the Introduction, IV (iii), IV (i), II (iii).

This is a psalm of swift transitions: the "immovable" (v. 6) much moved, the sick made well, the dying restored; anger turned to favor, a moment to a lifetime, weeping to joy, night to dawn; enemies are replaced by fellow saints, and mourning turns to dancing, sackcloth to finery, silence to song. A fragment of autobiography illustrates the vicissitudes of life!

A very sick patient despairs of his own life and is gloated over by enemies. In prayer he has argued with God with a child's simplicity: his death will bring neither of them profit! (vv. 8–10; the silence, shadow, and remoteness of Sheol are assumed). He is granted complete restoration. The next step is public acknowledgment, with thanksgiving (see Job 33:19–28). This poem is the result—perhaps a hymn for a formal "service for the healed" (v. 4).

The poet's *thanksgiving* recounts the immediate experience, calls others to join him in praise, acknowledges his fault (v. 5; and note "sackcloth," v. 11), but God's anger is brief, his favor for life; at evening, tears, at dawn, great joy (the original is extremely terse). Then the *testimony:* he had been overconfident, taking for granted the security he enjoyed (as he now acknowledges, enjoyed only by God's favor) as though it were some immovable mountain (the NEB reinterprets here: "But, Lord, it was thy will to shake my mountain refuge" — to rock my ivory tower). Somehow the poet lost God's favor, and all was changed. He learned his lessons the hard way. But now all is well again. Life is more glad—and especially more grateful (v. 12)—than it ever was before.

This is a beautiful tribute and testimony—but why "for the dedication of the Temple"? The Jewish Talmud confirms this usage at the Feast of Dedication (see John 10:22), which dates from Maccabean times. An earlier dedication, following the Exile, is recorded in Ezra 6:16, which also may have become an annual observance. This moving account of a sick man's forgiveness, recovery, and transformation could very fittingly be sung with the nation's sickness, near-extinction, restoration, and hope in mind. Israel, too, had learned her lesson the hard way.

New Testament echo: cf. 2 Corinthians 4:17.

31 "INTO THY HANDS..."

For headings, see the Introduction, IV (ii), IV (iii).

Out of seventy or so "lines" in this psalm, about fifty-five could well have been uttered by "the prophet of anguished faithfulness," Jeremiah. One phrase, "terror on every side" (v. 13), occurs five times in Jeremiah; verses 7–18 read like a commentary on Jeremiah 20:7–13; verse 12 recalls Jeremiah's parable of the potter; verse 6 reflects Jeremiah 8:19 and 10:8. Jeremiah constantly expresses in alternate moods, both complaint of ill treatment and the closest intimacy with God, varying prayer with affirmation of trust, just as this psalmist does.

Jeremiah is promised defense, a strong wall (cf. v. 21); he too has to contend with the "lying lips" (v. 18) of false prophets. He continually complains of the rejection, ostracism, and loneliness which loyalty to his mission entails for the faithful among the faithless.

No doubt somewhat similar parallels could be drawn between the Book of Jeremiah and other passages; these are sufficiently striking to suggest close resemblance in situation and feeling. The poet declares fifteen times his devotion to God's service; he especially rejects idolatry (whether the protest "I hate" or the acknowledgment "Thou hatest" is the true meaning of v. 6); and there is only one doubtful, and fleeting, reference to iniquity (v. 10; the Greek and Syriac versions have "misery"). Yet his sufferings—physical, mental, emotional, and social—are piteously described.

This raises for the poet a double problem: that of Job—Why, if human suffering is due to sin, should suffering fall so often upon the innocent?—and that of Jeremiah: Why should a life so selflessly dedicated to God's service so often meet with rejection and persecution from neighbors, acquaintances, and onlookers alike? (v. 11); why should the faithful suffer loneliness, contempt, and near-despair, fearful of becoming disillusioned, "confounded," and ashamed? (vv. 1, 17).

The psalmist has no answer, but offers a solution: to seek refuge in God, in his deliverance, protection ("fortress"), and favor ("let thy face shine on thy servant") as a privileged guest in the pavilion ("tent") of God—which, by Eastern rules of hospitality, ensured safety. So he committed to God his *spirit* (his inner self, v. 5), his *times* (his "fortunes" or circumstances; in 1 Chron. 29:30, "the times that went over David"—the way things turn out for him from day to day), and his *trust* (vv. 6, 14), knowing that God is aware of all his suffering (v. 7). This was essentially Jeremiah's answer. The psalmist, further, "holds on" to all he knows of God, especially to his steadfast love (mentioned three times), to his graciousness, his abundant goodness, and his remembered deliverances from panic and fear (vv. 5, 8, 19, 21, 22). This is essentially Job's reply: keep faith in God.

In that love and trust all faithful souls can "be strong," "take courage," and also "wait for the Lord" (vv. 23, 24). Waiting implies that God has some purpose, some future goal, worth suffering and waiting for; that was the reply of Isaiah, and later of Jesus—that the suffering of God's servant is redemptive, the means of saving the world.

New Testament echoes: Luke 23:46; cf. Acts 7:59; 1 Corinthians 2:9; Revelation 2:10.

32 ON BEING FORGIVEN

For headings, see the Introduction, IV (ii), IV (iii); for Selah, see IV (ii); for "Wisdom," see II (vi).

The gospel in the Old Testament!—this is an almost perfect expression of post-penitential gladness. Happy the man whose rebellion, missing the goal and turning off from the right way, has been "lifted" from him like a burden and "covered" from sight (literal Hebrew), his soul released from debt and his heart relieved of its inner duplicity (vv. 1–2).

Sickness had brought conviction of sin—his body shriveling, his vital energies ("life sap," literal Hebrew) fever-parched. At first unwilling, he at last took the simple steps required: he began to acknowledge his sin within himself; he resisted the further temptation to hide it; and he confessed fully to God and accepted divine forgiveness, of which healing was (to him) the sign and confirmation (v. 5).

With hindsight which only the forgiven possess, the poet encourages others to find rescue (from "floods" of distress) and to take refuge (vv. 6, 7; the Hebrew, "at a time of finding only," may warn that God will not always be available, as does Isa. 55:6).

Verses 8 and 9 are said to be in the style of the wisdom teachers, and thus spoken by *the poet* to any who will accept instruction in order to avoid sinning: "to keep the eye upon" will then mean "to look after," as the NEB and Jeremiah 40:4 have it. But so general an invitation seems impracticable unless offered by God; in that case, to "counsel *with* the eye," meaning "by a glance—one look enough," well expresses the sensitiveness of the pious soul to divine approval or disapproval. In contrast, the beast (or insensitive soul) needs curb and bridle to receive instructions.

A poignant memory stirs the final promise. The wicked find everything against them; the forgiven, trusting soul finds everywhere only steadfast love!

The psalm does not raise the problem of how such forgiveness is morally justified. Later moralists have insisted that forgiveness is a fiction, that nothing can erase the past. For Judaism the sacrificial system offered a form of atonement; Jesus gave his life as a ransom for many; Paul explains how God could be just and yet justify the sinner — because he "set forth Christ, an expiation for sin" (Rom. 3:21–26). So forgiveness *is* possible, and gratitude for it transforms sinners into saints.

New Testament echoes: Romans 4:6, 7, 8; James 3:3; cf. John 1:47; 1 John 1:9.

33 CALL TO WORSHIP

This psalm is a wonderfully neat, symmetrical poem (six lines, plus eight groups of four, plus six lines), calling to worship, saying why, and then worshiping, with an adequate "text" provided in verse 4, God's word and work. Whether some specific occasion called forth this "new song" to celebrate it (v. 3) is debated. It is at least possible that some invader, relying on horses (alien to Israel), on warrior leaders and armies (vv. 16, 17), has been foiled and the people delivered (vv. 10–11, 16–17; cf. 2 Kgs. 6:18; 7:6–7; 19:6–7, 35–36). But the psalmist reflects very calmly on God's way; the excitement and relief of a recent particular event are missing.

The call to worthy, "skilful," zestful ("loud shouts") worship rings with music and joy: "strike up with all your art," the NEB says(!). The first reason given is the character of God, his utter dependableness (vv. 4–5; note the suggestion in v. 5, an "earth-full" of love); the second reason, the amazing power of his spoken word (vv. 6–9; the "host" are stars; the "bottle" is strictly a goatskin, though the older text's "in heaps" is as intelligible if understood as "high waves"; the "storehouses" are secret treasure-chambers in wealthy houses — in his, God stores rain and winds, Jer. 10:13).

The third reason for worship is the work of the Lord: as his steadfast love fills the earth, so his purpose fills all history. His will prevails, he "counteracts" men's plans; the world he made "stands firm" and so does his program ("counsel") for human history (vv. 10–17). Especially happy, therefore, is that nation which is God's own "heritage," where his writ runs; but in fact he sees all men, moves the hearts of all peoples, from the lofty aerie of his throne. Proud, embattled men think they rule, but God gets his way.

And the fourth reason for worship lies in the watchful care of that same all-seeing God (vv. 18, 19), delivering his own from death and famine (another memory of war averted?). The closing verses offer the worship called for, in moving, heartfelt phrases.

For once, the individual complaining of his suffering, bemoaning his sins, is nowhere in sight. A fine sweep of objective reasoning sees in God's character, in his word in Nature and his work in history, sufficient incentive to lift the heart in thankful song. That is a healthy, mature response for Jew and Christian alike.

New Testament echoes: Hebrews 11:3; 1 Peter 3:12; Revelation 5:9; cf. Philippians 3:1; 4:4; 2 Peter 3:5.

34 THE OPTIMIST

For headings, see the Introduction, IV (iii); IV (iv); for "Wisdom," see II (vi); for acrostics, see III (iv) (b).

Despite the mechanical alphabetic framework of this psalm, the author has contrived to make his acrostic sound spontaneous and joyful. Curiously, the imperfections here (a letter omitted, a couplet added) are the same as those that occur in Psalm 25. Having himself experienced the deliverance of God (vv. 4, 6), the poet, with an outburst of praise, calls on others to share his thanksgiving and discover for themselves the goodness of God (vv. 3, 5, 8).

He encourages that discovery by emphasizing ten times the security and the reward of those who reverence God (vv. 7, 8, 9, 10, 12, 13, 16–17, 18, 19–20, 21–22; in v. 10 the Greek version has "wealthy men suffer want," in contrast with "those who seek the Lord"; the NEB interprets this as "unbelievers suffer want," because in later days only compromisers with alien rulers could hope to prosper; in v. 18 the NEB has "whose courage is broken...whose spirit is crushed"). This is plainly the main message of the poem: all goes well for the good; everything goes wrong for the evil.

The poet is, however, a teacher of "Wisdom"; the address "Come, O sons [pupils], listen to me..." (v. 11), the catch phrase "fear of the Lord" (vv. 9, 11), the question form (v. 12), and the proverb style (vv. 13–14), as much as the plain, practical advice and the seven or eight clear echoes of Proverbs, are all characteristic of the wisdom writers. If the thanksgiving of verses 1–11 implies a sharing congregation, the psalm will be of that later "wisdom" type whose religious insight and fervor had deepened. Likewise, the "guardian angel" concept usually betrays a later date (v. 7 — "The angel of the Lord encamps around those who fear him, and delivers them" — seems to combine Isa. 63:9 with 2 Kgs. 6:16–17). If the heading of the psalm is intended to refer to 1 Samuel 21:10–15, "Abimelech" must be a dynastic name or a mistake for "Achish"; more probably the whole incongruous reference is misplaced.

This is one of the most quoted psalms, even in the New Testament, and one of the most reassuring. Its optimism is founded on personal experience (vv. 4, 6), and it does acknowledge that "the good man's misfortunes may be many" (v. 19, NEB), though their consequences are invariably good (v. 18). All the same, it lacks the realism of other psalms. It needs the tempering honesty of the Book of Job and the frank warnings of Jesus that life's storms beat equally on the houses of the just and the unjust, while utter faithfulness to God may well lead to a cross.

New Testament echoes: John 19:36; Hebrews 6:5; 1 Peter 3:10–12; cf. Romans 14:19; 1 Corinthians 1:31; 2 Corinthians 3:18; 10:17; 2 Timothy 3:11, 12; Hebrews 12:14; James 1:26; 3; 1 Peter 2:3.

35 GOD OUR CHAMPION

For heading, see the Introduction, IV (iii); for theme, vindication, see II (ii).

All of the elements that mark psalms pleading for vindication are here present together, eloquently expressed. The poet calls God to do battle on his behalf (vv. 1-6), praying vehemently against his foes to the God who ever acts to defend the poor and defenseless against the slanders, accusations, and ensnaring of their adversaries (vv. 7–12).

In his own case such hostility is wholly unjustified in view of his former friendship and sympathy (vv. 13, 14), yet his enemies now gloat over his troubles with great cruelty (vv. 15–16). So again he pleads that God will intervene, promising to return thanks in the public worship (vv. 17, 18). Describing again his adversaries' conduct, the psalmist pleads still more boldly that God, who surely has seen it all, will bestir himself, wake up, and put the enemy in their place (vv. 19–26). Then will all the psalmist's friends rejoice, and he himself will ever tell how just and fair God is (vv. 27–28).

All this is clear. The details add fascination and, unfortunately, some difficulties.

The call to arms (vv. 1–3) mentions two sizes of shield, and a phrase which may mean "battle-ax" (literal Hebrew) or "bar the way" (NEB). The sevenfold prayer against pursuers ("Let them ...," vv. 4–8) shows no bitterness; it appeals to divine arbitration, the intervention of the Lord's "agent" (the guardian angel of later thought is here active in defense), and "poetic justice" (vv. 7, 8). Military tactics here change to poachers' slyness. The promised praise will involve the *whole* man and God's all-compassionate ways (vv. 9, 10).

False accusation and ingratitude make the psalmist's soul desolate (vv. 11, 12; the NEB changes this to "lying in wait to take my life"). For when his present enemies were sick, he grieved, fasted, and prayed for them as if for his own family (vv. 13, 14). "Prayed with head bowed on my bosom" may mean "humbly"; "my prayer turned back" ("returned to my mouth," Hebrew), equivalent to "was repeated"; "such as I could ask for myself"; or, as the NEB has it, "When my prayer came back unanswered, I walked with head bowed in grief...."

The poet's own stumbling is not explained, but enemies "crowd around" to gloat. Ingenuity, imagination, and very difficult Hebrew make a translator's playground of verses 15–21. People "smitten" (cripples, abject ones) or "smiting stealthily"; "impious mockers" or "clowns who enliven feasts for food"; "brutes who would mock hunchbacks"; sorcerers with evil eye and deceitful spells, leering in triumph and mouthing evilly and claiming to "see" things while circling their victim—all have been found in these lines. The hostile will not even give civil greeting ("Shalom!" — peace) to the inoffensive (v. 20). "Young lions" may mean avaricious collaborators with alien overlords; "my darling" (AV/KJV) means "my dear life." Patiently the suffering psalmist cries, "How long, O Lord?..."

But God, too, has "seen"; then let him bestir himself (v. 22). The plea reiterated in verses 22–26 had greater poignancy for a people desperate, at all costs, not to "lose face." Verse 27 asks the opposite of verse 26.

Attempts to find David, Jeremiah, another threatened king, and the orthodox confronting compromisers show that the poem's precise origin cannot be determined; it can only be said that it came from some loyal heart, hurt and afraid, calling upon God to champion his cause.

New Testament echoes: John 15:25; cf. 1 Thessalonians 5:3.

36 THE COUNTRY OF THE SEEING

For headings, see the Introduction, IV (i), IV (iii).
In this psalm the poet contrasts two things sharply but beautifully: on the one hand, the way and the man lacking all fear of God, and on the other, the country and the climate of the godly life. The ungodly lacks all vision except his own opinions, plotting in secret and in darkness (v. 4), speaking falsely, turning away from wisdom and all pursuit of good, and slipping into habits of evildoing, until by use and nature he no longer feels revulsion at anything he does.

All this follows, according to the poet's skillful analysis, because transgression like an evil demon whispers an oracle of darkness within his heart (where wiser men listen for the oracle of God). So deceived, blinded to moral truth, the ungodly man flatters himself that he can get away with anything (v. 2). The Hebrew of verses 1 and 2 is brief and uncertain, but "his transgression saith within *my* heart" (AV/KJV) is far less probable.

In contrast (and the brief, rugged style changes to lyric beauty), the whole landscape of life is different for the godly. *God's steadfast love* overarches all experience like the blue Mediterranean sky, glowing with silver by day, studded with stars by night. *God's faithfulness,* his unalterable loyalty to his own, fills the vault of heaven like the massed clouds. The *unvarying rightness of all God does* rises like a mountain range, the massive, immovable backdrop of human life, while God's *judgments* abide like the ever-moving sea, powerful, unfathomable, yet ever pressing forward his purpose in history like the slow, irresistible tide. Man and beast alike can depend on God (v. 6).

Sky, clouds, mountains, and sea form the background, while in the foreground of life are the grateful *shade* of God's enfolding care, the *feast* of good things that God provides, the refreshing *river* of divine delights, the springing *fountain* of life itself, ever renewed, and over all God's *daylight,* in which we perceive a diviner illumination. ("Thy house" may mean the sanctuary, and the "abundance" may mean the festal meals, but the psalmist appears to be thinking of all men, not Jews only.) The whole scene deliberately recalls Paradise; the word for "delights" echoes the name "Eden."

In such country, such climate, the godly live, bathed in God's sunlight while around is the darkness of "transgression." Too often the trampling "foot" of the proud and the violent "hand" of the powerful (v. 11) endanger godliness — hence the closing prayer that God's steadfast love may continue, and may triumph. The psalm ends with the dramatic exclamation that it shall be so: "There they lie, the evildoers..." (NEB).

The Christian name for that country of the seeing is the kingdom of God.

> *New Testament echoes:* John 8:12; Romans 3:18; cf. John 4:14; Romans 11:33; 12:9; 1 Peter 2:9; Revelation 22:1.

37 ON NOT GETTING "AGITATED"

For heading, see the Introduction, IV (iii); for "Wisdom," see II (vi); for acrostics, see III (iv) (b); for partial theme, vindication, see II (ii).

Despite its acrostic structure, this poem is vigorous, imaginative, and eloquent, a favorite with many readers. Addressed to men, not God, in a firmly didactic style by a venerable teacher (v. 25), it closely resembles Proverbs in part, and argues a case in the manner of the later wisdom writers.

The situation presupposed agrees with this form and date. It is a disappointing time. The faithful godly—the "meek," the "saints," the "poor and needy" (vv. 11, 28, 14, 16, 25) — are oppressed by the wicked, the enemies of the Lord (v. 20), who deny the right of the godly (v. 6); they prosper in their evil schemes (v. 7), plotting mischief, using violence, and corrupting justice (vv. 12, 14, 32; cf. Eccl. 5:8). All this they can do because they hold prominent positions with wealth and power (v. 35). The reins have fallen into evil hands; there is little hope of redress, for the sacred "heritage" of Israel has passed to enemies of right and truth (v. 18); it no longer "pays" to be faithful.

It is not surprising that the pious grew indignant and envious (literally "get not heated" for "fret not"), and fearful for cherished traditions and values. The simple, reiterated message of the teacher says four things. (i) The godly should cultivate assiduously their own convictions and lifestyle, resisting anger, trusting and delighting in the Lord, doing good, committing their way to the Lord and waiting in stillness before him for his time. (ii) The godly should recognize that the prosperity of the wicked, which they envy, is wholly insecure; they will fade like grass before the desert wind, be cut off, disappear, be destroyed by their own weapons, vanish like the smoke of sacrifice or (probably) of the furnace. God will frustrate their schemes, break their power.

(iii) The godly, meanwhile, may rely on God's help; he will grant their desires, act on their behalf, and vindicate their right. God "knows each day of the good man's life" (v. 18, NEB). The pious will have abundance even in famine (vv. 11, 19, 21—where the ability to be generous is the point); their children will be fed (v. 15). They will ever be upheld, even when they stumble (vv. 17, 24); sustained always by the wisdom of the law (vv. 30–31), they will finally win through to complete salvation (vv. 39–40).

(iv) As for the future, it is safe in God's hands. *Eight times* the vital promise is repeated: the godly shall possess, and dwell in, "the land," and the old word "inherit" is retained to recall the ancient promise. The future is with the pious meek and their descendants, their "posterity," for ever (mentioned six times); the wicked will be "cut off" (mentioned four times).

The godly, then, have nothing to get "heated" about, either in envy or in fear; if they wait for God's time, all will turn out well. When evil is triumphant, the teacher-poet would vindicate the ways of God with man not by argument but by simple assertion of faith in the justice of God, the permanence of whatever is good and true. His is no shallow optimism; he admits the destructive power of evil. His secret is *tenacity*, the supreme quality of the Jewish character.

Lacking an eternal horizon, the teacher gives to faith a far perspective by dwelling upon "posterity," where the deeper individualism of Christianity looks for vindication in personal immortality. At the same time, the Christian would—or should—think less of "abundance," "prosperity," and "the land," and more of the spiritual privileges and values he already possesses, *and envy no one.*

New Testament echoes: Matthew 5:5; cf. Matthew 6:33; 12:35; Luke 12:31; 2 Corinthians 4:9.

38 IN EXTREMIS

For headings, see the Introduction, IV (iii), II (iii).

In all of literature, few descriptions of physical, mental, and spiritual distress can rival this one for realism and poignancy. Physically the sufferer knows himself repulsive (v. 11), spent, panting, half-blind, and wholly helpless, "benumbed and broken" (literal Hebrew; cf. NEB), feeling already the chill of death (v. 8), "no part of my body unscarred" (v. 3, NEB), feverish, festering, on the verge of exhaustion (v. 17—yet not bedridden, as v. 6 shows; advanced leprosy may be indicated; cf. Isa. 53:3, 4).

Suffering being commonly "explained" by sin, repulsion was reinforced by condemnation. Here is Job *without* friends, alienated, avoided. "Those who wish me dead defame me" (v. 12, NEB). His enemies are "lively and strong" (RV, 1881 ed.; "living mighty," Hebrew), undeservedly hostile, and possibly using black art against him (vv. 19, 20; sorcerer's language is used in v. 12 in the Hebrew: "speak destruction," "meditate devices"). But he remains silent, appealing only to God (vv. 13–15) because he admits himself to be a sinner. His confession is candid, without excuse (v. 18); the flood that overwhelms him, the burden that crushes him, is his own iniquity (v. 4); the arrows that pierce and the hand heavy upon him are God's, and deserved (v. 2).

This is the poet's deepest bitterness and fear. He begs *not* that he remain unchastened but that he be chastened without anger, though he deserves that, too. And the grounds of his plea are his agony, his accepting patience, his penitence and prayer; now, at any rate, he purposes well (v. 20). His one hope is God—"my salvation" (v. 22). But no answer is recorded.

The title, "for the memorial offering," is usually linked with Leviticus 2:2, 9 and 24:7, and the psalm understood as part of a thanksgiving ritual, with incense. But it seems entirely inappropriate for such use. The original meaning of the title, later misunderstood, could have been "to put God in remembrance" of a desperate case. So intensely painful a poem could hardly be communal.

For all that, the psalm is highly wrought artistically; it is preserved now in Israel's hymnbook, and became part of Jewish liturgy. Isaiah 1:5, 6 and Lamentations represent the nation's condition as a guilty sickness, though not with such personal pathos. All too often Israel could have borrowed the individual sufferer's words to express the community's penitence and anguish—as many Christians still do on Ash Wednesday. The psalmist, whoever he might have been, speaks for humanity so long as humanity shall suffer, and shall sin.

New Testament echo: cf. Luke 23:49.

39 ''LORD, LET ME BE!''

For headings, see the Introduction, IV (i), IV (iii); for Selah, see IV (ii).
This sad poem almost defies interpretation. Some suppose that a

very sick man has previously sinned greatly with wild and bitter speech, in ways unspecified, and now resolves to be silent. Others think that verses 4–6 contain the questionings, irreverent and rebellious, hitherto repressed, now blurted out. Still others treat the psalm as wholly submissive and penitential, stressing verses 1 and 8.

It is simplest to recognize here a prayer of the dying. Realizing that his sickness is "terminal," the sufferer has struggled to suppress resentment and panic, lest he blaspheme, but to no avail (cf. Job 1:22; 2:10; contrast Jer. 15:18; 20:7). Increasing anguish and fever made his spirit burn with indignation and fear, so that he had to find relief in speech. He asks, in effect, "How long, Lord, before the end?" He describes in varied metaphors of smallness and evanescence — handbreadths, vanity, shadows, dream images, breath, vapor — the brevity of life and its futility at the end, when all that a man has striven for is left for others to squander.

But he submits, and waits for God's time (v. 7), asking to be forgiven and to be spared the scorn of fools who, by offering false sympathy or by gloating, may embitter the end. He repeats his submission (v. 9). And then he prays that God's "stroke" may be moderated; so severe can it be, sometimes, as to destroy, before death, all that is dear to a man (his senses? — or "all his beauty," a suggested emendation). The poet pleads for divine sympathy and for the protection afforded in the East to every passing traveler, for he is not only a "resident alien" in the land to whom Jewish law gave rights but also God's "passing guest" (see 1 Chron. 29:15). In deep sadness he begs that God will turn away his frowning face and let him smile a little before he goes hence to where there is no more *life,* but only darkness, shadows, and silence.

If we ask how such a poem came to be in the hymnbook, the answer must be that our own hymnbooks contain funeral hymns — but happier ones. A great deal of the difference between Judaism and Christianity lies in the contrast between this melancholy threnody and the verse by Saint Francis:

> And thou, most kind and gentle death,
> Waiting to hush our latest breath,
>   O praise him, hallelujah!
>
> Thou leadest home the child of God,
> And Christ our Lord the way has trod:
>   O praise him, *hallelujah!*

New Testament echoes: Matthew 6:19–20; Luke 12:33; Hebrews 11:13; James 4:14; 1 Peter 2:11; cf. Luke 12:20, 21.

40 ENIGMA VARIATIONS

For headings, see the Introduction, IV (i), IV (iii); for part-theme, vindication, see II (ii).

Here is an insoluble enigma! Rescued from the pit and set safely, joyfully on his way in verses 1–3, the psalmist slithers back into it by verses 11 and 17, having gotten involved in personal combat on the way. If the opening verses constitute an exultant "new song," inspired by a memorable experience of divine deliverance, the closing verses (13–17) are *either* a secondhand quotation, slightly altered, of Psalm 70 in Book II, *or* lines so detachable in meaning and manner from the great experience (not to mention so contradictory of it) that they became a separate psalm.

The miry pit, whether underground cistern (cf. Jer. 38:6–13), hunter's snare, road washout, or disused well, was a common hazard. Since mud hampers, stains, sticks, and slays, the pit provides an apt metaphor for adversity, shame, or sin (the "pit of Sheol," implying fatal sickness, is not elsewhere "muddy" or escaped by rock and pathway). The peril here is not specified; the long wait for a passerby ("I waited, waited for the Lord," NEB, does not imply patience; cf. Jer. 38:6), the calling-out, and the "inclining" of the rescuer to listen are vividly conveyed, along with the restoration to a firm footpath and the grateful song as the journey is resumed.

The witnesses of the poet's changed circumstance (whatever it was) share his wonder (v. 3). How very remarkable are all such deliverances wrought by God, too numerous to tell, and how useless, in comparison, is idolatry! (vv. 4, 5). As for thanksgiving, all four popular types of sacrifice are rejected in a strong repudiation of the whole sacrificial system; instead, true devotion lies in the ear "perfected" to listen to God; in the answer of a submissive servant, "Here am I"; and in acceptance of the recorded law, "prescribed *for* me" (vv. 7, 8; translation here varies with translators). But if sacrifice has not been offered, certainly grateful testimony has not been withheld (said three times), and neither will God "withhold" mercy and lovingkindness all the remaining way (vv. 9–11).

This is a truly warm and grateful act of worship, expressing considerable insight into "What doth the Lord require of thee?" (Mic. 6:6–8; cf. Ps. 51:16, 17). So Christ, our fellow traveler, plays "good Samaritan" to all who founder on the road of life, kindling endless, immeasurable gratitude.

Verse 12 seems unrelated to what goes before or what comes after it, a mere connecting link—but a very odd one.

Verses 13–17 (equivalent to Psalm 70 plus "Be pleased..." and a varying line in v. 17) are an urgent cry (vv. 13, 17) for help against enemies. A threefold imprecation — "Let them come to shame," "Let them through apostasy come to dishonour" ("turn back" is usually "to idols"), and "Let them be desolated" (paraphrase)— is followed by a twofold prayer for others and a plaintive plea for the poet himself. The one lovely, comforting line, "the Lord takes thought for me," becomes in the second version (Psalm 70) "hasten to me, O God."

Presumably, if one has enemies, it is better to pray against them than to curse them. Better still to pray for them—and always in any dispute, to pray for ourselves.

New Testament echoes: Hebrews 10:5–9 (following the *Greek* version); 1 Peter 5:7; cf. Romans 7:22; 2 Corinthians 3:3.

41 ''YOU PROMISED, LORD!''

For headings, see the Introduction IV (i), IV (iii).

With an Old Testament "beatitude," verses 1–3 state the Orthodox Jewish doctrine concerning the divine reward of almsgiving. "Concern" for the "helpless" had a very high place in Judaist ethics; a seventh promise — divine forgiveness — was later added to the six promises listed here. It is much debated whether the Hebrew in verse 3, "Thou *changest* all his bed," can fairly be translated, for that word and that age, "He nurses him...turns his bed when he is ill" (NEB).

Yet, as a man who is rich and conscious of having lived in good faith (v. 12), the psalmist's own experience has been different. He was ill. He prayed for healing and confessed his sin, yet his enemies treated him abominably (vv. 5–8; sharply described, they are "alert to gather bad news" and spread it, v. 6, NEB; the original terms of vv. 7, 8 suggest a spell cast upon him). Even his trusted friend, with whom he had exchanged the pledge implied in hospitality, had dealt treacherously with him, like a backward-kicking ox or ass lashing out suddenly at its master. Why his enemies or his friend should so grasp malicious opportunity is not explained; if the poet is a prominent, wealthy man, perhaps the king himself, envy and ambition could delight in his illness.

That would better explain, too, the psalmist's prayer that he might be healed to "pay them out" (v. 10, NEB) — that is, to re-establish his authority. Otherwise that odd request may be called unseemly, but human. Verse 11 in the NEB is the *future* consequence of this prayer; in the RSV it is a present assurance, along with verse 12.

The doxology, verse 13, is not part of the psalm but a supplied closure for Book I, the earliest collection of Hebrew psalms (see the Introduction, IV [v]).

Our author finds he has not made friends for himself by means of wealth, "the unrighteous mammon" (Luke 16:9). There is no guarantee that doing good will be well received. But the poet's final insight, that doing good is its own reward and "upheld" by God, is the ultimate, and satisfying, incentive.

New Testament echoes: John 13:18; Mark 14:18; cf. Matthew 5:7; Acts 20:35.

BOOK II
PSALMS 42–72

42–43 "CAST DOWN, BUT NOT DESTROYED"

For headings, see the Introduction, IV (i), IV (ii), IV (iii).
Whether these two psalms were originally one (as shared theme, style, and refrain suggest, and some ancient Hebrew manuscripts and modern translations show) or two (as shown by ancient Greek and other versions, followed by the modern Hebrew Old Testament) cannot now be decided. Some very close relationship is obvious.

The first stanza ("paragraph") of the poem (vv. 1–4) begins with a beautiful comparison of the soul's thirst for God with a fallow deer in desert-drought panting for water (cf. Joel 1:20). It passes to the poet's confession of intense sorrow at his absence from God and his admission that others can see his despondency and taunt him— "Where is your God?" His desolation is further deepened as he muses upon past joys in thronging festivals in God's house. The psalmist's phrase here is ancient, and vague: "the tent of the glorious one." If "I...led them in procession" (v. 4) is right, the author was probably a priest or a Levite (the NEB has "I marched in the ranks of the great").

The poet asks when he may share this again. His evidently enforced absence and consequent despondency lead to the self-questioning refrain (v. 5) and the assertion that the experience will pass; he will again praise God, his "help" and "his" God. (The Hebrew, "for the help of *his* countenance" or "his countenance is salvation," means God "will look with favor upon him"; the Greek and other versions have "the health of *my* countenance," presumably meaning "he makes me smile again." Modern translations give just the essential meaning, "my help.")

The second stanza (v. 6, "My soul...," to v. 10) resumes the poet's despondency, adding further remembrance, this time of God himself. He speaks now from the distant upper reaches of the Jordan, beneath the peaks of Mount Hermon (literally "the Hermons") and unknown Mizar. In that area of rushing streams, where melting snows create madly tumbling cataracts that echo to each other, filling the ravines with thunder, he thinks how storm and flood have indeed overwhelmed him. The "men" are now "enemies" who taunt him, wounding him deeply; their oppression occasions the deepest grief, the mood and aspect of one actually in mourning. Sharper still is the fear that though he remembers God, yet God has forgotten him (v. 9). (Verse 8 in Hebrew could be *present,* an assurance the author clings to, as the RSV and NEB have it; or *future,* a promise he treasures, as the RV, 1881 ed., has it; or, more probably, *past:* "The Lord used to command...," "his song used to be with me..." — a memory that saddens, prompting "Why hast thou forgotten me?")

The location and the enemies strongly suggest that the poet cannot attend his accustomed shrine because he is being carried captive, northeastward, after (possibly) Assyrian invasion of northern Israel or Babylonian invasion of Judah. The repeated refrain (v. 11) has, if anything, a deeper sadness now.

The third stanza (43:1–4) pleads for defense against a people now called "ungodly" (literally "unloved," outside the divine covenant, Gentiles). There is still fear of having been himself "cast off" (from Israel), still the air of mourning, but on the whole his tone is lighter, his faith firmer. God is still his God, his refuge; the poet's yearning takes form in definite and moving petition, that God would send his "guides," Light and Truth, to lead him back to Zion ("thy holy hill"), to the altar, and to God, who is his joy. The promise of praise and melody breaks like sunshine into the pervading gloom of the poem.

Strange, then, to meet the refrain again (43:5), unchanged, as though the sunshine were temporary. Curious, too, to note that the vague customary shrine has become Zion's hill and altar. The circumstances behind the poem are beyond recovery, but the unity-with-distinctiveness of Psalms 42–43 and some details *might* be explained by supposing the following: (i) that an early poet of the northern kingdom recorded his deep anguish at being carried into exile, away from home and sanctuary, and his struggle to hold on to faith and hope amid alien foes; (ii) that when later this sad poem was preserved in the treasury of national song, some later poet, with *Judah's* exile in mind, sought to relieve its profound melancholy with a "supplement," deliberately reproducing its style, pattern, and refrain but adjusting its final mood for congregational use within the temple.

It is possible to read that "brave refrain" the first time wistfully, the second despondently, the third triumphantly — but that, too, is speculation. One certainty amid much guessing is that both psalms are addressed, quite exceptionally, by the poet to himself. Such self-communing, self-examination, and self-understanding can often hold on to memory, faith, and hope where much clever argument only deepens perplexity.

New Testament echoes: cf. Mark 14:34; John 7:37; 12:27.

44 "I PROTEST!"

For headings, see the Introduction, IV (i), IV (ii), IV (iii); for Selah, see IV (ii).

Songs of social protest are familiar, but submissiveness and trust make songs of religious protest rare. This one is vigorous, said to be irreverent, a rebuke to the Almighty, impiously sarcastic; it is at any rate too clear to explain away.

Reciting the oral tradition, enjoined in the law, concerning Israel's settlement in Canaan (vv. 1–3), the poet stresses God's undoubted, and unaided, activity *then* ("set free," v. 2, means "caused to spread freely"; "the light of God's countenance" signifies his favor). The psalmist asserts his own generation's reliance on that tradition of faith (vv. 4–8). They know that any victories won by (the house of) Jacob are God's ordaining, that by divine strength alone the people have, like wild oxen, butted and trampled their enemies (v. 5; cf. Deut. 33:17; see the Introduction, III (ii), "the horn"). Here, the alternation of singular and plural pronouns ("I" with "our") well expresses the identification of some leader (warrior? king?) with the people as a whole.

Yet, in spite of the past and the promises, God has let Israel down (vv. 9–16), and badly. He has not accompanied the army; he has humiliated Israel before a plundering foe. Like a faithless shepherd, he has sold the sheep committed to his care for butchering, and at a contemptuous price ("next to nothing," NEB). All Jewish pride of "face" lies in the *eight* words used to describe the humiliation and scorn by which "the enemy takes his revenge" (v. 16, NEB).

For all this, the nation's conscience is clear. This is not divine punishment — not even fair dealing (vv. 17–22). For Israel has not forsaken God, that she should be "crushed as the sea-serpent was crushed" (v. 19, NEB; "the place of jackals," RSV, may mean the desert, which the devastated land now resembles, but mythological

overtones concerning the "dragon" or "monster of the abyss" conquered at creation may attend the language used—see the Introduction, II [iv]; "deep darkness" is literally "shadow of death"). The
people have remained faithful to God, as God well knows. Indeed,
their faithfulness has cost them dearly (v. 22), possibly by forbidding
alliances that could strengthen them.

"Why?" the poet demands, *why* hide, forget, reduce the nation
to mourners (vv. 24, 25)? "Rouse thyself! Why sleepest thou?... Rise
up..." (the scathing taunt that Elijah hurled at the prophets of Baal:
"Perhaps your God is fast asleep!"—1 Kgs. 18:27).

Only the last words redeem the protest from ungoverned
anger. No clear circumstances emerge; the danger of Jehoshaphat
(2 Chron. 20), the panic of Hezekiah at Assyrian invasion and his
boasting after his genuine reforms (2 Kgs. 18, 19), even the suffering
of the faithful Maccabeans—all illustrate the bewilderment of good
men who feel abandoned.

Beneath the daring and the indignation is a fine assumption,
that God *should be* consistently on the side of right. The psalm
faithfully represents one mood of religion: a moral protest at apparent divine inactivity. All the same, on our side of Calvary the protest
sounds superficial, immature. So often the theology in which we (like
the psalmist) were brought up has to be deepened by experience,
especially of the strength of evil and of "the long, long days of God."

New Testament echoes: Romans 8:36; cf. Romans 2:17.

45 ROYAL WEDDING

For headings, see the Introduction, IV (i), IV (ii), IV (iii); for "royal"
psalms, see II (iv).

A foreign princess (vv. 10, 12) is marrying Israel's king. The court
poet duly obliges with his expected eulogy and blessing, but offers it
as an inspired oracle and prophecy, implying divine authority (vv. 1,
16–17).

The king's beauty, wisdom, and martial skill are evidence of
God's blessing upon him. At one point Eastern flattery appears to
address the king himself as divine (v. 6); "Elohim" (God) is used of
"mighty ones," "gods" (Ps. 82:6), and of the Messiah (Isa. 9:8; for
the king as "son of God," see the Introduction, II [iv]). But the
NEB (and others) understand this as "your throne is like God's
throne, eternal." An anointing with oriental fragrances, amid music
and the attendant harem and in the presence of the new queen
adorned in "cloth-of-gold, richly embroidered," prepares the king

for an event whose issue shall establish his dynasty and his fame for all time (vv. 2–9; the "ivory palaces" *might* be "ivory harps," but see 1 Kgs. 22:39; the "ladies of honor" are literally "treasures," "jewels"—the royal harem; Ophir was probably in Arabia).

The bride is then addressed, urged to forget her own people, to submit to her new Lord ("when the king desires your beauty," NEB). She is promised, in return, honor and "all kinds of wealth." The poet calls the bride "daughter" in verse 10, suggesting that he is older; in verse 12 the RSV interprets "daughter" as "people" of (wealthy) Tyre, but the NEB has "daughter of Tyre" (as does the Hebrew), taking the whole sentence differently. (The only royal marriage with a princess of Tyre known in scripture is that of Ahab to Jezebel, recorded in 1 Kgs. 16:31; numerous other marriages of Israelite kings to foreign princesses have been suggested.)

The bridal procession is then impressively described (vv. 12–15) as it moves from the inner chamber into the presence of the king. The final promises (vv. 16–17, spoken to the king) are typically flattering.

The psalm may be ancient but adapted for later use, since a few "late" words occur and in places its text is uncertain. In a theocratic state the king's marriage was sufficiently charged with religious implications to explain the preservation of the poem. In any case, it would be a poor hymnbook that contained no wedding hymns — and it was a widespread custom to treat every couple as "king and queen" upon their wedding day.

But Jewish thought (e.g., in the Talmud) saw in some phrases of the psalm intimations of the glory of the Messiah, in spite of the more sexual references. Christian apologetics quickly accepted this offered "scriptural testimony" to Jesus, even accepting the notion of Christ's "marriage" to his "bride" the church. Only through that double adjustment of its original meaning has the psalm any significance for Christians.

New Testament echoes: Ephesians 5:25–32; Hebrews 1:8, 9 (based upon the Greek version); cf. Mark 2:19; John 3:29; Revelation 21:2; 22:17.

46 GOD IS WITH US

For headings, see the Introduction, IV (i), IV (iii); for Selah, see IV (ii); on mythology, see II (ii), II (iv).

The implications of this great psalm are undoubtedly far-reaching. Ritually, its constant use on festal occasions made the truth of the presence of God in Jerusalem "felt" with great power; whether it formed part of the annual "re-enthronement" ceremonies of the new year (see the Introduction, II [iv]) is another question. The refrain, probably sung *three* times (at *Selah,* after v. 3, and at vv. 7, 11) and possibly by the choir, affirms the presence of the Lord of "hosts" (originally "the stars," later "Israel's armies"), *the God of might,* and of "the God of Jacob" (who out of failure made good), *the God of mercy,* in Jerusalem, the holy city.

Prophetically (as dealing with "final things," "eschatology"), it is surprising how many ideas in the psalm come to have a place in later apocalyptic thinking: the destruction of the earth, as soaked in evil; the river out of Jerusalem (Isa. 33:13–24; Ezek. 47); the coming "golden age" of universal peace. But again, whether the whole psalm is eschatological and very late is another question. And the same must be said of attempts to find in it only mythological ideas: the conflict of God, at creation, with the primeval monster (Tiamat), here the raging sea; the triumph of God and the emergence of order, establishing the earth, so that even if it sway again in repetition of the struggle, we will not fear. Such ideas are discoverable in the psalm, but they hardly constitute its message.

Some recent emergency safely passed through divine intervention, ending the military danger (vv. 6, 8–9), occasioned the poet's profound reflection. The tempestuous sea, shaking earth, raging nations, shuddering kingdoms, and "melting" earth (nations in opposition) are then all metaphors for war's wide upheaval. The river which "gladdens" may be the inner resources of spirit by which little Judah can resist a mightier foe, but rivers were also *barriers* to ancient armies, and in Jerusalem's high, waterless situation, the water supply was a military problem. God took care of that, too—by rain?

The marvelous deliverance which God has wrought should teach Judah henceforth to banish fear; to "let be" (v. 10), to leave all in God's hands, to "learn that I am God" (NEB). So the nation will learn also to await the divine voice (v. 6) that will again intervene to end all conflict, destroy all weapons of war (v. 9).

Some details recall Hezekiah's deliverance from Sennacherib (2 Kgs. 18, 19), a massive invasion miraculously turned back: language resembling Isaiah's account (Isa. 37); a reference to divine help "at daybreak" in the NEB (cf. Isa. 37:36); the promise of a river (cf. Isa. 33:21, but this is possibly a reference to Hezekiah's aqueduct; see 2 Kgs. 20:20). Others think that Jehoshaphat's deliverance (2 Chron. 20) is the background.

The main purpose is unaffected. It lies in the opening and closing words: God is our refuge in all earthshaking events, and he is "with us," "in the midst," "letting himself be found exceedingly" (the almost literal meaning of v. 1). That is the central truth of Judaism and Christianity alike—"Immanuel," God with us.

New Testament echoes: Revelation 22:1, 2; cf. Matthew 1:23; Romans 8:31.

47 "GOD HAS GONE UP WITH A SHOUT"

For headings, see the Introduction, IV (i), IV (iii); for Selah, see IV (ii); for "enthronement" theme, see II (iv).

This is a poem for Judaism's Ascension Day. The contents (vv. 5–8) make it clear, even if the Jewish Talmud did not confirm it, that this psalm had a special place in the New Year Feast of Tabernacles. It celebrates, with great blasts upon the ram's horn (v. 5), the re-enthronement of the God of Israel as king of the whole earth. Verse 6 reminds us of Handel's "Hallelujah Chorus," and we should probably imagine various voices answering one another in this psalm, at some especially jubilant phase in the ritual of the festival. Handclapping (v. 1) originally beat out the rhythm for the sacred dance; later, primitive cymbals were used. "Terrible" (v. 2) simply means "to be feared," "awesome." The "pride" of Jacob is the promised land; "psalm" ("maskil," v. 7) is *here* really a skillful, complex poem. Verse 8—in paraphrase, "God takes his seat"—probably marks the ritual's climax.

The RSV makes verses 3 and 4 look back to Israel's settlement in Canaan; the NEB makes verse 3 present tense ("He lays the nations prostrate..."), as though it were a general truth, and verse 4 look back; still others make these lines into promises. The point of the whole psalm is that God did ordain a land and a people; he does, as king, continue to prosper them and love them. Now, enthroned once more, he will in his own time, as king of all the earth, bring the kings ("shields" means "rulers," "princes") of all nations beneath his throne, and the peoples of all lands to join with "the people of the God of Abraham" (with whom God's redemptive work began). Thus will Israel's "heritage" be extended (see Zech. 14:16–19).

In the excitement and exultation of the festival, this far-off future was felt as present, the ultimate purposes of God embraced as already realized. That is why the psalm is difficult to translate precisely. Small wonder that the church adopted the psalm for its own Ascension Day!

New Testament echoes: Romans 4:11, 12; 1 Corinthians 14:15 (based on the Greek version of v. 7); cf. 1 Peter 1:24; Revelation 19:6.

48 JERUSALEM THE GOLDEN

For headings, see the Introduction, IV (i), IV (iii); for Selah, see IV (ii).
This smooth poem closely resembles Psalm 46 in historical background and in the ritual and prophetic elements discoverable within it. Thus verses 12–14 may be read not as an invitation to pilgrim-tourists to explore but as a bidding to form a solemn procession of thanksgiving (or consecration). This would presuppose some festal occasion of worship. The testimony in verse 8, to having "seen" what others have previously told of, and the precise translation of verse 9 — "we re-enact the story of thy true love within thy temple" (NEB) — then suggest a ritual presentation of the truth that God in the midst of Jerusalem protects her. This could involve acting out a notable experience of deliverance, and the psalm would have a prominent place within it or following it.

Prophetic ("eschatological") foreshadowings may be found in the assertion that Jerusalem is the joy of the *whole earth,* established for ever, and that God is praised to the ends of the earth; in the assembling of kings against Jerusalem, and their subsequent panic; and in the limitless horizons of verse 14. A sacred mountain in the far north (v. 2; cf. Isa. 14:13) reappears in the apocryphal Book of Enoch as the place where the eternal King will sit when he comes down to visit the earth with goodness. The woman in travail (v. 6) is a constant feature of futurist prophecies (Mic. 4:10; Isa. 66:7; and the New Testament). It is, however, at least as likely that later apocalyptic thought would clothe itself in phrases already familiar as that the psalm itself must be "eschatologically" understood.

For the immediate impression of the psalm is convincing enough. The presence of God at once sanctifies, beautifies, and protects the holy city now, even as a reputed "mountain in the north" was sanctified and protected as a Phoenician, and Assyrian, "Olympus" of the gods. Jerusalem is in every sense above all rivals. The divine care of the city was powerfully demonstrated in the (recent?) miraculous deliverance from the assembled armies of the several conquered nations ruled by Sennacherib. For this, God is "exceedingly worthy" (literal Hebrew) to be praised (vv. 1, 4–8 recall Isa. 37 and Isaiah's doctrine of the inviolability of Jerusalem, 31:5; 37:33–35). Compare verse 12 with Isaiah 33:18; verse 7 refers to the east (storm) wind that could destroy even the larger ships built for the voyage to Phoenicia's colony at Tarshish in Spain; verse 10 suggests that God "lives up to his name"; in verse 11 "daughters of Judah" are surrounding villages.

Let the congregation hold this deliverance before their minds, perhaps by dramatically representing it, and then, imitating the freed inhabitants at the time, let them perambulate the circumference of the city, marveling at its undamaged towers, ramparts, and palaces. And let them see that the story never dies, for this God will be Israel's protecting high tower *for ever.*

So a famous victory has exalted Jewish pride in the delivered city, and written itself into Israel's worship as a supreme example of divine care, as in darker days of foreign overrule it fed prophetic hopes of similar exaltation over the whole earth in years to come.

Christians calmly transferred all this to themselves by the simple device of calling the church "Zion," "the City of God"—and using the psalm on Whitsunday, the church's birthday.

New Testament echoes: Matthew 5:35; cf. John 16:21; 1 Thessalonians 5:3; Revelation 21.

49 INTIMATIONS OF MORTALITY

For headings, see the Introduction, IV (i), IV (iii); for Selah, see IV (ii); on "wisdom," see II (vi).

"Death shall be their shepherd;...Sheol shall be their home" (v. 14) is the epitaph of this wisdom teacher for all who live in wealth and pomp, seeking to perpetuate their names in property (v. 11); they are overconfident, proud, self-congratulating, and flattered (vv. 13, 6, 18), yet have no understanding of the real meaning of life (v. 20; so the Hebrew has it; the RSV and the NEB repeat v. 12).

This psalmist is not envious of the wealthy, does not condemn riches, and is not perplexed by his own suffering in contrast with the prosperity of the wicked. But he is tempted to fear (vv. 5, 14) the influence and persecution of those who by compromise and lack of scruple continue to grow wealthy in "evil times" (v. 5, NEB). His "universal truth" ("riddle," parable, "moral of the story," NEB; one of several expressions that reveal the wisdom-school background) is that "man cannot abide in his pomp, he is like the beasts that perish" (the refrain of vv. 12, 20; cf. Eccl. 3:19). Neither wealth nor wisdom can purchase immunity from death (vv. 7–9): wealth cannot ransom either oneself or one's brother to live for ever (the text is ambiguous), and "even the wise die" (v. 10).

"Murmuring in spirit" (literal Hebrew) and "music" in verses 3–4 may imply divine inspiration—an "oracle" (cf. 2 Kgs. 3:15). The point is that since all die, none deserves to be feared. Death is the shepherd-king of the underworld whom none escape. This is clear, but there are uncertainties: the text is in some disorder and translation falters. "Their inward thought" (v. 11, Hebrew) should be "their graves" (as the Greek and Syriac versions and the Jewish Talmud have it). The Hebrew of verse 14 is almost unintelligible: we must beware of assuming that "the upright shall have dominion over them in the morning" (RSV margin) refers to the *resurrection morning*, a post-Easter phrase; the meaning here is probably irrecoverable.

Verse 15 is challenging, whether it is "an early announcement of belief in salvation beyond the grave" (J. H. Eaton), belief in the continuance of Israel, a marginal note by a later copyist, or (most probably) simply an assertion that God can arrest, overrule, or hold back Sheol, delivering from violent, premature death (in persecution?) those over whom he sets his protecting hand. Memories of Enoch, whom God "took" (Gen. 5:24), may shape the final words of verse 15. Though on verses 18–19, too, translators vary, the general meaning is not in doubt.

The emphasis upon the universal finality of death reflects here again the intense realism of Jewish thought, so often unrelieved by certainty of divine sonship or hope of resurrection; to this extent it anticipates the emphasis of some modern existentialists. To it, John Donne replies for Christians,

> Death be not proud, though some have called thee
> Mighty and dreadful, for thou art not so....
> One short sleep past, we wake eternally
> And death shall be no more; *death, thou shalt die.*

The main thrust of the poem is repeated by Jesus, pictorially, in the parable of the rich man and Lazarus.

New Testament echoes: Luke 12:19, 20; 16:19–20; 1 Timothy 6:7; cf. 1 Timothy 6:17.

50 THE DIVINE ASSIZE

For heading, see the Introduction, IV (iii); for Selah, see IV (ii); on God and Nature, see II (v).

The closing verse of this psalm perfectly recapitulates its message, and its clear twofold structure plainly applies that message, first to those who think God mainly requires animal sacrifices (vv. 7–15) and then to those who think God mainly requires knowledge of his law (vv. 16–21). True religion is neither ritualism nor legalism; it is a thankful heart calling upon God in trouble, vowing obedience, and faithfully keeping its vows (vv. 14, 15, 23).

This message and application are set within a court scene to which all the earth is invited to hear God's arraignment of his own covenant people. Earth is "summoned," God is judge, the heavens "testify" to God's righteousness, and God "testifies" against Israel. Heaven and earth are called as "assessors" (v. 4), and God "lays charge" against the wicked (v. 21; cf. Mic. 6:1, 2). The description of God's "coming into court" is based on traditional accounts of divine appearances (Exod. 19:16–19)—a magnificent preparation for God's indictment.

The basis of Israel's covenant relationship was sacrifice (v. 5; cf. Exod. 24:3–6), and law (Exod. 24:7–8). According to the psalmist, the sacrifices have been maintained (v. 8), but with a wholly wrong attitude of mind. Worshipers have supposed that their offerings have conferred some benefit upon God, as though he were hungry and needed to be fed (vv. 12, 13), as though *he* ought to be grateful to *them*! In truth, God owns all (vv. 9–11; following the Hebrew, the NEB has "cattle in thousands. . . . I know every bird on those hills. . . ."); man's worship, so far from leaving God in man's debt, only acknowledges man's gratitude, dependence, and obligation to serve and glorify God (vv. 12–15).

Similarly, the law which Israel accepted under the covenant was remembered, even recited (perhaps in some special service of covenant renewal), but again with a wholly wrong attitude of mind. For the heart remained undisciplined ("you . . . turn your back when I am speaking," NEB), and the law unfulfilled. Three examples are offered out of the "Ten Words" (commandments) of the covenant (Exod. 20): Israel habitually breaks those relating to stealing, adultery, and bearing false witness. In each example something worse than the bare disobedience is mentioned: they *defend* dishonesty; they *condone* adultery (by accepting adulterers into their social circle); they slander even their own natural *brethren*, despising all family loyalty (vv. 18–20; cf. Exod. 20:14–16).

Because in the face of such behavior God has so far been silent, worshipers have concluded that God, like themselves, has valued mere lip-service. This, the grossest of all mistakes in religion — imagining that God is man magnified, forgetting what God is really like—*must* be put right, lest God's judgments correct man's wrong opinions with finality (vv. 21, 22; v. 21 may be an ironic question: "Do you think? . . . Do you imagine? . . ." (literal Hebrew); or as the NEB has it, "Shall I keep silence? . . . You thought that I was . . .").

The danger of complacent formalism still besets the ritualist in religion, as the danger of intellectual hypocrisy — orthodox belief without loving obedience — besets the evangelical. To both, this forthright poet still speaks with undiminished clarity and power.

New Testament echoes: Acts 17:25; Romans 1:32; 2:21–22; cf. Romans 12:1; Hebrews 13:15.

51 GOSPEL IN POETRY

For headings, see the Introduction, IV (i), IV (iii), IV (iv).

An expression of penitence unparalleled even in Christianity, *the* religion of redemption, this psalm has voiced the repentance of countless generations. It analyzes the evangelical experience of conviction, penitence, forgiveness, and renewal so clearly that it is difficult not to read back into its phrases (e.g., "thy holy Spirit") the fuller meanings of Christian theology. The nearest New Testament parallel is very brief: "God, be merciful to me, a sinner."

Some serious sin is painfully regretted and confessed as a *transgression* by the will (rebelliousness), an *iniquity* of inclination (a distortion, twistedness), and a *sinful* consequence (a missing of the appointed mark), as something not external or accidental but innate (v. 5; this does not confess illegitimacy, make excuse, or offer a theory of the origin of sin; it expresses sinfulness of nature, something inward that answers to the outward temptation, in the only way that Hebrew can; cf. Ps. 58:3).

Emotionally repelled and even physically "shattered" (v. 8), the poet feels unclean (vv. 2, 7, 10), joyless (v. 12), intellectually astray, needing integrity and wisdom to avoid such blunders (v. 6; the NEB takes this as a comment on v. 5). He feels silenced (vv. 14, 15), helpless (v. 16; God was not to be so easily propitiated or "pleased"; see Num. 15:27–31), and afraid of repeated falling (v. 12). Most of all, he feels alienated from God, against whose just will and majesty the sin has been directly aimed, so that God is "proved right" (NEB) when he condemns (vv. 11, 4).

The salvation sought is likewise manifold. It involves several things: (i) the cancellation of the charge against conscience (vv. 1, 9; "Blot out" — that is, "erase the record," "annul the debt"); (ii) inward cleansing (v. 2; "wash thoroughly" was used of kneading soiled clothes at the riverside or burnishing metal — a brave prayer, that God would trample the stain from the fibers of personality and the fabric of life, a *process*, not, like forgiveness, an *act*; (iii) ritual purification, to allow access to God's presence (v. 7 pleads ritually what v. 11 asks spiritually; hyssop was a wild herb closely associated with cleansing rites, like those for lepers — Num. 19:6; see Exod. 12:22—and for leprosy, as in Lev. 14:4); (iv) the mind enlightened (v.

6), the imagination cleansed (v. 10), inward personality renewed (v. 10), the will upheld and strengthened (v. 12) by a right, holy, and willing spirit, joy and happiness restored (vv. 8, 12) — in short, "newness of life"; (v) restored testimony, praise, and usefulness (vv. 13–15).

And the ground of such a plea is not the poet's earnestness in repenting or promises of an amended life or, certainly, any ritual performance or payment (v. 16). It is *only* God's own lovingkindness and multitude of tender mercies answering a broken and contrite heart (v. 17, NEB: "*My* sacrifice, O God, is a broken spirit").

Altogether, this is a remarkably thorough account of the individual's transition from "sinful" to "saved" by the intervening mercy of God.

David's adulterous relationship with Bathsheba and his murder of her husband have for centuries been associated with this psalm, although there is nothing in 2 Samuel 5:6–11:27 to explain a ruined Jerusalem (v. 18; cf. Ps. 147:2) or a sacrificial system yet established there. Unless we invent qualifications for ourselves, verse 19 plainly contradicts verse 16. Such a justification of sacrifice as verse 19 would be a necessary later correction if an early poem were adapted for use in the temple service (it finds a place in some Day of Atonement ceremonies).

Other questions are not so easily answered. It is one thing to say, "I wronged others, but my sin was especially against thee, O God"; it is quite another to *deny* that any wrong was done to Uriah, Bathsheba, the child, the field commander, Israel, or the monarchy by claiming, "Against thee, *thee only,* have I sinned" (v. 4). In fact, no specific sin is named in the psalm: "bloodguiltiness" (v. 14) is literally "blood" and could mean "[Deliver me] from punishment by death"; a single letter changed would make it "deliver me from silence," which suits the context much better—note "tongue," "sing," "lips," and "praise." Moreover, it would be surprising to find David, around 950 B.C., analyzing sin and redemption so acutely and so accurately, devaluing animal sacrifices and extolling the broken, contrite heart, repudiating all self-justification and good works, and acknowledging the need for inward regeneration by a holy Spirit (an insight we thought Ezekiel originated—36:25–27; cf. later Isa. 63:10, 11). This thought would still be "advanced" for David, although it means simply a powerful, sustaining good influence from God, as "an evil spirit from the Lord," 1 Samuel 19:9, implies a contrary influence. All such ideas appear to presuppose the illuminating, searching ministry of the prophets, especially later Isaiah and Jeremiah.

Nevertheless, neither a later date nor liturgical use in the national hymnbook precludes a personal origin of the psalm. Both thought and feeling are far too intense and individual to be community products. In the contrite national mood that followed the Exile, the personal confession already at hand became an invaluable vehicle for corporate repentance.

The psalm anticipates, in a leap of faith, what is declared with infinitely greater assurance by the atoning death of Jesus: that God does accept the penitence of contrite hearts and totally renews the sinful soul. But the psalm eloquently and powerfully reminds us that the healing balm of forgiveness should be laid only upon a clean wound of genuine repentance, if the soul is to regain health. Far too often Christians emphasize faith but not repentance; peace, not purity; comfort, not cleansing; relief of guilt, not regeneration of personality. The consequence is years of struggle against sins never really left behind.

New Testament echoes: Romans 3:4; cf. Luke 15:21; John 3:6; Acts 3:19; 22:16; 2 Corinthians 3:17; Hebrews 9:19; 1 John 1:9.

52 ''LOOK ON THIS PORTRAIT, AND ON THIS...''

For headings, see the Introduction, IV (i)–(iv).

Abruptly addressing an individual, possibly representing a type or even a social group, the poet vigorously accuses him of misusing power and wealth (vv. 1, 7) to oppress and ruin "the godly," not by overt violence but by covertly using the forms of civil justice and social pressure, through treachery, lies, slander, and conspiracy. The portrait is repulsive: this man—a thrusting, malicious talker with a tongue "like a sharp razor" — is false, arrogant, and delights in evildoing; he is sheltered by his position in society, and purchases immunity with his great riches. The second line is in confusion: the RSV and the NEB both conjecture a rearrangement of words. With "tongue like a sharp razor," compare Psalm 57:4; for oppression practiced by the unscrupulous wealthy, see Amos 5:11–12; 8:4–6; Micah 2:1–2; 7:3; for the extreme importance of truthful speech in an illiterate society, see the discussion of Psalm 12.

Only the "fear of God" can curb such ruthless oppression of the defenseless. Verse 5 may be a prophet's threatening oracle, even a formal curse (a ritual "commination" or condemnation of evil: "May God break..."), which would explain the psalm's presence in the hymnbook. The divine reaction is itemized as "break down," "lay hold of" (or "snatch"), "pluck from" (a tent, a dwelling), "root up" (from life itself? — cf. Isa. 22:15–19). Except for "tent," the metaphors suggest removal of (social) weeds. Certainly "destruction" and removal await the oppressor, despite his imagined security (v. 7). The righteous, looking on, are "awestruck," laughing and commenting with the glad relief of despairing men at a sudden *right* turn of events (vv. 6, 7), when the God of truth intervenes to defend truth in society (note v. 9).

In contrast is set the true prosperity and security of those whose trust is not in riches, power, and deceit but in the steadfast love of God. Olive trees have long flourished within the temple precincts; "Wait for thy name" (Hebrew) sounds strange; "proclaim" (RSV) and "glorify" (NEB) are both conjectured improvements. If verses 8 and 9 sound smugly self-complacent, we must remember that the poet, too, speaks for a type, for the "godly" whose trust is deeper-rooted and whose boast is in the Lord.

The opening words could well relieve David's anger at Doeg's treachery, but it is not recorded that Doeg was a wealthy or a "mighty" man or an oppressor; he was a "chief herdsman" (1 Sam. 21:7), and he did but tell the truth (1 Sam. 22:9). The psalm heading probably records a well-meant effort to "locate" the psalm in David's story. As suggested above, its background is much closer to the time of Amos and Micah.

The two portraits continue to identify distinctive types in our own society, for where a man's deepest trust is placed still determines his behavior toward his fellows.

New Testament echo: cf. James 5:1–6.

53 WHAT FOOLS MEN ARE — AGAIN!

For headings, see the Introduction, IV (i), IV (ii), IV (iii).

This slightly different version of Psalm 14 varies somewhat in wording but not in meaning, except in the problematic and almost untranslatable verse 5 (as diverse modern translations show — all of them conjectural) and in the name used for God. The duplication of the psalm well illustrates not only the combination of different collections of poetry in our Psalter (see the Introduction, IV [v]) but also one remarkable difference between Book I and Book II. Throughout Book I God is usually called "Yahweh," more familiarly "Jehovah" or "the Lord"; but throughout Book II he is called "Elohim" (Book I uses "Yahweh" 272 times and "Elohim" 15 times; Book II uses "Elohim" 164 times and "Yahweh" 30 times). One might notice a similar distinction in preferred terminology between the hymnbooks of two modern "denominations."

54 THE LORD UPHOLDS

For headings, see the Introduction, IV (i)–(iv); for Selah, see IV (ii); for theme, vindication, see II (ii).

This brief, straightforward plea for help begins and ends with the divine "name," the sum of God's known character, upon which the poet's prayer and hope are based. Proud (or "insolent"), ruthless, and godless men seek his life; no explanation or circumstances are named. He calls upon God to help and uphold him. So confident is he in the power of God's "name" that he anticipates complete vindication, promises a thank offering (Exod. 35:29), and looks forward to "gloating" over his foes (v. 7; more than "triumphing"— "with delight," NEB).

An over-literal translation in verse 4 introduced into older versions the pleasant thought that "the Lord upholds those who support my soul," but the poet did not say that. If "strangers" is the correct word in verse 3, then presumably the "ruthless ones" are invading alien heathen, as in the phrases (similar in Hebrew) in Ezekiel 28:7 and 31:12. But Psalm 86:14 (like Jer. 15:21) similarly describes faithless Israelites, and it would appear that some copyists understood the poet one way, some the other. There seems no reason why the Ziphites' betraying David's hiding-place to Saul (1 Sam. 23:19–24; 26:1, 2) should prove them to be "insolent," "ruthless," and "godless" unless *some* setting in David's story has to be supplied for every psalm in the "David" collection.

The too-easy identification of one's own enemies with God's is very evident here; it is merely assumed. Moreover, Christians ought to bear in mind that when the Lord delivers, gloating over one's foes is always, and wholly, out of place—even when this psalm is used, as it often is, on Good Friday.

New Testament echo: cf. Acts 3:16.

55 LEADERSHIP
WITHOUT LOYALTY

For headings, see the Introduction, IV (i), IV (ii), IV (iii); for Selah, see IV (ii); for theme, vindication, see II (ii).

Violence, strife, mischief, trouble, and ruin stalk the city streets; oppression and fraud fill its market square; noisy crowds ("shouts," "shrill clamour," NEB) riotously perambulate the city walls (9–12), filled with resentment and plotting revenge, "alive with rumour and scandal" (vv. 3, 5, 11, NEB). Within the sanctuary the rightful leader of the people (king? priest?), fearing for his life (v. 4), has sought refuge and pleads God's help, confessing that he writhes, shudders, is horrified at the state of public life (vv. 1–5).

The leader himself nurses no great ambition for power; most gladly would he escape, like the solitude-haunting wild dove, and so be freed from the storm of rebellious passions that gives "no peace" (vv. 2, 6–8, NEB). But responsibility for others holds him fast. He prays that, as at presumptuous Babel (Gen. 11:9), God will confound the plans and confuse the counsels of those who are enemies of God, of the city, and of himself (vv. 9–11).

The crisis within the city is aggravated because the ringleader of insurrection was once of "equal rank" (literally), a companion, friend, and fellow worshiper (vv. 13, 14) of the psalmist. But he and his followers have proved treacherous, breakers of covenant, deceitful and sly (vv. 20–21). This adds personal bitterness to the public situation, and even to his prayer (v. 15), which is almost a curse — though in fact it requests the same punishment allotted to Dathan and Abiram, who revolted against Moses' leadership (Num. 16:1–33). In verse 15 (see the RSV margin) the Hebrew suggests they deserve to exchange their present homes, which are haunts of evil, for still worse homes — in Sheol! The breach of solemn covenant (v. 20) partly explains this severity, because God was witness to men's oaths and covenants, and the avenger of their betrayal.

Meanwhile, the beleaguered psalmist calls constantly upon God, and finds confidence: "he has heard my cry, he rescued me and gave me back my peace" (v. 18, NEB). Translations of verses 18–19 differ widely, partly because the troubled emotions of the poem occasion sudden transitions of thought (vv. 9, 14–15, 16, 22), and partly because the same words can be so differently understood. For example, "God will give ear" (v. 19) in the RSV becomes "Ishmael" ("God hears") in the NEB; Ishmaelites had a sad reputation for treachery, "their hand against every man and every man's hand against them" (see Gen. 16:11, 12). This, and the references to dwellers in the east, *may* refer to foreign mercenary soldiers brought into the city — but all is doubtful. The Hebrew word "he who sits *before*" is taken as referring to *time* in the RSV ("enthroned *of old*") — that is, God; in the NEB it is taken as referring to *place*, the usual word for "east" (before one, when facing the rising sun) — hence the translation "dwellers in the east" (that is, "the foes"). The word for "changes" (AV/KJV, RSV margin) is very obscure, but resembles an Arabic word for "oath." Only experts can decide the correct meaning, if anyone can.

With the final complaint against treachery comes another sudden change of thought and mood, almost an interruption, in the very gracious words of verse 22. Perhaps this was spoken by the sanctuary priest, or by a prophet to the distressed leader, or possibly by the leader to his downcast followers ("burden" means more accurately "lot," "condition," "what God has appointed you"). For a leader with responsibility for his people, however, even such personal consolation is not sufficient without the assurance that such violence and treachery shall at last be defeated.

Few things burden and embitter the heart more than heavy responsibility for others combined with base disloyalty and deceit. In such circumstances, *only* a sense that God carries the burden with you, and that you carry it for him, can sustain either courage or peace.

New Testament echo: 1 Peter 5:7.

56 "IN GOD I TRUST"

For headings, see the Introduction, IV (i)–(iv); for theme, vindication, see II (ii).

Because David was "much afraid" of the Philistines at Gath, someone has linked this poem on fear and faith with that incident, although in 1 Samuel 21:10–15 David was not "seized" by the Philistines but "fled" to them, and the psalm says nothing of David's feigned madness in Gath.

The meaning of the poem must lie in its refrain (vv. 4, 10–11; the second occurrence duplicates a line, probably by accident of the copyist, and so uses both names for God — see the discussion of Psalm 53; "man" — that is, "mere mortal man" — in v. 11 is little different from "flesh" — "mere mortal flesh" — in v. 4). Strangely, the Hebrew allows the translation "whose word I praise" (RSV), as though by oracle or promise God had spoken to reassure the poet; and "I will shout defiance" (NEB).

The familiar circumstances — foes who "all day long" watch, lurk, lie in wait, oppress, and "trample upon" the psalmist — prompt the cry for vindication and deliverance (v. 9); no identifying details are given. Apart from the comforting "word" (if that is the meaning of v. 4), the poet is assured that all his "tossings" of elation and depression (or "on his bed"; possibly his "wanderings") are known to God, all his tears treasured like the last drops in the desert-traveler's water-skin. (For God's "book," cf. Exod. 32:32; Mal. 3:16, 17.) He is sure, therefore, that God is "for him" (v. 9); he will live to fulfill his vows, pay his thanksgivings, and "walk before God in the light of life."

It is not impossible to read into the poem a ritual for crises of fear, with release of a "scape-dove" to placate the spirit of the distant wilderness (see the psalm heading), with prophetic oracle (v. 4), and with bowings and prostrations by the penitent ("tossings" of the head, v. 8), ending with formal fulfillment of vows and thanksgivings. But that reads much into few words. The one unexplained note in what otherwise seems a very human struggle-in-words between faith and fear is the reference to "nations" or "peoples" (v. 7), which seems out of harmony with verses 3, 5, and 6. Perhaps the poem was here adapted for congregational use, when Israel's dangers were more in mind than individual fears.

"In God I trust" and "This I know, that God is for me" constitute a powerful antidote to any form of apprehension, anxiety, fear, or foreboding: it lends to Christian hearts, as to Jewish hearts, an unconquerable courage.

> *New Testament echoes:* Hebrews 13:6; cf. Luke 10:20; Romans 8:3; Philippians 4:3; Revelation 21:27.

57 A NEST IN THE GREATNESS OF GOD

> *For headings, see the Introduction, IV (i)–(iv); for Selah, see IV (ii); for theme, vindication, see II (ii).*

The similarity of opening words (NEB) and some other phrases, and of structure and situation, has suggested that this poem is part of (or a supplement to) Psalm 56. But its tone is much more assured and positive. "My heart is steadfast" (or "fixed" — RV, 1881 ed.), said twice, as is "I will sing," the confident "He will send from heaven and save me," with the exulting refrain (vv. 5, 11)—all suggest that in comparison with Psalm 56 any struggle between faith and fear has ended with faith serenely triumphant, taking up its harp and lyre to "awake the dawn" (v. 8).

It is odd, however, that verses 1–5 differ sharply in tone from verses 7–11, despite the unifying refrain, and that verses 7–11 recur separately in Book V in Psalm 108:1–5. Possibly the poem was composed of familiar fragments, but given that caution, and with some attention to the flexibility of Hebrew tenses, it now stands well together. The conjectured link with David's experience, whether in 1 Samuel 22 or 1 Samuel 24:3, brings no illumination to the meaning.

In verses 1–4 a resolute sheltering beneath "God's wings" yields confidence in the intervention of God to save, alongside a realistic description of the dangers in which the poet stands — or, more accurately, "lies down" (the "fire-breathing lions" of the RSV margin become "man-eating" in the NEB — hence the mention of "teeth," "tongues"). It is just possible that the poet meant "I will [confidently] lie down amid the greatest dangers." There follows the truly worshipful, outward-looking refrain, revealing a heart without tension.

Verse 6 suitably introduces the second section only if it be understood as three lines of "complaint" and a fourth of *glad surprise* (and the familiar delight in "poetic justice"). In verses 7–10 the gladness, the unswerving confidence, and the stimulated spirit are obvious. "I will awake the dawn" means, more probably, "right early," "promptly"—hardly "I will anticipate deliverance" or "I will arise before morning."

Very impressive are the "dimensions" of God: love wide as the heavens, truth reaching the skies, God high above the heavens, his glory over all the earth—the nearest that Hebrew can manage to describe infinity. The poet is at least as concerned that praise be offered and glory be ascribed to God far and wide as that he himself should be secure. We are never delivered from our anxieties so long as we dwell upon them instead of upon God's goodness and glory.

58 FUTILITY AND FRUITFULNESS

For headings, see the Introduction, IV (i), IV (ii), IV (iii).

The longing of the sincerely good to see goodness triumph and evil fail has rarely been more forcefully and variously expressed than it is in this psalm. Despite its repellent metaphor for total victory, the close (vv. 10–11) well summarizes the poet's meaning. Only the details require examination, through the use of several very rare words and phrases (see the Introduction, III [iv] [c]).

The "gods" addressed (RSV; "rulers," NEB) pose a question, for *elohim*, "high and mighty ones," is used in Psalm 82, in a very similar context, for the gods of the nations or (better) guardian spirits appointed by God to superintend the life of each nation. This idea appears in Deuteronomy 32:8; 29:26; Daniel 10:13, 20, 21; and Sirach 17:17. In Psalm 82 they are clearly contrasted with human, mortal princes. The older idea, that *elohim* could be used of human judges, is now thought to be mistranslation, even in Exodus 21:6. In Psalm 58 these superintending spirits are rebuked for mishandling their authority, "weighing out" (literal Hebrew) in the scales of justice not good but evil, "gods" favoring ungodliness.

In protest, the psalmist insists first on the nature of evil as neither accidental nor gradual but *innate* (v. 3). The wicked in society are venomous as serpents yet willfully deaf to all appeal and example, as the Egyptian cobra ("asp") is to all enchantment (cf. Jer. 8:17). The wicked are not to be trifled with, therefore; the poet prays, with a remarkable series of metaphors, that they and their influence shall be thwarted:

like young lions ("unbelievers," NEB) whose jaw-teeth and front fangs are broken, frustrating their terrible destructiveness;

like water that is spilt, and evaporates in the hot sun (or, possibly, like the eastern wadi, a rushing torrent in spring when snows melt, but swiftly dried in summer);

like grass trodden by men and cattle in the dry season, and withering in the hour (the obscure Hebrew words here *could* mean "arrows diverted or broken in their flight");

like the snail, whose slimy trail shows it to be wearing away, "melting" in the sun, whenever it moves (again, rare Hebrew words *could* mean "an abortive birth," a good parallel with the next line, but do abortions "melt away"?);

like a stillborn, or malformed, child, hurried from the womb to the grave (cf. Eccl. 6:3,4; Job 3:16);

like the crackling thorns under the traveler's cooking-pot (see Eccl. 7:6), when a sudden whirlwind scatters raw ("green") food and blazing fire in seconds, sooner than "the pot can feel the heat," so may the sinners be swept away by the winds of God (The NEB understands this quite differently: [May they be] "rooted up like a thornbush," like "weeds which a man angrily clears away").

Such desire to see the end of evil is not vindictive (despite v. 10). To believe in the futility of evil and the fruitfulness of good (vv. 10, 11; "reward" is literally "fruit") is necessary to any faith in a moral universe, a righteous God, and the value of spiritual endeavor.

New Testament echo: cf. Luke 6:23, 35.

59 "THAT MEN MAY KNOW..."

For headings, see the Introduction, IV (i)–(iv); for Selah, see IV (ii); on theme, vindication, see II (ii).

A clever imagination made the link between the scavenging dogs surrounding the closed city each night and the assassins lying in wait around David's house (1 Sam. 19:11–17); but in this psalm the repetition of the attempt (vv. 6, 14), the prayer (v. 11, especially the impression of one praying for a wider circle), and the references to "nations" (vv. 5, 8, 13) make one pause. Ruthless enemies, intent on destruction in an attack wholly unprovoked (vv. 1–4), prompt the prayer that God, the "Lord God of hosts, ... God of Israel," will stir himself to act (vv. 4, 5). But "prowling about the city" (v. 6), the nations banded together (vv. 5, 8, 3), the "bellowing mouths" (v. 7, possibly "incantations," "propaganda," even "slavering mouths," but in v. 12 sinful *words*, "pride," "cursing," "lies," even "spells"), God's laughing derision (v. 8; recall Ps. 2:4)—all strongly remind us of Hezekiah's response to the Assyrian siege of Jerusalem, the Rabshakeh's foreign and offensive language, his challenges to God, and Isaiah's reply (2 Kgs. 18:17–19:8, especially vv. 22, 26, and 19:19–21; with Hezekiah's "that all kingdoms of the earth may know," cf. the psalmist's v. 13).

Hezekiah's experience, doubtless among others, may at least provide a plausible and appropriate illustration of what the poet means to say. A hard-pressed leader pours fine scorn upon his threatening foes of foreign tongue beyond the city walls. He likens them to the dogs that prowl by night, snarling (v. 7, unless Hebrew "swords" refers to "fangs"), among the city's rubbish, careless of who hears them, growling at being cheated of their prey (vv. 7, 15). The poet likes the image well enough to repeat it (vv. 6, 14). He himself is unperturbed, so sure is he that God will mock back at the scoffers (v. 8) and let him see the defeat of the foe (v. 10).

Through the night of howling dogs, the poet will praise (or, as the Syriac version has it, "will keep vigil for") God his strength until "the morning" (v. 16). For God in steadfast love will "meet" him and *lift* him high above these self-exalting enemies (v. 1, literally) upon the "high tower" (vv. 9, 16, 17, literally) of safety, and *cast down* the foe (v. 11). The strange, subtle prayer in verse 11 seems to mean that a lingering defeat will impress itself upon God's people more deeply than any sudden overthrow, though (v. 13) the enemies' defeat must be complete in the end. "Make them totter" (RSV), "wander" (RV margin, 1881 ed.), and "scatter" (NEB) are three shades of meaning of the word "to stagger"; "wander" might recall Cain's punishment (Gen. 4:13, 14).

Nowhere is the deepest motive of these repeated prayers for vindication more clearly expressed than in verse 13. And in few other passages is the essence of Old Testament confidence more plainly affirmed: God's steadfast *love*, God's invincible *strength*. Therefrom springs the marvelous resilience of Judaism and Christianity alike.

60 "WITH GOD WE SHALL DO VALIANTLY"

For headings, see the Introduction, IV (i)–(iv); on Selah, see IV (ii); "for instruction" seems inappropriate (see II, [iii]) unless it means "for military cadets," which seems fanciful.

Military defeat by immediate neighbors, probably Edom (vv. 1, 4, 5, 9, 10, 12), combined with an earthquake and its effects (v. 2), has kindled deeply superstitious fears that God is displeased and so is spurning his chosen and abandoning their armies. The people are bewildered, staggering as (in every sense) their world rocks beneath their feet. It is a bitter cup for God's elect to drain (v. 3); possibly the "banner" (v. 4) is also a bitter irony, a rallying point for fugitives from the dreaded alien "bows" of trained, professional soldiers such as Israel rarely possessed (the Hebrew here, "truth," is unintelligible).

Selah at this point, following the poet's introduction, suggests that verse 5, the people's plea, might well have been choral; if so, verses 11–12 might have been choral also.

Part of the divine response consists of an oracle (in different meter, probably indicating a quotation), possibly a traditional promise here recited or spoken under inspiration, by a sanctuary prophet (v. 6; the Hebrew, "by his holiness," implies a divine oath, as in Amos 4:2). The oracle is quoted again, as part of verses 5–12, in Psalm 108. If in the present psalm the quotation were by David, the words would be very old; but the story in 2 Samuel 8:5–14 and 10:13, 18, cited in the psalm heading, says nothing of defeat or earthquake, and needs considerable adjustment to form background for this poem.

The meaning of the oracle is clear: the whole land of Palestine, of Israel's neighbors no less than of Israel, is God's, to do with and to divide as he will. Shechem and Succoth (divided as spoil) embrace the land west and east of Jordan, and Manasseh the north; Ephraim, leader of the northern tribes, is God's military "helmet"; preeminent is Judah, God's royal scepter (cf. Gen. 49:10). Moab was (contemptuously) God's washbasin, and is said to look like it from eastern Palestine, a rim of mountains enclosing the Dead Sea. "Upon [or "at," "over"] Edom I cast [or "fling"] my shoe" is also contemptuous, whether signifying possession by purchase (see Ruth 4:7–8), the throwing of a shoe to slaves to clean, or the designating of Edom as the odd corner into which dirty shoes were flung. Philistia would hear God's shout of triumph; the NEB has, without explanation, "Philistia is the target of my anger." God's sovereignty over Palestine is unchallengeable.

Despite this, the poet does not rest upon the oracle but pleads to be led forward against the almost impregnable capital of Edom: Petra, the city of stone (Obad. 3, 4). He begs, too, that God will go with them, granting them strength to trample the foe like raging bulls, for the help of human allies is vain. It is not only that without God there is no victory, but that without God there is no valor, no heart for conflict, no courage to fight and die.

However we, Jew or Christian, love what "God has spoken," it is essential to remember that the ancient oracle will not save without present valor, nor present valor survive unless God goes forth with us.

61 TAKING SHELTER

For headings, see the Introduction, IV (i), IV (iii); for Selah, see IV (ii).
It is wisdom, sometimes, to run for shelter, like a child in a thunderstorm, unable to understand, resist, or change what is going on but sensible enough to seek safety.

This brief poem is such a "run for cover" — to the rock in the desert that affords shade from the burning heat, to the refuge in the fields that preserves when the storm threatens to destroy, to the strong tower that shields when foes press hard, to the tent on the lonely trail that offers hospitality and protection from brigands, to the warm, strong wings of the mother bird that give cover when the hawk flies high. For such shelter from danger the psalmist prays. "The rock higher than I" disappears in some translations in favor of "lift me and set me upon a rock," despite the parallel with "my shelter"; the "tent" is often the tabernacle (even the temple) of God — though here only protection is in mind.

The psalmist pleads "from the end of the earth" (which may be Sheol, exile, or simply a place far from home), and he is "faint." He has made vows to God, and (apparently) received the "heritage" of those who fear God's name. That is obscure, as is the sudden prayer for the prolongation and blessing of the king's life and dynasty (vv. 6, 7). A suggested correction, accepted by the NEB, changes "heritage" to "wish," and all is clear: verses 5–7 quote, in somewhat formal style (as the NEB setting indicates), the "wishful prayers" offered when the king made his vows and was crowned.

Thus, fainting, far from home, and under some pressure (whether of war, exile, or homesickness), the king remembers his promises and the prayers made for him, which God has so far graciously granted. So stirred, he prays for shelter in the strength of his God, and renews his promise of daily praise and devotion when the pressures have passed. (It seems unnecessary to suppose the psalm is that of a captive exile praying for himself and suddenly, without explanation, remembering his king, or to conjecture that it is two fragments of psalms clumsily combined.)

This is a very simple and earnest petition, no doubt preserved to help all those who, serving God's purposes, find hard days light-

ened by the memory of their own early vows and by the prayers of
their friends.

62 THE STRUGGLE
FOR POWER

For headings, see the Introduction, IV (i), IV (iii); for Selah, see IV (ii).
The burden of this strong affirmation of faith is very clear in verses
11 and 12. "Once...twice..." is a common form of solemn assertion:
"Power belongs to God; and...to thee, O Lord, belongs steadfast
love. For thou dost requite a man according to his work." Power,
love, justice — in the eyes of the psalmist these are not rivals but
facets, seen from different circumstances, of the unchanging character of God. Power, exercised in love to achieve justice for all, is
Israel's (and every society's) salvation.

   That unvarying character of God is here repeatedly affirmed as
rock, salvation, fortress, deliverance, "mighty rock," and refuge. In
God alone the poet trusts; to him alone he looks in silent, unques-
tioning confidence (the repetition of vv. 1–2 at vv. 5–6, thought by
some to be a copying mistake, is poetically effective, especially as
"shall not be greatly moved" in v. 2 becomes "shall not be shaken"—
"not moved at all"—in v. 6). In the serene assurance of the psalmist,
a particle word recurs six times meaning "surely and only," "It is so,
without alternative or question"; and what is so sure is his reliance
upon God's power, love, and justice as life's last word.

   That emphasis is the clue to the occasion of the poem. A
struggle for power is disturbing society; the speaker's leadership (v.
8, whether as priest, prophet, or, more probably, king) is threatened
(vv. 3, 4). There is a suggestion in "a leaning wall," "a tottering
fence," that his position was already precarious (because of age?),
and that enemies attack in numbers ("all of you") when he is down.
Moreover, his opponents are those who rely on falsehood and hypo-
critical professions of loyalty (v. 4); who, whether of high or low
levels of society, are in real substance weighed as mere wind (v. 9);
who rely on dishonest gain to reward their scramble for power (v. 10).
Such is the nature of their unscrupulous ambition.

   The people's rightful leader remains unshaken, and would have
his followers take heart (v. 8). He relies on neither such methods nor
such reward, but "only and surely" upon God. From him alone, in the
end, all power, love, and justice issue; on him alone all power, love, and
justice in society are based. On God, therefore, rests his safety and his
"honor" (v. 7); to be on God's side is to be invincible.

So fine an affirmation of social faith, so splendid a statement of the true relation of religion to politics, deserves a place in every hymnbook.

New Testament echoes: Revelation 19:1; cf. Matthew 6:19, 21; 16:27; Romans 2:6; 1 Timothy 6:17; Revelation 22:12.

63 "MY SOUL FOLLOWETH HARD AFTER THEE"

For headings, see the Introduction, IV (iii), IV (iv).

By taking full advantage of the freedom of paraphrase when exact translation is awkward or ambiguous, the NEB achieves a truly beautiful rendering of verses 1–8. Apart from several imaginative phrases, the one liberty taken with the meaning places the poet within the sanctuary, seeking the vision of God (v. 2), where the RSV finds a memory of past worship now denied him. The NEB has to assume that by verse 5 the vision has been granted; the feasting may allude to an actual sacrificial meal.

Less is assumed if we read verses 1–8 as a most moving expression of longing in spiritual drought, memories of past visits to the sanctuary only sharpening desire. We then hear the poet testify that, even beyond the limits of the homeland, without the help of formal worship and human fellowship, he has found the *steadfast love* of God still with him, stirring his praise; the lifting of hands in *prayer* a source of unbroken blessing; a *spiritual "feasting"* possible in private meditation and remembrance through the three watches of the night (Judg. 7:19); all the while the help and *overshadowing of God* have fed his joy continually. In short, while he remembers the sanctuary and its blessing with true gratitude, he has now learned that the fellowship of God is available wherever life has taken him. That is a "breakthrough" of spiritual discovery with very far-reaching implications.

The completeness and depth of the spiritual experience so revealed are equally remarkable. All of the poet is involved — soul, flesh, lips, hands, mouth, voice, and life — "as long as I live." The experience itself is many-sided, involving spiritual thirst (an intensive desire for God), the vision of God's power and glory, memories of shared worship, the sense of divine love, praise, prayer, the power of God's name, deep spiritual satisfaction, joy, meditation, help, shelter, the inner self "clinging to" God ("following hard after God," AV/KJV), even as God's right hand upholds the inner self. That is an impressive analysis of religious experience, of the two-way action and reaction of faith, which ever pursues rest and rests in pursuit, which always presses forward to attain and attains only to be drawn higher again.

From this high-toned testimony it is an abrupt descent to the forthright declaration that foes shall sink to Sheol, lying unburied on the battlefield, the prey of jackals, while the king rejoices in God (vv. 9–11); and another, almost inexplicable leap to the final verse, whose circumstance and purpose are lost to us. Guesses are very tentative.

The author is apparently exiled. He could be David, banished to the wilderness during Absalom's rebellion (2 Sam. 15–17; "king" in v. 11 could hardly mean Saul, so 1 Sam. 23–24 is inappropriate). In that case those who "swear by *the king*" (v. 11) are David's faithful friends, and the liars are the forsworn rebels. If the author is exiled in Babylon, he must in the midst of thanksgiving suddenly remember his king, also exiled. In that case those who "swear *by God*" are presumably the faithful exiles, set among those who "swear by" lies — that is, by idols. The former seems more likely, but it is not surprising that some take verses 9–11 to be a separate fragment which has lost its illuminating introduction and accidentally become attached to the splendid verses 1–8.

Because of the word "early" in verse 1 (AV/KJV, NEB) and the "night" recalled in verse 6, this psalm has been a morning hymn in Christian circles since postapostolic days. If we have rightly understood verses 1–8 as reaching the spiritual insight more fully elaborated in Psalm 139, then it stands on the very frontier between Old Testament faith and New Testament revelation with a gladness of discovery, a happiness of communion with God that not all Christians could claim to know.

New Testament echoes: cf. Matthew 5:6; Romans 3:19.

64 ON SLANDER

For headings, see the Introduction, IV (i), IV (iii).

This vigorous complaint about malicious tongues emphasizes especially the suddenness of the attacks launched (v. 4), and their secrecy (vv. 2, 4, 5 [twice], 6). Some leader, evidently an influential one, has drawn upon himself the base intrigue, the "cunningly conceived" plots (v. 6), of men whose minds and hearts are "deep" (v. 6 is a difficult verse to translate, possibly a proverb: "The inner man is the real man, and the heart is deep!"). Their spirits are hostile but cowardly. Not violence but "tongues like swords,"

"words like arrows" (v. 3), "wicked tales" (v. 8, NEB), possibly also sorcerers' spells, threaten the poet's "life" (perhaps threaten his physical life by falsely accusing him of a capital offense, or possibly his "life in society," his position and influence). For the immense importance of truthful speech in a nonliterary society and the vulnerability of leading persons to slanderous ruin, see the discussion of Psalm 12.

The resource of the psalmist is his faith that God likewise has his "arrows," his shafts of judgment (v. 7), and he too can act "suddenly." But his acts are not in secret; the wicked will be ruined by their own (reputation for) lies (v. 8), and "all who see their fate [will] take fright at it" (NEB). Men will draw their own conclusions; truth will endure; the righteous will rejoice; the upright will be honored within society and exultant within their own hearts.

This is a sustaining faith if one can hold it. But Christians have learned to fear when all men speak well of them, and to trust instead the blessedness of being reviled and spoken falsely against for the sake of righteousness and of Christ. Such is the lot, Jesus implied, of the prophets of truth in a world which so often prefers its comfortable falsehoods. Nevertheless, Christians also believe that men "cannot do anything against the truth, but only for the truth" (2 Cor. 13:8).

65 WHERE GOD IS KNOWN

For headings, see the Introduction, IV (i), IV (iii); on theme, God in Nature, see II (v).

Beginning in the sanctuary, moving out to the political and geographical scene, and ending with the charm and wealth of the productive countryside, this beautiful and remarkable poem is obviously appropriate to the Feast of Harvest Ingathering. It is possible that the "moving out" was quite literal, as a procession actually left the temple after worship to bless the growing crops and sprinkle water to simulate rain's beneficent, and wholly necessary, effects upon arid Palestinian soil (so vv. 9–10 have it).

Yet the theme of the psalm is unexpectedly wide-ranging. Some recent deliverance, by acts which inspired awe in all who beheld such signs ("tokens," RV, 1881 ed.) of God's power (acts which affected not only Israel but the ends of the earth and the peoples of the east and west — "portals of morning and evening," literal Hebrew, vv. 5–8), has stirred the poet to compose. It has been "a year of God's goodness" (v. 11, literally, not "*with* thy bounty"), a year of blessing, of abundant rains in spring (v. 10, a supposed overflowing of the celestial brook of God), of political deliverance in answer to prayer (v. 5), and crowned now by a splendid harvest "in preparation" (v. 9, literal Hebrew, which comes near to saying "it rained corn," vv. 11–13). Sweetness and abundance mark the passing of God in blessing through the land (v. 11; God's "paths" or "chariot tracks"); even the pastures of the open country ("wilderness") are fresh and luxurious. (There is no need to suppose two psalms are combined: Isa. 37:30 presents a striking parallel of deliverance in harvesttime; ripening crops so often tempted invaders.)

Thus the poem names three spheres where God is known: in the sanctuary, certainly; in praise, vows, prayer, confession, atoning sacrifice, and forgiveness ("covering") of sin; and in access to God. The poet is envious of those privileged to *dwell* there (vv. 1–4); deeply satisfying is the knowledge of God shared in such worship. But God is also known in the wider world as active in the affairs of men and especially in creation, as of old girding the still mountains with strength and setting bounds to the ever-restless sea, by his power subduing chaos to order in Nature and history alike (vv. 5–7).

All mankind feel awe and gladness at such divine activity. And nearer home, in the miracle and splendor of another autumn, the hills and valleys, fields and open countryside deck themselves ("gird," "clothe," "mantle" themselves) in white fleeces, joyful green and shining gold, shouting for gladness, singing for joy. For in the beauty and goodness of the world at our very doors God is known.

No Christian poet could surpass this tribute to the ways in which God makes himself known, except to add two things more to the quiet sanctuary, the teeming life of men, and the generous gifts of Nature: a cradle and a cross.

New Testament echoes: cf. Matthew 8:26; Acts 14:17.

66 EXPERIENCE
KINDLES WORSHIP

For headings, see the Introduction, IV (i), IV (ii); for Selah, see IV (ii).
This is a psalm of two clear "sections" (vv. 1–12, 13–20), each offering an invitation ("Come and see...," "Come and hear..."), each giving reasons for glorifying, praising, and blessing God—yet one calling on all the earth to worship because of what God has done for Israel, and the other calling on God's people to hear what God has done for the individual poet—in both cases, working "deliverance."

In the one instance the acknowledgment of God's power may be reluctant (v. 3; "cringe," RSV, and "cower," NEB, suggest enforced homage); in the other the very abundant offerings (vv. 13–15) and the testimony (vv. 16–20) are obviously given with heartfelt gladness. (Again there is no need for the suggestion that two fragments have been combined.)

"What God has done for Israel" (and truly, even the heathen say, "The Lord has done great things for them," Ps. 126:2) is defined in traditional fashion. He divided the Red Sea (Exod. 14:16–22) and the Jordan River (Josh. 3:9–17) during the exodus from Egypt. The obscure verse 7 may well recall the struggles of the settlement in Canaan under Gideon, Jephthah, and the rest. Verses 9–12 may describe the general and continuing discipline of Israel's life, but more probably recall, in language familiar at the time, the tragedy of the Exile and the deliverance from it (v. 9 well expresses the miraculous preservation of the nation when apparently destroyed; v. 10 reproduces Isa. 48:10; the "net" echoes Ezek. 12:11–13, as v. 12 recalls Isa. 51:23; 43:2; the affliction or burden in v. 11 is understood to mean "chain" in Jewish comments, as more appropriate for "the loins"). All these metaphors are used of the Babylonian exile, and the restoration is to a place spacious and delightful ("into liberty," NEB). In the face of such divine activity within Israel's history, the nations are urged to acknowledge the awe-inspiring power of God and to "shout" (literal Hebrew) his praise.

But Israel, too, must witness the thanksgiving of some leading figure in the community, evidently wealthy (vv. 13–15), as he also testifies to divine deliverance in individual experience, clinching the poet's argument (v. 16). For he has been in trouble (v. 14). If "under my tongue" (the Hebrew of v. 17) means "hidden" and not "on the tip," then at one time his praise was hindered. The only hint of the cause lies in the temptation to cherish iniquity in the heart (v. 18); some sense of alienation from God, now blessedly removed, is in verse 19. His prayer might have been rejected, but was not, nor was God's steadfast love "removed" (v. 20). His vowed thanksgivings shall not therefore be withheld ("incense" of rams means "smoke," a pleasing smell; Exod. 29:18). Like Israel as a whole, the poet himself has every reason to cry "Blessed be God."

Later centuries have indeed read the lessons of Israel's history, always to their great profit, and they have learned so often that testimony is the door to experience, and experience the spur to devout thanksgiving.

New Testament echoes: John 9:31; cf. James 4:3; 1 Peter 1:7.

67 AN ACT OF WORSHIP

For headings, see the Introduction, IV (i); for Selah, see IV (ii); on theme, God and Nature, see II (v).

Despite some debate, it seems clear that a good harvest throughout Palestine and neighboring countries has prompted this "poetic liturgy" — an act of worship rather than a simple hymn, if the pronouns be carefully observed. The double "internal" refrain confirms this impression (vv. 3, 5).

Imagine an autumn festival (the Feast of Tabernacles?) with the people gathered in the sanctuary, aware of the prosperous fields but knowing that other and deeper blessings are no less important. The presiding priest (later the ruler of the synagogue) recites the opening prayer (v. 1), echoing the Aaronic blessing (Num. 6:24–26); God's "shining face" means God's accepting favor. To this the people respond with verse 2; God's "way" or "ways" is his rule for living; "saving health" is an ancient and accurate phrase for "salvation." All — leaders, choir, and people — then unite in verse 3, thinking of neighboring peoples as well as themselves as equal recipients of God's harvest gifts.

The leader expounds this more fully, emphasizing that the neighboring peoples also are under God's law and within his purpose (v. 4), and the congregation again responds (v. 5). The leader declares plainly the success of the harvest, but here the RSV and the NEB part company. The NEB makes the leader add "and God, our God, will bless us," the act of worship closing with the prayer with which it began: "God grant us his blessing, that all the ends of the earth may fear him." The reason seems a little strange, unless "us" means "all men." More attractive, however, is the RSV's rendering, where the leader's announcement of a successful harvest is followed by its significance for pious hearts: "God, our God, has blessed us." To this the people respond with glad assent, "God *has* blessed us!" and the prayer "Let all . . . fear him."

Especially striking here is the embracing of neighboring nations in God's provision, guidance, and purposes; partly for this reason, the psalm is often used in the Christian church with missionary purpose.

New Testament echoes: cf. Acts 14:17; 17:25; Romans 1:20.

68 WHAT GOD HAS WROUGHT

For headings, see the Introduction, IV (i), IV (iii); for Selah, see IV (ii).

A Jewish poet of the Middle Ages imagined all commentators on the psalms gathered before David in Paradise to compete for a prize. When Psalm 68 was assigned for the test, "what a thick vapour arose!" Variously ascribed to periods covering a thousand years, dismissed as a medley of quotations and fragments from well-known war-poems yet also described as "magnificent," this poem's use of words (some archaic, some very late), uncertainties of text (as foot-notes show), and difficulty of translation (as widely differing modern versions illustrate) make all opinions tentative, every interpretation debatable.

The theme is clear: what God "hast wrought" (v. 28) — namely, a series of "deliverances" (v. 20; literally "our God, a God of deliverances"). The purpose is to call all people to extol the might, the victories, and the glorious character of the God of Israel (vv. 3, 4, 32–35). Several phrases recalling prophets of the restoration from Babylon suggest a deeper purpose: to rekindle the faith and hope of returning exiles. But since the temple still stands (v. 29), that may be a later use of the psalm rather than its original intention. At least verses 24–27 imply a ritual procession celebrating God's victories (see v. 18). This may well indicate the psalm's immediate *use*, and explain its disjointedness, as a kind of running commentary recited or sung at successive stages of the ceremony. The ritual would link traditional fragments (jealously preserved but not easy now to interpret) and new songs with symbolic actions into a coherent seqence.

Assembling at some distance, probably with the Ark of God, the celebrants raise the cry Moses enjoined when the ark went forth (Num. 10:35), adding a warning to opponents to flee before him who disperses enemies like smoke or melting wax. They exhort God's people to be joyful in praise and to "cast up a highway" (v. 4, Hebrew; cf. Isa. 40:3) before the all-conquering Lord. This would be the signal not for literal road-mending but to form the procession, singing as they go. And the opening praise is of the gracious character of God, of his compassionate justice and protection (vv. 5–6, memorable verses), which make his victory beneficent.

The singers make their way toward the sanctuary, reciting or singing the past victories of God: those in the Exodus from Egypt to Sinai and through the wilderness (vv. 6–8), and in the settlement in Canaan (where God's power as creator was shown in the fruitfulness of the land; the rainfall continues to be, even yet, all-important in Palestine, vv. 9, 10; alternatively, Exod. 16:4 speaks of "raining manna"). The intervening and ensuing wars are passed over in silence, except for the assertion that they fulfilled God's command; the news of triumph, like the spoil, was committed to the women. This clearly echoes one of the oldest of all victory songs, that of

Deborah (Judg. 5; see vv. 28–31, and cf. 1 Sam. 18:6); it also recalls the victory song of Miriam and her women (Exod. 15:20–21). The silver-golden dove appears to be some famous emblem captured in battle (v. 13); the "snowstorm" on the "dark mountain" near Shechem pictures the whitening bones and sun-bleached equipment of a defeated army (v. 14).

With such ancient glories in mind, the procession approaches the rise to "Zion's hill" (or a vantage point on the road, as in Luke 19:41), and the song changes to a defense of God's choice of Jerusalem for his dwelling place, in spite of the envy of older shrines on loftier mountains in the north (vv. 15, 16; probably three-peaked Hermon). This song recalls the coming of David's army to take Jerusalem, with God's mighty help, and his establishing the Ark there (vv. 17, 18). Again praise bursts forth at this recalling of God's many deliverances and his great care of Israel. To him belongs escape from death itself (vv. 19, 20), while his victories continue over rebellious foes.

Here (v. 21) a quoted fragment declares how God will subdue "the long locks streaming free" affected by "dedicated" soldiers (Judg. 5:2, literal Hebrew; and Deut. 32:42, with the example of Samson's Nazirite vow). A more primitive spirit breathes in the expectation that God will bring back any escaped foes to satisfy Israel's revenge (vv. 22, 23; cf. Ps. 58:10; 1 Kgs. 21:19).

The procession arrives, apparently described by those waiting within the sanctuary, who welcome the celebrants with more song (vv. 24–27). Benjamin, the smallest tribe, and Judah, the more numerous tribe, with Zebulun and Naphtali, represent the whole land from extreme south to farthest north; "those of Israel's fountain" are presumably true Israelites born of the Patriarch (cf. Isa. 48:1 in the Hebrew: "from the waters of Judah"). The united congregation then sing to the might of God, asking that it be manifest in universal victory (vv. 28–31). The hippopotamus represented Egypt (cf. Job 40:15–24); the bulls with their following calves are apparently other peoples who like war, greedy for richer "tribute."

The celebration closes with a far-ranging call to all nations to praise the Lord, whose power overarches the world like the sky, whose voice sounds in the thunder, whose might strikes awe into enemies but lends power and strength to those who are his. "Blessed be God!"

Whatever illumination such "ritual interpretation" brings to this difficult psalm, much remains obscure. It is said that the psalm was especially favored by Christian Crusaders, Protestant Huguenots, Puritan Ironsides, and Scottish Covenanters—with little awareness, apparently, how ill the nationalistic and militaristic spirit native to Judaism accords with the universalistic and reconciling spirit of Christianity. Christians share Judaism's faith in God's triumph, but they seek no victories that are not Christlike.

> *New Testament echoes:* Ephesians 4:8 (a Rabbinic commentary of Paul's day has "gave" for "received" gifts); cf. 2 Corinthians 1:3; Revelation 9:16.

69 IN DEEP WATERS

For headings, see the Introduction, IV (i), IV (iii); for themes, complaint and vindication, see II (i), II (ii).

The author of this moving prayer of complaint suffers deeply in God's service, but in place of a sustaining belief in his own rightness he possesses an undermining sense of folly and guilt (v. 5; "guilty deeds," NEB). His situation so resembles Jeremiah's that a case can be made for the prophet's authorship; thirty or more phrases would apply well to Jeremiah (cf. with Jer. 11, 15, 17, 20). Supporting this idea are the psalmist's tender intimacy with God (vv. 17, 18), his zeal for proper use of God's house (v. 9; Jer. 7:1–15; 11:25; 12:7), the thought of God's smiting him (v. 26; Jer. 15:17, 18; 17:17; 20:7), some reminders of the prophet's language (vv. 9, 20; Jer. 23:9; 11:19; 15:15), promises concerning the cities of Judah (Jer. 33:16–17), and words of vengeance on opponents (Jer. 11:20; 15:15; 17:18).

On the other hand, while Jeremiah was humble and often unsure, there is little in him parallel to the folly, guilt, shame, and dishonor (vv. 5, 19) confessed by the psalmist, nor of detailed, strong imprecation (vv. 22–28). The conditions behind the psalm resemble those of Jeremiah, and Jeremiah provides an excellent illustration of a servant of God suffering in evil days. But there have been other periods — not least the period when Jewish patriots resisted Persian and Greek influence, and the terms "poor" and "meek" (underlying vv. 29, 32) were synonymous with "faithful" — for which the psalm speaks as eloquently. This explains its place in the national anthology and its frequent echo in the New Testament situation.

In the description of the poet's need, images of sinking, mire, flood, and abyss occur ten times, suggesting a dreaded insecurity. Wounds, pain (vv. 26, 29), and the danger of the pit (Sheol? — v. 15) may imply sickness also. Much is said of opposition by numberless foes attacking with lies, reproaches, and insults, so that marketplace gossips slander him and drunkards invent scurrilous songs about him (vv. 10–12, 20). The intensity of opposition breaks his heart, makes him despair (v. 20), for he is not only unpitied and friendless but alienated from his family (v. 8) and unvisited even by God (weary of crying to God, tired of waiting for him, vv. 3, 17).

He is also anxious lest others should be brought to share his fate (v. 6, perhaps by his example). Even his attempts at repentance (prob-
ably personal, not mourning the nation's sinfulness) have led only to further reviling (vv. 10, 11); he can only cast himself upon God's steadfast love and mercy (vv. 13–18; "thy great affection," v. 16, NEB), on God's faithfulness to a servant, and on the need that the godless shall not triumph. So he may find "redemption," freedom and salvation.

Nevertheless, the immediate occasion of the poet's suffering is his loyalty to God (v. 7; "I am thy servant," v. 17, NEB), especially in some way to God's house. The slightly derogatory reference to animal sacrifice (v. 31), though echoing Leviticus 11, may reveal an attitude which angered fellow worshipers (v. 9; "zeal for thy house" is literally "burning...has burned me up"; the NEB takes this as "burning ones," "bitter enemies" of thy house, parallel to "those who reproach"). The poet shares the reproaches heaped on God in his day. The number and ferocity of his foes, like his concern for those who follow his example, show that he is in some way the leader of a party or pious "movement" ("sect") in Israel, at present violently unpopular (note "those in bonds," v. 33). His plea is for deliverance from danger, for comfort in deep distress, and for vindication as one who is truly God's servant, in this sense "set on high" (v. 29) above all deep waters.

Like many such pleas for vindication, his other prayer becomes an imprecation, a prayer against opponents. The psalmist's own identification with God's cause (v. 9) makes these opponents God's opponents, too; when they keep "sacrificial feasts," may they be trapped in their own conspiracies (v. 22). Much of the "cursing" simply returns the wrong done upon the wrongdoers (emphasize "upon *them*," "overtake *them*," and so on). These enemies are so spiritually insensitive to divine judgment that they add to others' chastening instead of taking warning for themselves (v. 26). In spite of all this, however, the prayers for their punishment go beyond desire for vindication of right within society, seeking not reform but requital.

With the need in mind to encourage others to suffer for righteousness' sake, the psalmist ends (vv. 30–36) with the promise of grateful and tuneful praise, more acceptable than slaughtered beasts, and with a call to have confidence not only that God will hear but that eventually he will have his way in all the earth, to the great comfort and *security* (suggested by "inherit," "dwell") of all who love his name. The references to rebuilding Judah may be postexilic adaptation, but if a struggle of the "orthodox" against the "liberals" is behind the psalm, this assurance that the future lies with the godly is wholly appropriate.

A few striking phrases are also puzzling. The end of verse 4 is probably a proverb protesting innocence (but the NEB has "How can I give back what I have not stolen?"). Verse 13 means literally "faithful salvation"; in verse 21, an unusual word, used also in 2 Samuel 12:17 and Jeremiah 16:7, is said to mean "neighborly gifts of food carried in sympathy to mourners," but here poisoned! Others think this another proverb for mocking the hungry and thirsty. On the book of the living (v. 28), compare Jeremiah 32:31–33 and Ezekiel 13:9.

The psalm voices the pain and longing of the "faithful remnant" of God's people in every age. Christians reject the harsh prayers against the sinful, the absence of the will to save. But only because Jesus, dying for us, prayed "Father, forgive them...."

> New Testament echoes: Matthew 27:34, 48; Mark 15:36; Luke 23:36; John 2:17; 15:25; 19:28, 29; Acts 1:20 (Greek version, adapted); Romans 11:9, 10 (Greek version); 15:3; Philippians 4:3; Revelation 20:12, 15; 21:27; cf. Matthew 10:30; Luke 10:20; 12:7; 2 Corinthians 6:2; Hebrews 12:2, 23; Revelation 3:5; 13:8; 17:8.

70 FOR A SPECIAL OCCASION

> For headings, see the Introduction, IV (i), IV (iii); for "memorial offering," see II (iii).

This "extract" from Psalm 40 (vv. 13–17) in Book I, where already it sat awkwardly (see the discussion of that psalm), is here preserved, with few changes, for the liturgical use indicated. "Elohim" is twice substituted for "Yahweh"; "unto me" is omitted from verse 3, generalizing the expression; in Psalm 40 the third-to-last line is "but the Lord takes thought for me"; in Psalm 70 it is "hasten to me, O God!" For the fragment lacking a beginning, the RV (1881 ed.) supplies "Make haste..." (from v. 2); the NEB supplies "Show me favour..."; the RSV supplies "Be pleased..." (from Ps. 40:13). See the discussion of Psalm 40:13–17.

71 "IN THE TIME OF OLD AGE"

Testimony mingles with prayer, memory with promise in the richly stocked mind of this old man. His poem is somewhat shapeless and full of quotations from treasured psalms, some imperfectly remembered (vv. 1–3 are equivalent to vv. 1, 2 of Ps. 31; vv. 5, 6 are based on Ps. 22:9, 10; vv. 10, 11 recall Ps. 22; most of vv. 12, 13 could be borrowed from Pss. 22, 35, 38, 40; "O God, who is like thee?" in v. 19 echoes Ps. 35:10; the last lines closely resemble Pss. 35:4; 40:14). The old man knew his Psalter!

Apart from verse 20, where the evidence is divided between "me" and "us," there is no indication that "the personified nation" is speaking. Any individual could, of course, note the parallel between his own checkered career and his nation's story. If, as suggested by the virulence of his enemies and the significance of his life's "example" (v. 7, that is, "sign" or "token" of spiritual loyalty, as in Isa. 8:18, rather than the modern meaning of "portent of doom"), he has been a leader of his people, that parallel would come more readily to mind. As always, the use of the poem in the nation's worship came to lend a representative function to the words.

Now age, gray hairs, and failing strength (vv. 9, 18) leave the poet vulnerable to "wicked," "unjust," "cruel" men who watch for his increasing weakness (vv. 10, 11) to "accuse" and "hurt" him (vv. 13, 24). But he meets his fears bravely, *hiding* in God as refuge, towering crag, stronghold (NEB; the text, though confused, apparently includes "to which I resort continually"); *calling* upon God for rescue (v. 4); *relying* on God's righteousness (v. 2) and his promise never to forsake (v. 9); and *pleading* with God to draw near (v. 12). But most of all, age turns back to memory for support, and the poet testifies to God's utter faithfulness to him from his infancy (v. 6) and boyhood (vv. 5, 17, NEB; note youth's hope and instruction) to his present age.

The psalmist does not idealize his experience. There have been many "sore troubles" and possibly a danger of death (v. 20; "depths of the earth" probably means Sheol, but the tenses are doubtful; the NEB has "thou *dost* revive…lift me"; others have "thou *didst* keep me alive…*didst* bring me up…," following the ancient versions). Honor and comfort need to be "restored" (v. 21, NEB); God has "rescued" his soul (v. 23). Nevertheless, through darkness and light God has done great things (v. 16), and the old man's heart, over-full, exclaims, "O God, who is like thee?"

That is why "praise" (used seven times) and "testimony" (used thirteen times) dominate the psalm. His praise is continual, day-long, increasing (v. 14), exclusively God's (v. 16), musical and complete (vv. 22–24; note "harp," "lyre," "lips," "soul," "tongue"). His testimony, too, is long-standing (v. 5), and he will "come" (v. 16; "into the sanctuary"?) to tell all that God has done. He longs to make sure that coming generations share what he has known of God (v. 18). An intriguing question arises in verse 15 because the original has "righteousness," not "righteous deeds" as the RSV has. "For their number is past my knowledge" can hardly follow "righteousness," though it could echo, a little clumsily, Psalm 40:5. The NEB ventures to take "numbers" as meaning "meters," "verses," and translates accordingly: "Thou shalt ever be the theme of my praise, although I have not the skill of a poet."

So, with resolute faith and hope (v. 14), the aged saint will "sing and tell" to the end of his days, for he has a lifelong story to share of the faithfulness of a great God. Jew and Christian rejoice together in the steadfast testimony of a godly life, well lived, triumphantly completed.

New Testament echo: cf. Matthew 27:1.

72 THY KINGDOM COME!

For headings, see the Introduction, IV (iii); on "royal" psalms, see II (iv).

To mark a coronation, possibly of a young king (v. 1; "a king's son," NEB), the court poet prepares for recitation an expression of the prayers and hopes of the people for this new reign. The psalm was no part of synagogue liturgy, but was preserved, doubtless long after the monarchy disappeared, as expressing the prophetic ideal of justice and compassion in society, under a God-fearing king. Numerous phrases echo the books of the prophets, and the Jewish commentaries come later to treat the psalm as "messianic," though with so many references to the poor, needy, and oppressed, and so little about the Messiah himself, the psalm could not have been intended as a description of the messianic age.

The association with Solomon (absent from some ancient copies) probably arose from verses 1 and 15. The main question about the psalm is whether to translate it as a prayer, wish, or statement. The RSV has in verses 4–11 "May..."; makes verses 12–14 statements ("He delivers...," etc.); and in verses 15–17 returns to "May...." The NEB has in verses 4–7 "He shall..."; in verse 8, "May..."; in verses 9–12, "He shall..."; in verses 13–17, "May..." and "So shall...." The difference is not so great as it might appear; such wishes turned to prayer become prophecies. But the psalm is probably better taken as throughout a prayer for the new king.

Divine "justice" is requested for the king, that he might govern as God's representative and "oracle." So the chief dangers of Eastern absolute rule — fraud, oppression, the devaluing of human life — will be avoided, and the poor and the defenseless be royally protected. Such was the prophets' dream of justice and compassion ruling upon earth even as in heaven (vv. 2–5, 7, 12–14; if, in v. 5, "fear thee" is right, following the Hebrew, it would mean "may the people fear *God*").

The second description of the coming just rule (vv. 12–14) will apply to the larger kingdom beyond Israel, extending from the Dead Sea (or less probably the Persian Gulf) to the Mediterranean, and from the Euphrates to Egypt (the southern limit of known territory; 1 Kgs. 4:21). Tarshish was in Spain; the "isles" include the Mediterranean islands and coasts; Sheba meant southern Arabia; Josephus says Seba was in Ethiopia; "the wilderness dwellers" (v. 9, Hebrew) were the Bedawin, who owned no master; with verse 8, compare Zechariah 9:10.

The requested "long life" of the king (vv. 5, 15, 17) really means of his dynasty, through which his life still flows. The prayers that shall be made for him, the benedictions invoked upon him, will keep in mind the religious basis of monarchy, the dependence at all times upon divine blessing. (When the Jewish Targum made the psalm messianic, v. 15 came to mean prayer "to" him.) The abundant harvest will show God's blessing also upon Nature, a return to Paradise. Grain on ("to," NEB) the tops of the mountains shall "wave" (or "rustle") like the trees of Lebanon Forest. Men shall fill the cities with busy life (the countryside fertile, the cities populous constitute prosperity), though the NEB changes the phrase to "sheaves be numberless." "Men blessing themselves by him" may mean praying to be prosperous like him, or using his name in formulae of blessing — either way fulfilling the Abrahamic promise (Gen. 22:18). Such shall be the universal glory of the kingdom God shall bless.

(For the doxology, vv. 18–19, closing Book II, and the subscription, v. 20, see the Introduction, IV [v]).

Although, surprisingly, the psalm is never quoted in the New Testament, it has nevertheless been closely versified in one of the best-known Christian hymns, which begins, "Jesus shall reign where'er the sun / Doth his successive journeys run...." This hymn preserves the court poet's noble vision through many generations. Even so, come, Lord Jesus!

BOOK III
PSALMS 73– 89

73 DOES RELIGION PAY?

For heading, see the Introduction, IV (iii); on theme, vindication, see II (ii).
That "God is good to the upright, to those who are pure in heart" is
the poet's capsule summary of the teaching of the prophets that the
world is under the moral government of a just and holy God (v. 1; the
same letters, divided differently, give "to Israel," but the parallel
"pure in heart" shows the meaning intended). The sharp contradiction between this teaching and everyday experience is dealt with by
Job, who knew that the upright suffer grievously and counseled
submission; by Habakkuk, who found the wicked in great power and
counseled faith; in Psalm 49, which emphasizes that all human
conditions are transient anyway; and in Psalm 37, where envy is
deprecated and confidence in God enjoined.

The author of Psalm 73 is especially troubled about the prosperity (vv. 3, 7, 12), the peace (vv. 5, 13, 14), and the pride (vv. 6, 8,
9, 11) of the wicked. They escape "pangs," even in death (cf. Job
21:23–24); they grow fat and sleek (v. 4; wealth in the east means
ample food!); they know none of the doubts and misgivings of the
godly (v. 5). "Their eyes gleam through folds of fat" (v. 7, NEB; or
"iniquity issues — oozes — from their grossness"); their minds
indulge in fanciful schemes. They blaspheme God and slander men,
yet people flock after them (v. 10, a difficult verse; the RSV and the
NEB almost agree on this meaning, though the text is sometimes
amended to "sated with bread...water"). Arrogantly, they even
charge God with ignorance and stupidity (v. 11).

Yet God is silent, and wickedness prospers (v. 12). "As for me,"
complains the psalmist (in paraphrase), "this tripped me up — I
almost slipped from faith; for I preserved my innocence, and all I got

was affliction and chastening" (vv. 2, 13, 14). "My striving was in vain; I grew envious" (v. 3). "I kept quiet for others' sakes" (v. 15; to have spoken out would have "betrayed the family of God," NEB). "So I set myself to think this out" (v. 16, NEB), but "I found it too difficult to understand, and wearisome." Religion did not pay, wickedness did; life is unfair.

The poet found his attempts at understanding wearisome "until," he testifies frankly, "I went into God's sacred courts" (v. 17, NEB, plural), possibly seeking an oracle, an inspired insight. There he learned (i), with Psalm 37, that the wicked, too, stand in slippery places, their prosperity as insecure as dream images (vv. 17–20). He also learned (ii) how very different was his own lot: "as for me" (again), he was befriended, upheld (from slipping), guided, and counseled by God (vv. 23–24). So he learned (iii) how stupid, "brutish" had been his envy, how soured his attitude (vv. 21–22). For, having God, he has all he can desire (v. 25, a magnificent verse); the gain in godliness lies just in having God. This settles the problem: to be "far" from God is to miss the highest good and end in "perishing"; to be "near" to God is to be safe ("my refuge") and have a faith to tell.

That is the Old Testament's supreme answer to the question, Does religion pay? God himself is its reward. How far does the poet's assurance take him? "Afterward...receive me to glory" (v. 24) may mean only "bring me to honor"—"receive me *with* glory"; or it may adumbrate immortality, arguing from the reality and joy of fellowship with God here to the confidence that God will not let him go, "for ever." That is the deepest biblical argument for immortality (Luke 20:37, 38; Rom. 8:38). Even if in verse 26 "fail" means "decline," "become enfeebled" and not "cease," "die," so that the strength — the (inner) "rock," as the Hebrew has it — of God will replace his dwindling powers, yet the phrase "my portion for ever" surely implies something more than "a strong death."

Certainly Judaism came eventually to faith in immortality; it is significant that, with Job, the psalmist approaches this conviction by way of the inexplicable suffering of the godly. He has God, and for ever; religion does pay!

New Testament echoes: cf. Matthew 7:24–27; Luke 12:15; Philippians 3:8; 1 Timothy 6:6; James 4:8.

74 SAD DAY FOR RELIGION

For heading, see the Introduction, IV (ii), IV (iii).

The situation so vividly described in verses 3–8 could have obtained just after Nebuchadnezzar's deportation of Judah to Babylon (cf. Jer. 41:4–5, though the city and people are not mentioned in the psalm); or in the time of Antiochus Epiphanes, who defiled the temple and set up heathen standards (v. 4) against Maccabean resistance (1 Macc. 4:36–41, where "gates" recalls the psalm's "doors," v. 6, Greek version); or, more probably, in the early days of the return from Babylon (cf. Hag. 1:7–9; Zech. 7:3–5).

The havoc in the sanctuary was not the only tragedy: verse 9 reflects a still deeper decline and danger. This and the absence of other "meeting places" for worship (though the Greek version necessarily uses "synagogue," the Hebrew word never meant "buildings" but "assemblies"), together with the *retrospective* viewpoint of the psalm (vv. 1, 3, 5–8, 10), support the date at the early days of the Return, and the sad discoveries then made. Once written, of course, the lament and prayer applied, unfortunately, to several other occasions of persecution and destruction.

The poet wrestles with the contradiction between the divine *anger*, leading to rejection, which this tragedy reveals (though without explicit acknowledgment of sinful desert), and the *love* which originally made Judah the Lord's "sheep for pasturing" (not for butchering), which created and redeemed her to be God's own "heritage" (vv. 1, 2), his "turtle-dove," now in danger of beasts (? — "falcons," v. 19). He pleads that God will come and look (v. 3), as if the sight will soften God's heart. He describes with grievous detail, as if to move God to feel pity and to "remember" his former pride in Zion (vv. 2, 3). "Perpetual ruins," which begs the question "how long?" in verse 10, probably means "total, utter ruin." The tumult and the alien "standards" (NEB) or ensigns (v. 4) break God's law and Judah's heart. Verse 5 is difficult to translate; it probably likens the foe's wild vandalism to the woodmen's brandishing of axes in a thicket. The covenanted land is far from what it ought to be: its "black spots" are full of violence and crime (v. 20) — but this interpretation is doubtful.

As he surveys the long-standing devastation, the moving cry of the poet is "How long, O God? . . ." (v. 10) — "Is it for ever?" (v. 1, NEB); "We cannot see what lies before us; we have no prophet" (v. 9, NEB). It is not, surely, that God has no power. Surprisingly, the psalmist draws at length upon the Babylonian tradition (fresh in the minds of returned exiles: see the Introduction, II [ii], II [iv]) concerning the pre-creation conflict in which Marduk clove Tiamat in two to make earth and sky. He subdued the forces of chaos, the monster of the abyss, slaying the great Leviathan, the seven-headed serpent of the deep, and cut the deep channels by which the raging sea was tamed, controlling the mighty rivers. Into newly ordered Nature he brought light, the sun and stars, day and night, the seasons, the boundaries of the nations. All this *thou* (very emphatic, ten times), "God my King," has done, and not another, not Marduk! (vv. 12–17; "from of old" means "in the beginning," "originally"). "Creatures of the wilderness" (v. 14) may be jackals or "sharks" (NEB); possibly, though, the waters were given to the desert itself to "absorb."

All this God has done, achieving victory in far greater battles against cosmic foes. Why then should the enemies scoff now at God's inactivity (vv. 18–19, 23), and his people "turn back" from him, disappointed and ashamed? (v. 21, literally).

So the psalmist argues and pleads. He would *remind* God, seven times, not only of the people he first purchased and the glory of his former dwelling (v. 2) but of the vaunting of the enemies in their wicked triumph (twice—vv. 18, 22), of his former love for Judah and care for his "poor" people (twice — vv. 19, 21), and of his covenant with the nation of old (v. 20)—all strong arguments for God to "take his hands out of his pockets" (v. 11), so to speak, to arise and maintain his own cause (v. 22). This last argument expresses the psalmist's deepest perplexity of all. It is God's house and people, God's sanctuary and name (vv. 10, 18), God's chosen (v. 19) and covenant (v. 20), God's cause and personal majesty (v. 22; note "thee") that are at stake, still shamed by the persisting ruin. Why then does God not act?

Can it be that God is still angry? (v. 1) — and if so, for how long? (v. 10). A paraphrase suggests the psalmist's insistent plea: "Remember, O Lord....Arise...and defend your own name, stand up for your cause!"

In the end God will both forgive and triumph; so Jew and Christian believe.

New Testament echo: Acts 17:26.

75 THE WINE CUP OF GOD

For headings, see the Introduction, IV (i); for Selah, see IV (ii).
The changing voices in this warning poem (see the Introduction, III [i]) betray a liturgical dialogue; a litany of judgment, spoken, intoned, or sung with the assembled congregation; and a leader (priest or prophet) speaking God's word and another (or possibly the congregation) speaking about God. The theme is clearly God's judgment against the arrogant. If verse 3 preserves an allusion to an actual, nerve-shattering earthquake (note Amos 1:1), the poem may well have originated in a prophet's moralizing upon a recent traumatic experi-

ence; reference to a myth concerning some primeval cosmic blunder that God repaired seems farfetched (for "pillars," see 1 Sam. 2:8).

We should envisage, then, a moment in the worship service after the traditional reading (or recitation) of previous great deeds of God when the people give thanks, acknowledge the sense of divine presence and power kindled by the record, and then wait for a word from God. (So v. 1 in the NEB has it; "name" is probably a reverent circumlocution for God's personal presence, as in Isa. 30:27–28; "we call on thy name," RSV, requires amendment of the awkward Hebrew.) A leader then speaks on God's behalf, either reproducing a familiar oracle or speaking under inspiration a new message (vv. 2–5). The significance of the earthquake is spelled out. God, at his chosen time (without warning), acts to shake the hearts of men, to warn the proud and "pushing," the arrogantly self-willed (v. 5; for the metaphor of "horns," see the Introduction, III [ii]; "stiff neck" is a common Hebrew phrase for obstinacy, but with some support from the Greek version it may mean here "your rock"; the NEB has "your Creator," parallel to "high heaven").

Another speaker then comments (vv. 6–8) on this word of the Lord. Only God can "lift up" and "put down" as the earthquake did, in his unanswerable judgment lifting up one and putting down another. Such intervention comes not from east or west or south (the wilderness of Judea) but only from above. Then follows a dreadful picture of God the host, in his hand the foaming wine-cup "hot with spice" (NEB), which he passes round to his guests. It is the ancient "cup of ordeal," the cup which the guilty will find poisoned, and so to them a cup of judgment (Num. 5:11–31). All the living, who sit daily at God's table, must drink of it; the arrogant and guilty will perish by it (cf. Isa. 51:17; Jer. 25:15; contrast Pss. 23:5; 116:13).

The leader, perhaps with the congregation also, replies. So far from being arrogant, seeking his own glory, he will declare the praises of God ("will glorify...sing praises to the God of Jacob," NEB). The spokesman closes the solemn lesson by reiterating the main point: judgment is, and will be seen to be, the Lord's alone!

We modern Christians have lost the sense of "dwelling with the everlasting burnings" in a world where God's judgments are about us all the time. We are morally and emotionally feebler as a result. The psalmist's imagery may repel, but the truth behind the words is inescapable. Yet we rejoice that there was one who did not insist that the cup pass from him; in consequence we drink the cup of the new covenant in forgiveness and in peace.

New Testament echoes: Revelation 14:10; 16:19.

76 "TERRIBLE ART THOU!"

For headings, see the Introduction, IV (i), IV (iii); for Selah, see IV (ii).

When Sennacherib, latest of the *kings* of Assyria (Isa. 37:11, 18), threatened Hezekiah, Isaiah promised that God "would put *a spirit* in" Sennacherib so that upon hearing a rumor he would return to his own land and there be slain. Concerning the force left to besiege the city, the prophet promised that neither "*arrow, shield,* nor siege mound" should attack the city; God would defend it for his own sake. Then "an angel of the Lord slew a hundred and eighty-five thousand in the camp," and "when men arose early in the morning, behold, these were all dead," and the siege was suddenly over (Isa. 37:33, 35, 36).

Reading this psalm and noting especially verses 2, 3, 5, 6, and 12, it is difficult not to feel within it the awe and gratitude of a city so marvelously delivered. In Judah-Israel (v. 1) God's name (character, power) has been plainly manifested; his dwelling place ("battle-quarters," NEB) at Salem (an abbreviation for Jeru-Salem) has been miraculously saved (vv. 1–3). More glorious, more "terrible" to an enemy than the steadfast protecting hills about Jerusalem is her "terrible" God (so, apparently, the NEB has it, following Jewish commentaries and omitting difficult words; one Hebrew word for "prey" in "mountains of prey" means also "eternal"; there has been some confusion). "Men that lust for plunder stand aghast, the boldest swoon away, and the strongest cannot lift a hand" (v. 5, NEB).

So "terrible" is God when he is roused (vv. 7, 12, and also in vv. 4, 11, Hebrew). The earth is stilled as God interferes against the mighty to protect the "oppressed" ("poor," "meek") state of Judah (vv. 7–9). By such a manifestation of his "name" God turns even the warring passions of men to his own glory, and this will yet be confirmed by his subduing any "residue" of rebellious men. Mighty and irresistible indeed is our God! (v. 10).

The only adequate response to so revealing an experience is heartfelt homage, the faithful performance of vows, and the offering of gifts to him who is "terrible" even to the mighty among men (vv. 11–12; Hebrew idiom allows the interpretation "perform faithfully now the vows you made in the hour of crisis" or "make and keep new vows").

This explanation seems more straightforward than the one that sees the poem as a "liturgical commentary" accompanied by a mimic battle in the sanctuary. But some think it too simple, partly because the word "oppressed" ("meek," "humble," NEB) in verse 9 does not readily suggest small, bullied Judah; partly because vows are introduced unexpectedly in such a context; and partly because this exposition oversimplifies verse 10—which is almost unintelligible by any interpretation. The Hebrew letters can be so divided as to yield "for all her fury, Edom shall confess thee, and the remnant left in Hamath shall dance in worship" (the NEB, with help from the Greek version). What that means is left unexplained; it would be hard to reconcile with a "Sennacherib invasion" setting of the poem.

The "terror" of God is not a notion that sits comfortably in Christian minds, although a Christian writer can warn that "it is a fearful thing to fall into the hands of the living God" and "our God is a consuming fire" (Heb. 10:31; 12:29). The poet is, however, entirely right in relating our sense of God's "fearful might" with the sincerity and depth of the *homage* we pay him.

New Testament echo: Revelation 6:17.

77 "IN THE DAY OF MY TROUBLE"

For headings, see the Introduction, IV (i), IV (iii); for Selah, see IV (ii); on part-theme, God and Nature, see II (v).

The description of one in dire trouble (v. 1; literally "tossing," v. 2), crying aloud to God in earnest prayer through the long, sleepless night, murmuring over to himself "the remembrance of things past" that now only intensifies his feeling of desolation, is too intimately felt to be other than (originally) individual. Doubtless, as so often happens, the individual confession came to express in the hymnbook the nation's own need, but "us" in verses 7 and 8 of the NEB is not original. The odd expression in Hebrew, "hand outpoured," gave rise in Jewish comments to "eye outpoured"—that is, weeping; the NEB takes this as "lay sweating"; "refuses to be comforted" apparently means "refuses [superficial] comfort."

Memory and meditation bring no consolation, only regret, groaning, sleeplessness, and wandering, restless thoughts (though the NEB has "eyelids tightly *closed*," v. 4; the RSV follows the Syriac version for "search my spirit"; the Hebrew is more intelligible—"my spirit searches"—for endless internal questioning). The result is a string of six questions (vv. 7–9) doubting whether God's favor and compassion will ever return.

This deep spiritual depression underlies verse 10, though

translators despair of showing just how. The RSV, following Jewish commentaries and the Greek version, is full of pathos, especially if "grief" be understood as "what wounds me." The NEB paraphrases it as two more questions: "Has his right hand...lost its grasp? Does it hang powerless, the arm of the Most High?" Other amended versions go further afield: "It is my sickness makes me think that the right hand of the Most High has changed" (though no physical sickness has been mentioned). What is clear is the psalmist's unrelieved and deepening despondency.

His resource is to "remember" or "consider" (used six times) God's self-revelation in history and in Nature, the traditional springs of faith for Israel in all dark days. Though the tone changes at verse 16, the unity of argument makes it improbable that this poem is two psalms combined. The *history* is not here recounted in detail (vv. 11–14), but only the resolve to cease meditating, considering, remembering, and communing about his own spiritual state, and instead to "call to mind," "remember," and "meditate on" what God has done, his mighty works, his unparalleled "way" in history (v. 13).

The manifestation of God in *Nature* is affirmed in the description of a great storm coming across the sea: the drenching rain, the roll and crash of thunder, the tearing whirlwind and lightning arrows that illumine the world—though as God in tempest went by, none could trace his footprints, so mysterious was his approach and passing. This is the probable meaning of verses 16–19; there is no direct reference here (as in Ps. 74) to the primeval conflict with chaos, though every storm doubtless re-enacted for Jewish minds the victory of God over the forces of Nature. Some think that verse 18 (literally "what goes round") refers not to the whirlwind but to the chariot wheels of God heard in rolling thunder (cf. Ps. 29; Hab. 3:7–12).

Nevertheless, the psalmist's question was not of God's deeds of power but whether God's favor continued, whether his compassion had failed, his right hand been withdrawn. The answer is—Never! For all the mighty deeds of God in history centered in this, that he redeemed his people, all Israel (v. 15); and all the mighty power of God in Nature finds its focus in this, to shepherd Israel (v. 20). It is an audacious affirmation. But the psalmist knew that he was embraced within that purpose, and knew, too, that the only claim that men can ever make upon God is that he will perfect that to which he has once set his hand.

Self-communing rarely brings comfort. To look out of ourselves to what God has done, and is doing, in the wide earth is to catch again the vision of what he will do, and take heart.

78 "A STORY WITH A MEANING"

For headings, see the Introduction, IV (ii), IV (iii).

What appears to be a recited review of Jewish history — introduced by eight verses claiming attention in the sanctuary for the sacred tradition of the great deeds of God, which God himself commanded to be passed from generation to generation — turns out to be a somewhat self-righteous moral lesson drawn for Judah (the southern kingdom) from the ignominious collapse and deportation to Assyria of the northern kingdom. The poet undertakes to "expound the riddle of things past" in a "story with a meaning" (v. 2, NEB), according to the solemn charge given by God (v. 5) that each generation should set their hope in God, not forget his works, and keep his commandments.

To this is added a fourth purpose with a distinct edge to it: "that they should not be like their fathers" (v. 8, RSV), "a generation with no firm purpose" (v. 8, NEB). Of the remaining sixty-four verses, no less than thirty-five contain sharp condemnation of Israel. The reason for such emphasis is that "Ephraim" (a general epithet for the northern kingdom), though well armed, failed utterly in the day of testing because of a previous total failure in spiritual loyalties (vv. 9, 10) and an ignorance of God's mighty deeds (v. 11). This was plainly the occasion, or at least the "text," of the original poem.

Those great deeds (or an argumentative selection of them) are then recounted, interspersed with sharp contrasts, highly derogatory to "Israel," between God's patient goodness and "Israel's" persistent unfaithfulness. Curiously, throughout this historical sermon the name "Israel" is used as though from earliest days it signified only the northern tribes, so that Judah, the surviving kingdom, had no part in "Israel's" rebelliousness.

God's "marvels" are retold, with some exaggeration, from the Exodus from Egypt to the giving of water from the rock (vv. 12–16; cf. Exod. 17, Num. 20; Zoan was in northern Egypt). Ungratefully, the "Israelites" at once put God to a further test, demanding whether he could provide bread and meat. This kindled God's anger, yet he commanded the "rain" of manna and "winged birds" — quail (vv. 17–29; "they tried God's patience wilfully," v. 18, NEB; with v. 19, cf. Ps. 23:5; it was believed that manna resembled white corn, so vv. 24, 25 gave Christianity the phrase "panis angelicus"—"the bread of angels"—to describe the Lord's Supper; "like dust" in v. 27 means "like a dust storm"; in Exodus and Numbers the manna and quail were given before the water from the rock). In spite of this provision,

God had occasion yet to be angry with "Israel": "they still sinned," and did not believe, so death spread among them (vv. 30–33).

For a while the subdued people sought God, realizing their need of him, but their repentant speeches were "flattery" and "lies," and their hearts were not steadfast (vv. 34–37; v. 37 possibly refers to the failure to enter Canaan). God's tireless patience with this recalcitrant people is beautifully described: God wiped out their guilt, "restrained his anger," remembered their frailty, yet they continued to provoke him (vv. 38–41). Perhaps to provide a contrast to this "restraining anger," the poet reverts to describing some of the terrible plagues which God, without such restraint, sent upon Egypt, things "Israel" too readily "forgot" (vv. 42–51). In verse 46 note locusts and their young, "grubs"; for "frost" the NEB has "torrents of rain"; in verse 48, "plague" and "pestilence." God's "anger," "wrath," "indignation," and "distress" are probably not destroying angels but "messengers of evil" who prepare the way for God's fury ("angel" means "messenger"). "Ham" is the ancestor of Egypt in Genesis 10:6.

The leaving of Egypt, the deliverance from Pharaoh's army, the journey through the wilderness, and the settlement in Canaan occupy only verses 52–55, though it is emphasized that God was the people's shepherd, leading them in safety to his "holy land," "the mountain his right hand had won" (? — Canaan, Sinai, or Zion, as the sequel might suggest). Even still, "Israel" tempted God, being rebellious, treacherous, twisting in the hand like a slackened (or unseasoned) bow. She provoked his anger with her hill shrines and her idol worship; with this reference the poet briefly summarizes the period of the "judges" and later apostasy (vv. 56–58; after Josiah's reforms, a Judean psalmist would condemn any shrine but Zion).

At last God's patience gave out. "He utterly rejected Israel" ("put them out of mind," NEB); forsook his earliest shrine-dwelling at Shiloh in Ephraim; surrendered the Ark, the symbol of his power and glory, into the hands of enemies (vv. 60–61; cf. 1 Sam. 4–6 for Philistine possession of the Ark; Jer. 7:12–15); and permitted all kinds of tragedy to follow — upon young men, brides-to-be, priests (Eli's sons?), and mourners. It was as though God awoke from a drunken sleep in a rage — a daring metaphor — to put his enemies (Israel) to flight into Assyria, in everlasting shame (vv. 62–66; the RSV's "strong man shouting" becomes in the NEB " a warrior heated with wine"; in v. 66 the NEB restores the AV/KJV with "striking his foes in the back parts" — a contemptuous kick!).

So the northern kingdom had ended in complete rejection. The divine "choice" ("election") was withdrawn so far as "Joseph-Ephraim" was concerned (v. 67) — but not from Judah, God's chosen tribe, or from Mount Zion, which he loves (and to which David brought the Ark, 2 Sam. 6 — unaccountably omitted here). There *God* built his sanctuary (following the model "in the heavenly heights," 1 Chron. 28:19; cf. Exod. 25:9, 40 — "in the mountain-heights" or "high as the heavens"), "founded like the earth to last for ever" (NEB). There God chose David the shepherd to continue the shepherding begun by God in the wilderness; "Israel" now has its usual meaning, parallel to "Jacob," as the nation descended from Abraham to be God's people. And with what upright heart and skilled hand David tended them! (vv. 68–72).

There, suddenly, the summary ends, because there the poet's intention is fulfilled: to "explain" and justify the rejection of the northern kingdom and the passing of the divine choice to Judah, to Jerusalem, and to the dynasty of David. It is history retold with patriotic zeal for religious propaganda, and a solemn warning to all future generations (even to Judah, who preserved the poem) against the dire consequences of apostasy.

Doubtless it is well to learn from other men's failures — even better to do it humbly, and with regret.

New Testament echoes: Matthew 13:35; John 6:31; Acts 8:21; cf. 1 Corinthians 10:3, 9; Hebrews 3:16, 17; Jude 5.

79 DISASTER!

For heading, see the Introduction, IV (iii).

This wail of grief, passing into prayer for pity, deliverance, and revenge, speaks eloquently for itself. Although it is impossible to be certain which disaster to Jerusalem occasioned its composition, the background situation closely resembles that of Psalm 74, the first years of the Exile or the early years of the Return. (Jeremiah 41:4–5; Haggai 1:7–9; and Zechariah 7:3–5 were there adduced to illustrate the existence of the ruined but not destroyed temple.) A Maccabean date, when Antiochus defiled the temple, is less probable, since verse 3 is quoted as scripture — "in accordance with the word which was written" — in 1 Maccabees 7:16–17.

The psalm is full of familiar phrases and quotations: verse 1 recalls Micah 3:12; verse 2 resembles Jeremiah 19:7 and other passages; verse 4 is the same as Psalm 44:13; verse 5 is like Psalm 89:47; verses 6 and 7 are the equivalent of Jeremiah 10:25 slightly altered, where the words are original; part of verse 10 is in Psalm 115:2; verse 11 is very like Psalm 102:20; and verse 13 has a phrase resembling Psalm 100:3. The language of the catastrophe was probably familiar to many.

The situation is dramatically described (vv. 1–4; the NEB has "The heathen have *set foot* in thy domain.... They have *thrown out* the dead bodies"). It is God's land ("inheritance"), sanctuary, city, servants, and covenant people that are despoiled by pagans and mocked by neighbors. This was an intolerable insult in Eastern eyes; for the dead to remain unburied (v. 3) was the final indignity, outrage, and calamity, since it precluded "rest" in Sheol. The horror expressed is meant to appeal to the divine pity (so vv. 8, 11 show).

Though the heathen did it, the event embodies *God's* wrath (v. 5). The implied admission that punishment was deserved, though repeated at verse 9, is somewhat perfunctory. God should pour his anger instead upon the truly heathen, who have done this wrong to Jacob (vv. 6, 7). Behind this suggestion lies the feeling that to punish sinners through greater sinners is less than just (cf. Hab. 1:12, 13). It is equally unfair to punish one generation for another generation's sin (v. 8; cf. Ezek. 18).

Moreover, God's own "character" (reputation, "name") is at stake in the fate of his people (vv. 9, 10), but desire for the wrong to be "avenged," not in the distant future but "before our eyes," quickly mingles with concern for God's honor. The brief prayer for pity upon the prisoners taken and those condemned to death (v. 11; literally "sons of death," which may mean "living as already dead") passes into a prayer for sevenfold requital (v. 12). Then, when justice is seen to have been done, "we, thy people, the flock of thy pasture [an ironic reminder of old promises?], "will give thanks...will recount thy praise."

It expresses a very human mood, this half-penitent, half-complaining cry to be better treated! Jeremiah had struggled hard to achieve a deeper penitence than this, lest the humiliation of the Exile should produce no lasting reform. But that wholly "new heart and new spirit" is not yet reached in this psalm. Without it, salvation is not complete, in Jew or Christian.

New Testament echoes: Revelation 16:1; cf. 1 Thessalonians 4:5; 2 Thessalonians 1:8; Revelation 11:9.

80 "TURN AGAIN, O GOD OF HOSTS..."

For headings, see the Introduction, IV (i), IV (iii).
This psalm has a "growing" refrain (vv. 3, 7, 19) possibly sung by the congregation between solo voices; note "O God," "O God of hosts," and "O Lord God of hosts." It is *possible*, too, that it should appear

after verses 10 and 13. This refrain well summarizes the prayer of the poet for the northern kingdom of Israel (v. 2) in its last days before the deportation to Assyria. The people are still in the land and "salvation" is still possible (contrast Ps. 78 and cf. 2 Kgs. 15:17–22). But enemies, tears, plunder, and destruction have brought the people low (vv. 6, 5, 12, 13). The poet prays that God will "turn" the misfortune to deliverance (equal to "restore," literally); will also "turn" himself to look down with concern (v. 14), and "turn his face" from frowning disfavor to welcoming acceptance (vv. 3–4). In return the psalmist promises that the people will never "turn back" from God (v. 18). This assumes that behind the ravages of the enemy lies the anger of God (vv. 4–6); the surprised poet cannot understand why (v. 12).

Much here is shared with Psalm 78 and with later psalms reflecting upon Judah's similar experience. What is unique here is the appeal to the "blessing" pronounced upon the tribe of Joseph in Genesis 49:22–24, whose sources, at least, may be very old. There it is promised that Joseph shall become "a fruitful bough by a spring," whose "branches run over the wall...his arms...made agile...by the name of the Shepherd, the Rock of Israel...."

For the frequent figure of the shepherd with Israel as his flock, compare Psalms 23 and 74 and Ezekiel 34; this poet feels that God has acted most un-shepherd-like! (vv. 1, 5). The Ark, or sacred chest, originally kept in northern Israel, had carved cherubim (winged, probably sphinx-like creatures representing heavenly throne-bearers) guarding or supporting its throne-seat (see Exod. 25:19, 20; cf. Gen. 3:24; Isa. 6; Ezek. 1). "Shine forth" means "manifest thyself"; only here is Benjamin included with the northern tribes led by the sons of Joseph; "stir up thy might" implies "from slumber" — the shepherd's task included defending the sheep; "come" is literally "go," to fight.

Dropping the metaphor, the poet pleads that God will no longer be "angry with thy people's prayers" (the NEB has "how long wilt thou resist thy people's prayer?"; also, "tears of threefold grief," v. 5). He protests Israel's total loss of face among her neighbors (v. 6; if the Hebrew "strife," for "scorn," is right, it means presumably "cause of strife").

The other metaphor in the old blessing, the "fruitful bough" (note v. 11), is here elaborated into another frequent figure, that of God's vine. Transplanted from Egypt, tended with care, flourishing from the mountains of the south to Lebanon's cedars in the north, from the Mediterranean to the Euphrates, "filling the land," it is now abandoned to passing (Assyrian) vandals, to wild boars and other creatures ("swarming insects from the fields," NEB, vv. 8–13; cf. Isa. 5:1–7; 27:2–6; Hos. 10:1).

"Why?" demands the poet, adding, "take thought for the vine, for your right hand planted it" (paraphrase)—a bold address to God. The RSV relegates to the margin the Hebrew phrase "and upon the son whom thou hast reared for thyself," presumably because "whom thou hast *made strong* for thyself" occurs in verse 17 to describe "the man of thy right hand," "the son of man," or "son" ("heir") of Adam. (The NEB makes verse 15 read "this stock which thy right hand has planted," and verse 17 read "Let thy hand rest upon the man at thy right side, the man whom thou hast made strong for thy service.") The possibility that the phrase has been accidentally repeated in copying is complicated by the further consideration that "son of the right hand" is, in Hebrew, "Benjamin"! The significance of this pun can now only be guessed at, but the prayer for the Joseph vine, perhaps especially for the Benjamin tribe, is clear, for the enemy has cut it down and burned it. Ezekiel points out that the wood of the vine is useful for nothing but fuel (15:2–5). If the prayer for "a right hand of blessing" and "a gift of life" is granted, then the poet promises faithfulness henceforth.

As sheep among domestic animals need more care than others, so the vine among cultivated plants needs the most tending. A feeling of dependence, of weakness, is suggested here, which promises greater faithfulness in the future — though northern Israel had no further opportunity. Those who are saved must never forget that they needed, and still need, to be saved; the sheep must still follow, the branches abide closely in the vine.

New Testament echoes: John 10:11–12; 15:1–11.

81 "IF MY PEOPLE WOULD BUT LISTEN"

For headings, see the Introduction, IV (i), IV (iii); for Selah, see IV (ii). Modern translations tend to rewrite and rearrange this poem (as does the NEB), to "correct" some phrases and leave others unintelligible (as does the RSV, vv. 16, 5, 10), or to treat it as fragments of two or three psalms, ill-matched in tone and meaning (as commentaries do). The undoubted difficulties may better be approached by understanding verse 3 to refer literally to "the" pilgrim feast (NEB; the New Year Feast of Tabernacles held in autumn, prepared for at the new moon of the old seventh month—later, "the beginning of months"— and formally begun at the full moon, about the fifteenth; see Num. 29:1, 7, 12; 10:1–2, 10; Lev. 23:34, 42, 43; ram's horn and silver trumpets, there mentioned, were not always rigidly distinguished in use). Jewish tradition confirms this liturgical use of the psalm. It certainly becomes easier to follow in this light.

A resounding call (by the officiating priest?) to keep the festival and to hail the presence of God with shouting, hand-drum (tambourine), lyre, harp, and trumpets, as appointed by God from the days when Joseph "came out *of* Egypt" (NEB), gathers a rejoicing and expectant crowd within the sanctuary to celebrate the "remembrance" (symbolized by "booths" or tents about the city) of the pilgrim past. At a given moment one spokesman (a ritual prophet?) bids attention for "a voice I had not known"—no familiar speaker, but God himself (for this experience of a divine "oracle," cf. Num. 24:3–4, 15–17; 2 Sam. 23:1–3; Job 4:12–16).

The spokesman proceeds to recall the salient features of Israel's exodus from Egypt. (i) He mentions the release from slavery in answer to the people's distressful prayer, from the "burden" of forced labor and the "builders' baskets" of brick-makers (v. 6). God had answered, as at Sinai, either by thunder or from the thunder cloud. (ii) The testing at Meribah by thirst and the gift of water from the rock he cites as typical of the years of discipline and care that followed (see Exod. 17:1–7; Num. 20:2–13). (iii) He recites the essential elements of the covenant at Sinai — remembering their deliverance by God, renouncing other gods (vv. 8–10 recall the Ten Commandments of Exodus 20 and the daily "Shema," Deut. 6:4–9). This was a mere "sample" of the covenant's obligations, but reasserting to the law was an essential part of the festival rite. (iv) He notes the corresponding covenant blessing, the promise of bounty to an obedient people (the end of v. 10; this is very debatable, but without such reminder the festival's "remembrance" offers no incentive or promise; the NEB transfers this to verse 7 and amends it to "where I opened your mouths and filled them"; a Jewish commentary understands it to mean "take in my commandments as your food: be teachable, and I will teach you my law").

Either the same spokesman (as the RSV has it) or possibly another "applies" the oracle to contemporary conditions. Taking up the words "if you would but listen to me," he reproaches Israel for "not listening" to the conditions of the covenant accepted in those far-off days now being celebrated (vv. 11–16; v. 11 appears also in Jer. 7:24, perhaps as a quotation from the ritual). "Stubborn hearts" appears in ancient versions as "lust"; in verses 13–14 the NEB has "If my people would but listen...I would...." In verse 15 the NEB amends to "Let those who hate them come cringing to them, and meet with everlasting troubles." Then, whatever the pronouns should be, verse 16 (here in paraphrase) echoes and elaborates the ancient incentive-promise of verse 10, quoting Deuteronomy 32:13,

14 (a fuller version of "flowing with milk and honey"): "I will feed you with the *cream* of the wheat [literally "the fat"] and the honey from wild bees" in the fissures of warm rocks.

So the sacred festival commemorating ancient events was given, by a courageous exponent of its meaning, a contemporary and urgent relevance, as all such religious occasions should be given—not least the Christian "holy days."

New Testament echoes: Romans 1:24, 26 (based on the Greek version).

82 ON JUSTICE

For heading, see the Introduction, IV (iii); for Selah, see IV (ii).

This psalm, a magnificent soaring of poetic imagination and insight, yields two invaluable and timeless principles. The background ideas and language were considered in the discussion of Psalm 58; a parallel picture of God presiding over "spirits," "sons of God," in the heavenly court is in Job 1:6–12 (cf. 1 Kgs. 22:19–22). To understand "gods" (v. 1) not as "guardian spirits appointed by God to superintend the life of each nation" but as "gods and goddesses worshiped by heathen nations" would imply not merely rival gods (as in Exod. 20:3,4; Pss. 95:3; 86:8) but an actual pantheon of many gods, among which Israel's God had a recognized place—an idea alien to the Old Testament and difficult to reconcile with the "death" of these gods in verse 7.

As chief judge of the universe's "court of final appeal," God hands down his verdict upon the way the appointed guardian spirits of the nations have dispensed justice on earth, "lifting up the face of the wicked" (literal Hebrew), neglecting and perverting righteousness (vv. 1, 2). The sole test of true justice is positive discrimination in defense of those who cannot defend themselves—those "brought low" (literal Hebrew), those without parental guardians, the afflicted and the destitute. The Book of Amos testifies to how rare such justice was in the ancient East (Amos 5:7, 12; 6:12, 23–24). Lack of justice leaves society "in the dark," its foundations crumbling (v. 5, NEB; in the RSV this is apparently an intrusive comment, interrupting God's verdict; in the NEB, perhaps God speaking about, instead of to, the heavenly judges). Then God pronounces his verdict: though they are "gods, sons of the Most High" (v. 6; cf. Job 1:6; "sons of a high god," NEB), yet shall they die as any human "prince" (? — judge) dies who displeases his king. Life is at all times the gift of God; for God's punishing the host of heaven, see Isaiah 24:21; compare Job 4:18.

The concluding reflection (v. 8, as likely to be by the poet as by "some pious reader") pleads that God will himself take over the judgment of the earth, for all the nations belong to him (or "for thou dost pass all nations through thy sieve" — NEB, without explanation).

That comment says it all. (i) In Israel's eyes it is God's own task to administer justice on earth, and only he can be trusted to do so with equity. "The judgment is God's" (Deut. 1:17). (ii) Justice is the foundation of social order, and the quality of justice lies in its compassion toward the vulnerable and the deprived. By that alone will "a just society" be recognized (Deut. 10:17, 18). In these two principles lie the social message of the Bible and the hope of the world's salvation.

New Testament echo: John 10:34–35.

83 THE USES OF HISTORY

For headings, see the Introduction, IV (i), IV (iii); for Selah, see IV (ii); on theme, vindication, see II (ii).

The confederacy of neighboring tribes listed in verses 6–8 entirely encircles Judah. The tent-dwellers are nomadic tribes, Bedawin; the children of Lot are Moab and Ammon. Gebal may be a nomadic people near Petra. "Assyria" ("Asshur," NEB) could be another Bedawin tribe (Gen. 25:3), a late name for Syria (a country otherwise omitted), or the imperial overlords who, displeased with Judah, have moved surrounding vassal states to seek her destruction (vv. 8, 4; cf. Jer. 48:2). These uncertainties prevent our relating the psalm to the confederacy against Jehoshaphat (2 Chron. 20), to that against Judas Maccabeus, when six of these neighboring peoples were involved (1 Macc. 5), or to any specific moment of similar danger.

But that Judah is besieged is clear. Her foes proudly toss their heads and roar like beasts — how then can God keep silent and still (vv. 1, 2)? For it is against God that they conspire (v. 5) as well as against his "protected ones" (or "hidden ones," as treasures; other versions have "hidden thing" — namely, the temple, Ezek. 7:22; the Greek version has "favoured ones").

Therefore the psalmist prays that God will do to "them" (the besiegers, v. 9 taking up v. 5) what he did in two former outstanding instances of deliverance from conspiracies. One was that led by Barak and Deborah against "the kings of Canaan" (vv. 9, 10; Judg. 5:19, though Judg. 4 names Jabin king of Canaan and Sisera his general; the flooded wadi Kishon helped carry away the enemy,

Judg. 5:21; Endor, not named in Judges, is at the foot of Tabor; the NEB suggests En-harod, named in Judg. 7:1; so great was the slaughter that the corpses evidently remained unburied). The second remembered deliverance was led by Gideon, who defeated the Midianites (vv. 11, 12; see Judg. 7, noting v. 25, and 8:5–12; the Midianites came mainly to plunder; "the pastures of God" presumably means "pastures of God's land and people," but other versions have "God's altar," "sanctuary," or "temple").

Doubtless this appeal to history implies encouragement in a somewhat similar crisis. But the immediate purpose of the appeal is more vindictive: that God will do to the new confederate enemies what he did of old, with great severity, to other conspirators. This prayer is elaborated in several vivid metaphors. May the enemy be driven like dust before the whirlwind ("thistledown," NEB; more probably, as the RSV margin has it, "tumbleweed"), like chaff before a gale, like a blaze in the forest, like fire (in summer-dried thorn and brier) across the mountainside; may they be pursued by tempest and hurricane, their faces burning with shame, dismayed for ever, perishing in disgrace.

This is a fierce prayer! The last thoughts, whether by the poet relenting or by a later adapter, dilute the vindictiveness: may these things so happen to them that they may seek, and come to know, God most high.

Religious zeal, especially in controversy, too often forgets that one cannot both destroy and convert opponents. To defeat a foe means very little compared with winning him.

84 THE IMMEASURABLE PRIVILEGE

For headings, see the Introduction, IV (i), IV (iii); for Selah, see IV (ii).
At the end of the hot, dry summer, before the early rains herald another growing season for crops and birds, with the whole land "panting" for new life and refreshment, pilgrims from all parts of Palestine gather for the "autumnal" festival. They come to proclaim God creator and king — here, "Lord of hosts," "the Lord," "the living God," "my King and my God," "the God of gods," "Lord God of hosts," "God of Jacob," "God," "my God," and "the Lord God." They come to pray for rain upon the parched land and for blessing on the king and his people. Such a lyric as this, in which the seasonal metaphors abound and the joy of worship overflows, well fits the beginning of another festival.

The first stanza ("paragraph," vv. 1–4), marked by anticipation, longing, and thirst for God and for his house, is appropriate to the journey and the first entry into Jerusalem, perhaps the first sight of the Holy Place. Immediate reactions are an exclamation at its beauty, a sense of coming home, as the bird to its nest, and envy of the immeasurable privilege of those ministers in the temple who actually dwell there, spending their lives in unbroken praise. The "dwelling places" (literally) may include the whole cluster of buildings—hence "courts"—and the nests of birds in colonnades open to the sky. It is debated whether the poet meant to envy the birds or simply to delight at arriving at the soul's "nesting place," even God's altars (ever a sanctuary, Exod. 21:13, 14), as the birds delighted in theirs. (The number of altars in each successive temple is too doubtful to assist in dating the poem; verse 9 implies existence of the monarchy.)

The second stanza acknowledges, however, the almost equal privilege of those who make the journey to the festivals, "who love pilgrimage" ("in whose heart high ways," Hebrew; the words "are" and "to Zion" are not original; "cast up high way" in Ps. 68:4 suggested a pilgrim procession; here the NEB has "whose hearts are set on the pilgrim ways," with the margin supplying "whose hearts high praises fill"; some would amend the words to "in whose heart is confidence," parallel to "strength"). Moreover, the gathering pilgrims *impart* blessing, too. Passing the valley of Baca (baca being a species of balsam that, like cacti, thrives in drought conditions; see 2 Sam. 5:22–24), they find it "a place of springs" and leave it covered with the welcome pools that signal the awaited early rains (v. 6; the NEB says the Hebrew is obscure, and without explanation translates "the Lord provides even men who lose their way with pools to quench their thirst").

So the pilgrims go "from strength to strength"—not to weariness—as the journey lengthens, inspired by the assurance that "the God of gods" will be seen in Zion (v. 7; understanding "strength" as a strong place or wall, the NEB changes it to "they pass on from outer wall to inner," marking the pilgrims' progress through the city). Perhaps a fear of being disappointed after all prompts the earnest prayer of verse 8.

The third stanza (vv. 9–11) is marked by the joy and privilege of arriving at the shrine and sharing in worship. Unexpectedly, it begins with prayer for the king, shield of the people and anointed of God. Such prayer was usual at this festival, but just possibly it was evoked at this point by a first view of the royal palace. (For the king as shield, note the parallel with "thine anointed" in Ps. 89:18.) The visit is no disappointment. As verse 10 declares, even one day is glorious, especially when "elsewhere" (RSV) is understood as "at home" (NEB), and "rather be a doorkeeper" is taken, probably correctly, as "rather lie a beggar on the threshold" (cf. Acts 3:2; a temple doorkeeper was a responsible and respected official — another to be envied). "I would rather lie begging on the threshold of God's house than live as guest in the tents of the wicked" (paraphrase).

But the great joy and blessing of the temple is God himself, a sun and shield, giving grace and glory, withholding no good from those he can trust. The NEB preserves the parallelism by translating "sun" (nowhere else used to describe God in the Old Testament, perhaps because of prevalent sun-worship) as "battlement" (cf. Isa. 54:12; "pinnacle" as reflecting the sun). The lesson of the whole wonderful experience is in verse 12: "blessed," "happy" indeed is he who trusts in God.

The joys of shared worship here mentioned are perennial: the "tabernacles" of God give rest, his "courts" grant audience, his "altars" renew forgiveness, "the Lord's house" offers fellowship with God. So may all worshipers ever find how happy are the privileged.

New Testament echo: cf. 2 Corinthians 3:18.

85 IS FORGIVENESS ENOUGH?

For headings, see the Introduction, IV (i), IV (iii); for Selah, *see IV (ii).*
The apparent contradiction between verses 1–3, where God has forsaken his anger, and verses 4–7, where the people pray that God *will* do so, presents a puzzle which the assurance of happier times ahead (vv. 8–13) does not resolve. Some, therefore, would make all the verbs "prophetic perfects" and argue a highly technical meaning for "didst restore the fortunes" (namely, "bring back the golden age," "restore the primeval bliss"). This makes the psalm (with a few other adjustments) wholly apocalyptic, a prophecy of the dream future, when history will return to its beginnings and the world will be young again. On that interpretation, nothing here refers to contemporary history. But much has to be amended to support that meaning.

On the other hand, one historical situation would illumine the poem considerably: the earliest years of the return from Babylonian exile. This would accept "brought again the captivity of Jacob" (v. 1, Hebrew) in its simplest meaning. The apocalyptists' objection is that verses 1–3 in no way describe the conditions of that return or those years of intense disappointment, struggle, and poverty which Ezra,

Nehemiah, Haggai, and Zechariah depict. But this seems precisely the psalmist's point.

The return from exile established one thing clearly: the changed attitude of God toward "Jacob" (an endearing name for Israel). Verses 1–3 concentrate upon this — "favour" in place of rejection, "the turned tide of Jacob's fortunes" (NEB), life in the nation's homeland, not in exile. The people's "iniquity," "sin," is now "lifted," "covered" (literal Hebrew); wrath and anger are ended. Religiously, as before their God, they are pardoned, accepted again, as their great prophets had promised they would be (Isa. 40:2; Jer. 31:31–34; 53:5, 6; and elsewhere). The people's return demonstrates their forgiveness.

But a people cannot live upon forgiveness. The conditions of the Return — to ruined cities, wasted fields, overgrown pastures, untilled and unproductive soil — were such as to break the people's heart. "Consider how you have fared," says Haggai. "You have sown much, and harvested little; you eat, but you never have enough; you drink, but you never have your fill; you clothe yourselves, but no one is warm; and he who earns wages earns wages to put them into a bag with holes" (1:5, 6, 9, 10; 2:16, 17). "Theologically" pardoned, they were still being economically punished.

That is the background of the psalmist's prayer (vv. 4–7): "restore us," "revive us" (RSV), "give us new life" (NEB), "that thy people may rejoice in thee. Show us thy steadfast love, O Lord, and grant us thy salvation" (RSV). It is a plea, in three plaintive questions, that the pardon assured by the fact of the Return shall now be demonstrated by full reacceptance into blessing, prosperity, and joy. This also had been promised repeatedly (Jer. 30:18, 19; 31:4, 5; 32:43, 44; 33:7, 10, 11, 29; Isa. 35:10; 51:11; 65:17–25).

To this challenging prayer the poet gives an answer. It is introduced with the old formula of the "oracle" (v. 8; the Hebrew states a condition, "but let them not turn back to folly"; the NEB has "...words of the Lord: are they not words of peace, peace to his people and his loyal servants and to all who turn and trust in him?"). There follows a magnificent sketch of the coming renewal, salvation, and glory, when God's steadfast love, righteous government, and bountiful giving will meet and "join hands" with (NEB) or "kiss" (RSV) man's newfound fidelity, peace, and prosperity. Then indeed God will come, righteousness extending wherever he is present, like a shining pathway prepared for his hallowed feet.

That vision of universal reconciliation is hardly surpassed elsewhere in scripture, nor is the promise that "the Lord will give what is good, and our land will yield its increase" in the least out of place. The Bible never pretends that pious people can live on feelings, nor does it ever forget that the earth, too, is the Lord's.

The nation's preservation of the psalm shows that its words did not apply only to the situation that produced it. Later, in corporate worship, a single voice might utter verses 1–3, the congregation answer with verses 4–7, and a leader reply with the promise of verses 8–13. So heartening a vision of the kind of world which God intends, when all man's futile rebelliousness is healed, will never, never be out of date—until it be fulfilled.

New Testament echo: cf. Matthew 6:33.

86 ''SHOW ME A SIGN...''

For heading, see the Introduction, IV (iii).

A near-literal translation of this poem falls into an almost monotonous rhythm, resembling some of our more pedestrian hymns. In verses 1–7 eight petitions follow one upon another, each accompanied by its reason; "for" occurs six times and is twice implied. Each petition is too general to stab the mind with urgency. Verse 5 almost says that it is God's nature and function to forgive! One imagines recited, formal prayers, a passage set for intoning—almost a litany.

With a slightly brisker tone, verses 8–10 and 12–13 change to acknowledgment of God, but the phrases are familiar. Indeed, most of the psalm is so like other passages in the Old Testament, from Exodus to Jeremiah, that to list parallels would be tedious. The psalmist is not quoting, but his language is conventional, almost hackneyed. (In verse 8, for "gods," meaning subordinate "angels," see the discussions of Pss. 58 and 82, but the mention of heathen nations here and the comparison made suggest that rival gods are meant.) In verses 11–17 the prayers are for guidance, for pity, for strength against (unspecified) "insolent" and "ruthless" foes ("a mob of ruffians," NEB), and for some sign of God's favor that shall confound his enemies.

The poet says or asks (so to speak) all the right things, but without warmth, without kindling mind or freshness of expression. Even the phrase "the depths of Sheol" is conventional, and may be used here metaphorically of deep trouble, not of rescue from death. Not until verse 14 do we gather any hint of special circumstances to light up "the day of my trouble" (v. 7). The lovely verse 15 (echoing v. 5) repeats Psalm 103:8. In verse 16 "thy servant, ...the son of thy handmaid" ("thy slave-girl's son," NEB) is, we are told, merely variant parallelism and does not mean "servant of the lowest class, impossible to liberate," as Exodus 21:4 might suggest. Another fine phrase, "Unite my heart to fear thy name" (v. 11, AV/KJV), turns out *not* to mean "grant me a wholly integrated personality" but "let me be one in heart with those who revere thy name" (NEB; so Jer. 32:39 promises that the whole people shall have one heart and one fear; in the next line the psalmist already possesses "a whole heart"; Greek and Syriac versions have "let my heart rejoice").

The last request, for a "token," a sign, or proof of divine favor, seems entirely characteristic of a soul lacking sparkle, a religious experience somewhat formal; it is "rationalist" in tone and largely secondhand. For some reserved, "cold" natures, that might be as far as religion can take them—to their great loss.

Not all readers of the psalm will share this impression that it is pedestrian, repetitive, "rationalist," borrowed, and long in coming to the point, but most will recall, at any rate, how often that is true of our prayers when, like this psalmist, we concentrate entirely upon our own "day of distress." "Show me a token, Lord" is ever the plea of a spirit too dulled to find God everywhere, and all the time.

New Testament echoes: cf. Mark 12:29; 1 Corinthians 8:4.

87 CITIZENS OF NO MEAN CITY

For headings, see the Introduction, IV (i), IV (iii); for Selah, see IV (ii).
In its main message this is one of the greatest of the psalms. It declares that eventually men of all nations shall be reckoned by God, and shall be proud to reckon themselves citizens of the City of God. They shall testify, with music and dance, that all their deepest sources of inspiration are in Zion—this, because God loves Zion and has spoken glorious things of her. All nations shall at last be "registered" in the City of God (so Isa. 2:2; 44:5; 45:22–25; 66:23; Zech. 2:11).

That much is clear; the attempt to reduce the poem to an announcement extending homeland citizenship to Jews born in distant centers of the Diaspora, as increasing numbers migrated to areas around the Mediterranean, is not convincing. Nevertheless, some details are uncertain, to the great confusion of translators, rearrangers (NEB), and commentators. The RSV has plausibly "mended" the broken opening sentence and linked verse 3 with the opening praise of Zion; verse 3 *can* be taken as introducing the divine pronouncement in verses 4–6. The RSV has also, in spite of Paul's quotation, ignored the Greek version's introduction of the word "mother" in verse 5, which with other small changes yields "Each one calls Zion mother, and in it was each one born." The NEB has "Zion shall be called a mother in whom men of every race are born." It seems probable that the RSV is not far from the poet's original intention.

"Gates" (v. 2) signifies a city, as distinguished from open towns and villages. "Rahab" (v. 4) is here a name for Egypt, as in Isaiah 30:7, and not for Tiamat in the Babylonian creation myth; this verse defines the political horizons of Israel. For God's "register of the living," or book of life, compare Exodus 32:32 and see the discussion of Psalm 69:28. The text of the last verse is obscure, but in general it affirms that with song and dance (cf. Ps. 26:6; 2 Sam. 6:16) Jerusalem's citizens proudly proclaim the city the source of all their joy.

To Christianity no less than to Judaism, Jerusalem has indeed become a mother-city for people of every part of the world. More important, "the City of God," the sacred community, has captured the minds and hearts of many generations, glad to claim their noble birthright and to confess that in the present and future "Jerusalem which is from above" lie all their springs of faith and worship, and of hope for the world.

New Testament echoes: Galatians 4:26 (based on the Greek version); Revelation 21:2; cf. Luke 10:20; Ephesians 2:19; Philippians 4:3; Revelation 21:27.

88 WHEN GOD IS SILENT

For headings, see the Introduction, IV (i), IV (ii), IV (iii); for Selah, see IV (ii); on theme, complaint, see II (i).

This psalm has been described as the gloomiest in the Psalter, despairing, a litany of suffering and death written with the heart's blood! In attempts to avoid the psalm's impression that religion itself could ever fail to impart relief, courage, peace, or hope, could even intensify distress, it is variously suggested that closing verses of reviving faith have been lost, that this poem belongs to the next, or that it is the nation in exile that is complaining. The last suggestion probably explains the preservation of so unhappy a poem in the hymnbook (and so Jewish commentaries assume). But its intensity and pathos are unmistakably individual. The poet has had an exceedingly hard life and complains bitterly about it; he has found no help in God and says so.

It began in his boyhood and has continued until now, when he is at the threshold of Sheol (vv. 15, 3, NEB). His segregation from society ("I am in prison and cannot escape," NEB); his separation from "lover," "friend," and "companions"; his being "loathsome," a "horror," to those near him, afflicted through the years and now failing in strength (v. 4) — all suggest that the basic trouble is advancing leprosy. In addition, his sight is failing (v. 9). He knows death cannot be long delayed; already he is counted as good as dead (vv. 4, 5) and hardly remembered. He has had his "fill of woes" (v. 3, NEB), but three things add bitterness to his lot: the loneliness of his life, God's refusal of his prayers, and God's anger toward him.

Day and night he has prayed (vv. 1, 9, 13), but there is no reply; God is turning away (vv. 2, 14; in v. 1 the Hebrew has "God of my salvation," which suggests he has found help, but so understood the sentence is too broken to yield meaning). The poet has therefore no hope, no future (vv. 3–6), only Sheol, land of the forgetting and forgotten (v. 12), the abode of shades. What healing wonders or praise or love or help is *there*? (vv. 10–12).

Still more startling are the twelve declarations that all his trouble is due to *God's* actions, disfavor, anger, wrath, and torment. *God* has appointed him for Sheol, overwhelmed him with the ocean-breakers of his displeasure (cf. Ps. 42:7), isolated him from friends, attacked him from all sides (v. 17), and left him completely alone, to bitter memories and to darkness. The poet can only ask "Why?...Why?..." (v. 14).

It is a heartrending lament, not truly appropriate for Christian use on Good Friday. A few phrases only are unclear. "Free among the dead" (v. 5, Hebrew and other ancient versions) possibly means "free from pain, as the dead are," but the Hebrew word is associated with a house for lepers. The NEB's "lies dead" perhaps means the leper's "death in life." The strange phrase could mean "cast off — freed — like an unwanted slave, left in age or sickness to fend for himself." Sharp irony is suggested by the phrase "my *ringing* note" (v. 2 — not the usual note of joy but one of pain); "sated" (v. 3, literal Hebrew — not with pleasure but with grief); and the possible reply (v. 5) to Job 3:19 (where in death the slave is at last free of his master, whereas in death the leper is at last "free" of society's harsh laws). The last phrase (v. 18) is difficult. The NEB amends the text to "parted me from," but Job 17:14 has a parallel, the *company* of one's family present in the *darkness* of Sheol — the only place where the poet will find friends?

Seven echoes of Job evoke comparison with that pitiable sufferer. But here is a "Job" without submission, faith, or a glimmering hope of immortality. The psalm expresses all that sense of the unfairness of life and of the hopeless, useless, God-forsaken existence of Sheol that was to lead faith eventually to belief in immortality. It is striking that the psalm contains no contrition, no awareness of sin—only recognition of God's anger, "burning fury," and unkindness.

Some people are deeply, desperately afflicted and yet find no comfort in religion, partly because their faith is secondhand, "impersonal," formal, or legalistic—or simply ill-informed. The poet surely needed spiritual instruction on the faithful love of God, his nearness and compassion—needed, in short, the gospel of Christ.

New Testament echo: cf. Luke 18:7.

89 "LORD, WHERE IS THY STEADFAST LOVE?"

For headings, see the Introduction, IV (ii), IV (iii); for Selah, see IV (ii); on "royal" psalms, see II (iv).

A poetic meditation on the story of David's accession to the throne (vv. 19–37; cf. 2 Sam. 7:4–17) is sandwiched between a splendid festal hymn to God the universal king (vv. 5–18) and a strong complaint that the great promises made to David have not been fulfilled, with a plea that God would remember, and keep his word. This curious arrangement is now prefaced by a statement of the double theme: God's steadfast love and firm faithfulness, and the "unbreakable" covenant made with David (vv. 1–5). Some versions, such as the NEB, transfer verses 3 and 4 to introduce the "David" passage (vv. 19–37). It makes little practical difference whether we think of this psalm as three psalms now combined to make a forceful argument; as a festival hymn celebrating divine and human monarchy, to which a sad supplement has been added in view of the fall of David's line; or as a lament at Judah's failure, to which an old hymn and a related meditation are deliberately attached in sharpest contrast, so enforcing the demand, "Lord, where is thy steadfast love of old, which by thy faithfulness thou didst swear to David?"

As the psalm is now preserved, the standpoint is that of Judah's downfall. A poignant "But now..." turns from past to present (v. 38), to the situation facing the poet—rejection, wrath directed even against the Davidic king, the supposedly unbreakable covenant renounced, the crown defiled to the dust, the walls of David's sheepfold broken down (so the Hebrew implies), his stronghold cities in ruins, so that passersby vandalize his property and scorn his weakness (vv. 40, 41 echo Ps. 80:12; there this is said of the northern kingdom). God has sided with the enemies of the king,

David's successor, strengthening their hands while diverting the king's sword, leaving him to suffer defeat.

God has removed the scepter of kingship from the hand of David's "son" (Hebrew "cleanness," meaning "lustre," equal to "lustrous thing," such as a scepter). He has overturned his throne, cut short the days of his youth, and covered him with shame (? — a reference to Jehoiachin, last of the free Davidic line, appointed when he was eighteen and after three months taken to Babylon; 2 Kgs. 24:8). The whole picture seems far too somber and final for a mere occasional military reverse.

In immediate contrast with this catastrophic outcome is set the strong covenant which God made with David "for ever." From verses 19 to 37 the poet keeps very close to the vision given to Nathan ("thy faithful one," 2 Sam. 7) about the terms of the kingship: God's setting the crown upon a warrior "from the people"; David's anointing with consecrating oil, being promised sufficient strength and continuing victory; God's declaring faithfulness and steadfast love to defend and exalt him (for "horn," see the Introduction, III [ii]). His kingdom shall stretch from the Mediterranean to the Euphrates (v. 25); his relation to God shall be filial (2 Sam. 7:14; see the discussion of Ps. 2 and the Introduction, II [iv]); he shall be supreme among human monarchs.

And all this is "for ever" — reiterated *eleven* times. Though David's descendants misbehave and are punished (with "men's" stripes and lashes, 2 Sam. 7:14), yet the covenant with David's house shall hold, as permanent as "the days of the heavens," as long as sun, moon, and skies endure. It is so sworn on God's faithfulness, word, holiness, and steadfast love (cf. Isa. 55:3; note too the reiterated "seed"—descendants—and promise of security in vv. 4, 29, 36; in v. 37, "witness" is probably a Hebrew misspelling).

In spite of all, the covenant has failed. David's throne has fallen, and his dynasty ended! (v. 38).

Nor is that the deepest problem. What have generations of the fathers sung, repeatedly, at the New Year Festival of the re-enthronement of God and the blessing of the king? What else but the magnificent hymn, in verses 5–18, celebrating God's glory. The heavens themselves and all the divine council of the "holy ones" acknowledge the majesty, the supremacy, of God (see the discussion of Ps. 82 and cf. Job 1–2). Nature, too, acknowledged his power when in the primeval conflict with chaos he (and not some foreign deity) slew Rahab (Tiamat; see Job 26:12 and the discussion of Ps. 74:12–15; also the Introduction, II [ii], II [iv]) and established "cosmos," the orderly universe, stilling the abyss and claiming all earth, from end to end, from mountaintop to mountaintop, as *his* (in v. 12, the NEB preserves the Hebrew as [unknown] place-names).

Such is God's mighty hand, such his glorious character as righteousness and integrity uphold his throne, and steadfast love and faithfulness herald his way, that the people who share his festal enthronement are blessed above all. They walk in his favor, exult in his name, for God is their glory and their strength, their Lord and their king (so the NEB has it; the RSV makes the hymn lead directly into the meditation with "For our shield *belongs* to the Lord, our king to the Holy One of Israel"). For the "festal shout" of verse 15, compare 1 Samuel 4:5.

This is truly a fine hymn to the majesty and faithfulness of the eternal King, whose representative and vicegerent David was to be. But look how it has all ended!

Hence the psalmist pleads that God will look upon David's house, will no longer hide his face nor maintain his anger. Man has not long in life — none lives for ever — and cannot wait indefinitely for the fulfillment of divine promises (vv. 46–48). Where then is the faithfulness the fathers sang about and the prophets promised? Let God remember how David's successor (so the NEB understands "footsteps," "those who tread after") is insulted, taunted, and mocked (as by Edom, Moab, and the captivity). For all such insults fall equally upon God himself, who undertook that David's throne should last for ever!

From this forthright argument with God it was a natural movement of thought to ask how, even yet, the ancient covenant would be kept, God's faithfulness vindicated, God's oath fulfilled. The answer lay in a Messiah of David's line, who would indeed rule all lands, and for ever. Though the psalm scarcely *sounds* "messianic," it is in fact one of the most cogent arguments for messianism. But only Christians can answer the strong challenge of verse 49 — by pointing to the Christ.

The "final verse" of Psalm 89 is a simple doxology, closing Book III of the Psalter (see the Introduction, IV [v], and cf. Ps. 41:13).

New Testament echoes: Acts 2:30; Revelation 1:5 (also 1:5 and 3:14 based on the Hebrew version); cf. Acts 13:22; Revelation 19:16.

BOOK IV
PSALMS 90–106

90 ETERNITY AND TIME

For heading, see the Introduction, IV (iii); for "Book IV," see IV (v).
Man's sense of "the hurrying years" (v. 10, NEB) has rarely been more poignantly expressed: all the metaphors are of brevity, insecurity, and imperfection. What is man's life? — a journey across the wilderness; a returning to the dust from which he came (Gen. 3:19); grass springing fresh and green in the dawn only to wither and bleach by evening; a passing bird, swift and silent; a rushing torrent in the quickly flooded, quickly dried wadi; perhaps (in older versions) a tale soon told; a short, dream-filled sleep beneath the stars; a sentry's wakeful vigil before being relieved to take his rest. In the end we pause and are gone, "like a sigh" (v. 9, RSV; a "murmur," NEB).

Thus in swift and vivid strokes the frailty of life is beautifully drawn. But there is hardship, too: years of affliction in which we see evil. We live under God's judgment, our iniquities fully known, our hearts dismayed at his displeasure. For all of the futility and finiteness of man's life is due, in Jewish thought, to man's ill-deserving (Gen. 3:17–19), which only adds to the wistful pathos, even melancholy, of this softly sung lament.

Yet God has "put eternity into man's mind" (Eccl. 3:11, RSV). If brief and passing time is man's, eternity is God's, from everlasting to everlasting, through all generations, since before the world "was born" (cf. Gen. 1:12, a suggestion of the ancient idea of "the earth mother"; these echoes of Genesis, and others of Deuteronomy 32 and 33, probably account for the link with Moses' name). So a thousand years are in God's sight but the "passing yesterday" (literal Hebrew). Endlessly working (v. 16), timeless and changeless, the permanent background to all man's fleeting, fussing busyness and regret, stands the Eternal, the "I am." For his immutable constancy there are no metaphors, for earth affords no parallel.

What then is the relation between man's passing time and

God's ever-steadfast eternity? Is any real relation possible? The poet replies that, for one thing, the eternal God is man's home, his origin, shelter, and goal (v. 1; the Hebrew has "dwelling place"; the Greek version and Jewish tradition, "fortress"; the NEB, "refuge"). God is where man "belongs" and finds satisfaction (v. 14; "in the morning"? — of each day; "that men may rejoice...all the day," according to literal Hebrew and the RV, 1881 ed.; or "soon," "in good time," while man still has time to enjoy his life).

The eternal God is also man's hope of justice, of a life in which gladness will fairly balance affliction (v. 15) — no exalted hope, perhaps, but the maximum that the psalmist can anticipate, and all that the unselfish individual has a right to expect. Without God, his life would be "nasty" and "brutish" as well as short. The eternal God as man's background gives continuity and purpose to the passing generations, rescuing life from final futility (v. 16). Within that ongoing purpose, even mortal man can find, through God's favor, a worthwhile work for his hands that shall not be extinguished by death (v. 17; for "favor" others suggest "God's loveliness," "beauty"; the NEB, "May all delightful things be ours"). It is God's eternity that thus gives background, refuge, "order" (v. 12, NEB, or "discipline"), perspective, and value to man's brief existence; to be aware of this, and live by its light, is "wisdom" (vv. 11, 12).

The Christian misses here any clear conviction that the eternal God shall prove at last also our eternal home, though the poet comes to the very brink of that all-transforming horizon. It is not surprising that this beautiful and profound poem has been adopted wholly into Christian worship ("O God, our help in ages past...") and into Christian hearts, not only in bereavement but in worship. The eternal God has indeed set eternity in the mind of man.

New Testament echoes: 2 Peter 3:8; cf. Romans 8:20; James 1:10, 11.

91 IN THE SHADOW OF GOD

The strong rhythm and calm beauty of this poem must not hide from us the questions it raises. The change of pronouns ("he who," "you," "he," "I") prompts some to find three speakers, each speaking twice, or two speakers with God answering (vv. 14–16). The RSV makes verse 1 describe who speaks, verses 2–13 give what he says, and verses 14–16 record what God answers; the NEB makes the psalmist address verse 1 to the hearer. The person addressed (v. 7) seems to be anyone who cares to hear and fulfill the description given. If the promises are given only to the king, seated in the secret place at God's right hand (as some think), that is not clearly stated.

A bigger question is whether one can honestly believe these promises of total immunity. It will hardly do to say, "None of these expressions, of course, must be understood as saying that the believer will be untouched by worldly calamities," for that is precisely what they do say—which gives us pause.

The psalm can, in fact, be understood in two ways. (i) In Jewish literature it is called "a song for evil encounters" and recommended for averting attacks of demons. In verses 3–7 a catalogue of demonic dangers may be discerned: "the destructive word" (Greek version) or spell; "the terror by night," Lilith the night-hag (cf. Isa. 34:14); perhaps "the arrow that flies by day" means the meteor-stone, in Jewish tradition the "arrow of Lilith"; "the pestilence that stalks in darkness" may be Namtar, the night-demon of plague; "the destruction that wastes at noonday" (in the Greek version, a demon) may be Qeteb, in rabbinic literature "a hairy, scaly demon who stalks from 10 am to 3 pm" (Jewish Midrash). One ancient Jewish comment reads, "If a thousand evil spirits assemble at thy left hand... ten thousand at thy right...they will fall..." (angels will overcome them—cf. v. 11; "the snare," v. 3, is probably in this context the net ascribed to pursuing witches). The ancient association of demons with wild animals, especially serpents, may underlie verse 13 ("lion" is probably —note "tread"—a misspelling for "asp" in Hebrew). It is at any rate certain that the psalm was so understood.

On that interpretation, its purpose was to protest against the people of God turning to magic formulae, charms, wizards, and "black" rituals for protection instead of taking refuge only under the shadow (a *protection* from the sun in Isa. 32:2) of the almighty ("Shaddai") from the demons ("shedim") — safe from all "winged dangers" under the wings of God. The wicked are vulnerable (v. 8), but to those who "dwell" and "trust" in God he will prove shelter, refuge, fortress, deliverer, and mother-bird (v. 4), long shield and short shield — what more can be needed? Person and home (v. 10) shall be safe; angels shall guard and carry lest you trip. God's "name" is the only charm you need. God promises to "set inaccessibly high" (v. 14, literal Hebrew), answer, befriend, rescue, honor, satisfy with long life, and save; why then seek the help of sorcerers? So read, the psalm raises no question as to the truth of its promises.

(ii) Most readers understand the psalm as offering the believer refuge from and comfort in all the ordinary ills and dangers of daily life —slander, pestilence, disease, and death (in plague or battle, vv. 7, 8) —whether he is at home or on a journey (vv. 11–13); *nothing* shall ever go wrong! If that be the meaning, it seems probable that verses 14–16 are God's correction. The godly person is not promised such total immunity — only a limiting of calamity, ultimate deliverance, and salvation, and especially the hearing of his prayers and the granting of God's presence *in the midst of trouble* (vv. 14–16). We cannot be immune to, untouched by, or insulated from the ills that affect our fellows; but we are not abandoned, and we shall win through.

Which interpretation is true? Probably both. A protest poem, calling the superstitious to put their faith in God, could pass into general use in worship in less specific form. Modern Christian congregations still sing with Bunyan about "hobgoblins and foul fiends" without analyzing precisely what the words mean. The truth of the whole matter of divine protection from the ills of the world still lies in the house that endures the storm and remains standing when wind, rain, and flood have passed away.

New Testament echoes: Matthew 4:6; Luke 4:10–11; cf. Luke 10:19.

92 THE RIGHTEOUS FLOURISH, TOO!

For headings, see the Introduction, IV (i), II (iii).

Immemorial usage follows the Greek version and Jewish commentaries in making this a Sabbath-day song, though it is hard to see why. Morning and evening sacrifices, with praise (v. 2), were offered *every* day, and though Sabbath worship certainly remembered the great works of creation-week (cf. v. 4 with Gen. 2:2–3), that may not be the "works" in mind here, but something deep, hidden from the foolish, like the ways of God with the evil and the good.

It is not fair to say that the psalmist thinks he has solved the much-examined problem of the prosperity of the wicked. His point is that the problem can be exaggerated. Psalms 37, 49, and 73, besides Job and Habakkuk, deal in different ways with the seeming injustice of life — that is, of God's ways with men (see the discussion of Ps. 73). The present poem begins by emphasizing that there is no oppressive problem, only good cause for thankful, happy, melodious praise of the steadfast love, faithfulness, actions, and accomplishments (literally) of the Most High (vv. 1–4). Admittedly, God's ways are "deep," but that man is "dull" and "stupid" who does not know that the prosperity of the wicked is short-lived; they are doomed for ever, while God sits on high for ever.

Besides, it is not true that only the wicked prosper. The poet's own strength has been vaunted like the horn of the wild ox (see the Introduction, III [ii]). He luxuriates in ever-fresh anointings of aromatic oil, a sign of great affluence — not the oil of official appointment but a word meaning "mixture," implying costly fragrances. He has seen his enemies outwitted and the righteous flourishing into old age (vv. 10–15). It is just not true that "the unrighteous flourish, the righteous suffer," or that God — the foundation-rock of the good life—is ever unjust in his rewards. There are exceptions, no doubt, but let those who are righteous and flourish *say so*, and give thanks for it (v. 15, equivalent to Deut. 32:14).

The main metaphors are familiar but freshly used. The wicked are like grass, quick-sprouting under the spring rains but soon withering under sun and wind (cf. Isa. 40:7, 8). The good are like trees, planted not here by the river (Ps. 1) but in the very precincts of the temple (cf. Ps. 52:8), and flourishing, if not exactly like "the green bay tree" (as the wicked are said to do), yet gracefully, like the palm, with stateliness like the cedar, fresh and fruitful into old age (for the palm, up to two hundred years).

This is a needed lesson. We exaggerate our problems and sometimes we deny God's goodness to show how "realistic" we can be. Let us be honest: the righteous flourish, too, very often. They would never change places with the wicked!

New Testament echoes: cf. Romans 9:14; 11:33.

93 A MINIATURE SEASCAPE

For theme, enthronement, see the Introduction, II (iv).

It is tempting to see here an artist-poet's reaction to a great storm at sea —wave after wave after wave (v. 3), the thunderous crash of "breakers" (literally), the irresistible surge and return of mighty waters, and over all, source and controller of all this power, "the Lord on high," who also is mighty. Such a scene could well have evoked declarations of God's majesty and strength, the enduring firmness of his handiwork and his throne, in spite of all the raging tumult. Storm or calm, what God says and wills stands quietly secure for ever (v. 5). This is a profitable meditation, as the poet took shelter on the shore.

That is tempting, and not impossible, as the *origin* of the poem. But there is no doubt that for Jewish minds, especially after the sojourn in Babylon, every storm had at least faint echoes of God's primeval wrestling, with majestic power, against the original chaos, "the monster of the deep," the struggle out of which the order of the world was born. What poet could resist that imaginative double-reference?

Moreover, the phrase "the Lord reigns" (the NEB has "the

Lord is king"; cf. Pss. 47:8; 96:10; 97:1; 99:1) was the worshipers' rapturous cry at the New Year Festival of God's re-enthronement, part of which focused upon that story of ancient struggle (see the Introduction, II [ii], II [iv], and the discussions of Pss. 74:12–17; 89:10). From that creative struggle issued the firmness of the solid earth, the order of the universe that reflects the "decrees" of God, stamped with his immaculate character (perhaps a deliberate contrast with the Babylonian gods figuring in the older myth). For such a festal occasion the poet's evocative meditation, with "lifted up" used three times (as though against the heavens), would serve admirably as a hymn of acknowledgment that God, robed in majesty, girded with strength, deserved to ascend his throne. Is he not the Conqueror of chaos, matchless ruler of the world, "while time shall last"? (NEB).

Wherever the main idea first took its rise, the Christian accepts gratefully its deepest truth: that where the Lord reigns, there tempest and chaos subside, the wind and sea obey, and the effect of righteousness is quietness and assurance for ever.

New Testament echoes: cf. 1 Corinthians 3:17; Revelation 19:6.

94 "GOD ALSO IS WISE"

For theme, vindication, see the Introduction, II (ii); for the "wisdom" school, see II (vi).

The abrupt, urgent call to the God of vengeance to "shine" (show himself) reveals that something is seriously wrong. The proud, wicked, arrogant, boastful, and "swaggering" (NEB) are exulting, crushing the Lord's people — especially the defenseless (v. 6) — afflicting God's "heritage," creating "days of trouble" (v. 13), banding together against the righteous and condemning the innocent (v. 21). They cause even the poet to fear for his life (v. 17; "slept in the silent grave," NEB, or "to be tempted to keep silent about wrongs"). He felt in need of "upholding" amid many "cares."

The use of "thy people" and "his chosen nation" (vv. 5, 14) in the NEB suggests that Israel herself is oppressed by foreign and unjust domination, and that the cry is for national deliverance.

On the other hand, the RSV's use of "thy people" and "thy heritage" while singling out especially "the widow," "the sojourner," and "the fatherless" (whom the prophets had often charged rulers to protect); the blasphemous claim that the God of Jacob neither sees nor perceives (v. 7; literally "understands not"); the appeal for supporters in withstanding prevalent evils (v. 16) — all suggest that

the true situation behind the psalm is oppression by a proud (? —
rich), godless, boastful, and ruthless ruling class such as Amos,
Micah, Isaiah, and later prophets too often confronted.

This view is confirmed by verse 20, where the fundamental
problem of misgovernment *in a theocracy* appears to be raised. Can
wicked rulers (royal or priestly) claim to be acting with and for God,
as Israel's rulers had always claimed? (Cf. Isa. 10:1–4; the question
does not arise about alien, pagan overlords.)

The plea, then, is that God will come forward to defend and
vindicate the defenseless and innocent faithful among his own
people, oppressed and exploited by the godless in society, the
wicked who are in power. Three additions to this plea are especially
striking.

(i) The answer given here to the familiar claim that God does
not see or understand what is going on is a superb piece of simple
logic, arguing that "God also is wise" (Isa. 31:2). From the change
of meter (vv. 8–11), this is possibly a quotation in the style of the
"wisdom" school; in verse 10, for "chastens" the NEB has "instructs," suggesting that he who made eye and ear awakens also the
minds of men, and reads men's thoughts as "but a puff of wind" (v.
11, NEB).

(ii) There are resources for living courageously through harsh
and unjust days, in the instruction (v. 12, NEB) and the law of
God, in the assurance that God has not forsaken and will not do so,
and in the promise that justice shall yet return (vv. 12–15; v. 15 is
obscure; the NEB has "For righteousness still informs his judgement"; others offer "the righteous may come to his own" or "to his
right"). So the good may endure with quiet heart, and hope.

(iii) The poet seeks supporters ("Who is on my side against
these sinful men?" NEB). He testifies that the Lord has sustained
him so far, amid dangers and anxieties. God cannot uphold the
wicked tyrants who misuse legal processes for their own schemes (the
NEB introduces "sanctimonious calumny" here). But he does uphold the righteous who protest, and he will remove the wicked in his
own time.

A prayer to the God of vengeance! Our first impression is that
such should have no place in Christian scripture — until we think
again. Christians are so reluctant to learn that one cannot actively
defend the weak or long uphold compassion or work patiently for
peace without a steel-tempered faith in the judgments of God, and in
his strong vindication of the oppressed and wronged.

New Testament echoes: Romans 11:1, 2; 1 Corinthians 3:20; cf. Romans
12:19.

95 PREPARING FOR REST

On Psalms and worship, see the Introduction, II (iii).

To suggest that this was originally two poems (the second, vv. 8–11, a mere fragment) is to miss entirely its forceful thrust of meaning. Ancient (and modern) Jewish liturgy, closely followed by early (and modern) Christianity, uses this psalm, with its promise and hope of rest on the day God rested, to begin Sabbath worship. But one unforgettable incident in Israel's wilderness journey cost Moses and Aaron, and a whole generation, their rest in Canaan. The poet says, Let the assembling congregation remember that, every Sabbath.

The call to assemble and to enter and the references to "ringing cry" and "loud shouts" (literal Hebrew, possibly implying trumpets to make a joyful noise *accompanied* by songs) both set the scene for congregational worship. Acknowledgment that God is king above all gods, holding the depths and the peaks of the earth in his hands ("farthest places" in v. 4 in the NEB follows the Greek version but spoils the parallel), adds weight to the argument that he who *made*— the sea, land, and people—necessarily *owns*. The creation story is, of course, the appropriate theme for the seventh day. To come to worship, to bow, to kneel, is but fitting, for he is our God, and we are his, the flock he chose to shepherd. So come, hold Sabbath, and share God's rest!

But as the joyous opening praise dies away, a voice is raised. It may be the voice of a prophet speaking the divine oracle for the service (cf. Ps. 81:7–13, especially v. 5), or it may be that of a priest at the entrance to the sanctuary: "Today...." The NEB conjectures that the words are the close of the invitation: "You shall know his power today if you will listen to his voice"; the RSV takes the words as introducing the "lesson" from the past; the difference is unimportant. The assembled congregation is reminded that others seeking rest failed to find it: God "swore" in his "anger," the culmination of "loathing" (v. 10; the NEB has "indignation"), that they never would find rest.

The psalmist says this happened at Meribah and Massah, names which mean "contention," "testing." Exodus 17:1–7 tells of Israel's complaining about thirst and the gift of water from the rock at a place near Horeb, apparently bearing both names. Numbers 20:1–3 places the experience at Kadesh, consequently called "Meribah" (Deut. 32:51 names Meribath-kadesh; it is said that a rock-spring is still nearby). The Exodus story says nothing of the banning from the land of rest; the Numbers story tells how Moses and Aaron were excluded from the land for disobedience at Meribah. The exclusion of that first generation of pilgrims is recorded in Numbers 14:20–23, and it was due to a failure of faith in the report of the spies forty years later (v. 10), and to not hearkening to God's voice.

Evidently the Sabbath exhortation ignores historical niceties and concentrates upon the lesson: that rest in God always depends on hearkening to his voice with "soft," receptive hearts not given to wandering "astray" (v. 10, NEB). Without that earnest listening for God's word, all the cries and shouts and noise are merely emotional indulgence. Without such spiritual preparation, Sabbath and sanctuary can do nothing for us. Too many fruitless Sundays remind us how true that is.

New Testament echoes: Hebrews 3:7–18; 4:3–7.

96 ENTHUSIASTIC WORSHIP

On enthronement psalms, see the Introduction, II (iv).

All the elements of planned worship (v. 9) are here: jubilant songs of praise (vv. 1, 2), homage (vv. 7, 8), testimony (vv. 2, 3), creed (vv. 4, 5), entrance to the shrine, offerings (v. 8), and sacred garments ("holy array," v. 9; the NEB has "in the splendour of holiness," but the conscientious margin offers the sober, accurate "holy vestments"). One version of verse 9 adds prayer ("entreat his favour"); another, "dance in his honour"; yet another, "tremble [shake]" before him." Verses 3 and 10 mention also a declaration, or gospel, to the waiting world. It may be fanciful to recognize four "acolytes" attending (so the NEB has it) the Lord in his (heavenly or earthly) sanctuary: Honor and Majesty, Strength and Beauty. The thrill and exuberance of joyous worship still move us in the "sing — sing — sing," "ascribe—ascribe—ascribe," "tell—declare—say." The poet likes such excited repetition (v. 13).

Despite the use of this psalm in the Chronicler's late history (1 Chron. 16:8–36; the Greek version of the psalm links it with *both* the removal of the Ark *and* the rebuilding of the temple), the original occasion for such enthusiasm is probably the festival when God was "re-enthroned" (see Pss. 47, 93). The usual festal features of God's greatness — his superiority over all other gods (he is greater than "idols"; in Hebrew, "feeble things," "nothings") and his creative power — are mentioned (vv. 3–5), and the announcement is sent out to all the world that "the Lord is king" (v. 10, NEB; see the discussion of Ps. 93:1). But the somewhat incidental reference to these features suggests that this is another "new song" (v. 1 — despite echoes of Pss. 29, 105, 106) composed for a later point in the ritual, when the great "enthronement" moment has passed and the news with its implication for all men must now be carried forth (vv. 3, 10).

For the earth, the implication of God's re-enthronement is the thrill of great joy, as all Nature, sympathizing with Israel's rapture, bursts into praise with the nation (vv. 11, 12). For mankind, the implication is stability and justice, for the God now enthroned will judge all men with equity, righteousness, and truth (vv. 10, 13; another repetition appears here: "judge — judge — judge"). In communal worship in later years, this emphasis upon God's coming to reign would of course take on a messianic dimension, and the psalm would rekindle Jewish hopes of glory.

That hope, the joy of the whole earth when God through Christ is king of men, still thrills Christian hearts and lights the Christian's future.

New Testament echo: Revelation 19:6.

97 HUNGERING FOR RIGHTEOUSNESS

On enthronement psalms, see the Introduction, II (iv).

The opening words, "The Lord is king" (NEB; see the discussion of Ps. 93:1), link this poem, too, with the "re-enthronement of God" ceremonies, and several ideas of Psalms 96, 47, and 93 recur, varying only in expression. The whole earth, to the coastlands of the Mediterranean, should rejoice at God's taking his throne. Traditional language describes his mystery, majesty, and glory (vv. 2–5, recalling Sinai); if past tenses are correct in verses 3–5, as some think, the brief phrases may review God's primeval conflict before creation (see the Introduction, II [ii], II [iv]; mountains that "melt like wax" suggest volcanic lava). God's superiority over all other gods (cf. Ps. 96:5) is emphasized, this time with no reason being given (vv. 7–9), while the closing thoughts of Psalm 96, God's coming to judge in equity, are here echoed in the promises to deliver the righteous from all evil. Many of the psalm's phrases as well as its thoughts are found elsewhere.

Yet one distinctive emphasis captures attention. In twenty-six fairly short verse-lines the idea of righteousness-justice-judgment occurs six times, together with the declaration that "the Lord loves those who hate evil; he preserves the lives of his saints" (in v. 8, "judgments" probably refers to historic events revealing divine justice, such as the fall of Babylon). Amid the mystery and thick darkness that surround God's throne, this at least is sure: it is built upon righteousness and justice (v. 2). In some symbolic way the overarching, impartial heavens proclaim the universal righteousness of God (v. 6). Idolaters are here not destroyed or even punished but "put to shame," their gods bowing (like Dagon) before the Lord; they are not annihilated but converted (v. 7).

The righteousness of God toward his own is manifested (v. 8), and "light dawns" (literally "is sown," to spring and flourish in God's time) for all the righteous, who ought therefore to rejoice and be grateful. Let men give thanks, not just for the earth-shattering power and majestic glory of the re-enthroned God but for his "holy repute" (v. 12, his "name"—literally his "memorial").

This thought is not new in these "enthronement" psalms, but the emphasis upon it is greater. Here is a "theophany" in the moral realm, as other enthronement psalms have described one in the sanctuary, in Nature, and in world history. What strikes this poet, as one who hungers and thirsts after righteousness, is the effect of God's enthronement on the revelation and establishment of *right,* the attainment of public righteousness. Thus the psalm looks directly toward Christ's message of the kingdom and his exhortation: "Seek ye first the kingdom of God and his righteousness, and all things shall be added unto you."

New Testament echoes: Romans 12:9; Hebrews 1:6 (Greek version); cf. Hebrews 12:29.

98 THE FESTIVAL SYLLABUS

For heading, see the Introduction, IV (i); for enthronement psalms, see II (iv).

Any prolonged religious festival rich in ideas needs a collection of hymns, songs, and patterns of worship sufficiently alike in language, thought, and exhortation to give unity to the occasion, and yet not entirely repetitive, allowing for change of meter and variety of mood and possibly of tune. A "new song" each year adds interest to the well-worn themes (v. 1; cf. Ps. 96:1). (Christmas with only one carol would seem sadly impoverished, yet in one sense there is only one carol, rehearsing in many forms the one story.)

This carol celebrating God's re-enthronement and the New Year Festival has all the required reminders, exhortations, and rejoicings:

— the announcement that the Lord is again king ("acclaim the presence of the Lord our king," v. 6, NEB; cf. Pss. 96:10; 47:2, 5, 7; 93:1–2; 97:1)

— the call to praise (v. 1; cf. Pss. 96:1; 47:6)

— the victories of God (vv. 2, 3; cf. Ps. 96:4, 5)

— God's covenant relation with Israel (v. 3; cf. Ps. 47:4)

— the summons to exuberant (and orchestral) rejoicing (vv. 4–6, where the Hebrew may imply trumpets in v. 4; cf. Ps. 47:1)

— the recall of God's primeval wrestling with chaos and the abyss (echoed in vv. 7, 8, Ps. 93:2–4; see the Introduction, II [ii], II [iv])

— the gladness of Nature herself (v. 8; cf. Ps. 96:11–12)

— the promise of a reign of righteousness and peace now that God is once more enthroned (vv. 9, 10; cf. Ps. 96:13).

The poet has put it all together again somewhat briefly, even tersely — perhaps for impatient younger pilgrims! If there is any special emphasis, it may be upon the whole world's interest in the divine enthronement (mentioned seven times in ten verses). One is reminded of the brevity of the Christian creed, endlessly repeated in Christian worship.

But, after all, one cannot meet too often a family of such great and such important ideas, or say them over to oneself too frequently. That is a secret of religious education, and of disciplined moods, that not all Christians appreciate sufficiently.

New Testament echoes: Romans 3:25, 26; cf. Luke 1:54.

99 ALL AUTHORITY IS GOD'S

For enthronement psalms, see the Introduction, II (iv).

This is yet another variant psalm for the divine "re-enthronement" festival (see the discussion of Ps. 98). The familiar notes occur: the announcement of God's kingship in verses 1 and 4, the call to praise in verse 3, the special relation to Israel in verses 4, 7, and 8, and the supremacy of the divine righteousness in verse 4 and perhaps verse 8. The effect upon Nature (Pss. 96:11, 12; 98:8; etc.) is here replaced by references to history; the victories of God, including those over primitive chaos (Ps. 98:2, 7, 8), are omitted. "Rejoice" becomes here "extol," "worship" (v. 9), and the earth, instead of being called to ascribe glory (Pss. 96:1; 98:4), is here bidden to tremble and quake. It is for Zion and to Jacob that the greatness of the enthroned king is cause for praise; there his righteousness has accomplished judgment and a just society. Clearly, as political conditions overshadowed a particular New Year Festival, so the tone of the accompanying hymns would reflect the people's fears.

In Zion God is enthroned "upon the cherubim" (see the discussion of Ps. 80:1, and contrast the imagery of Ps. 97:2). There, too, God is known as "holy" — the special emphasis of this psalm, mentioned four times, three times in a responsive refrain (v. 3, where it interrupts the meaning, and in vv. 5, 9). Like verse 6, this may suggest a priestly author for whom the holiness of God was at least as important as the righteousness of God was to rulers.

No one has satisfactorily explained the sudden introduction of Moses, Aaron, and Samuel, or what precisely is said about them. Moses is not elsewhere called a priest; though he exercised priestly functions (e.g., Exod. 24:6–8; Lev. 8:10–12), he set aside others for the purpose. While all three cried unto the Lord, it is puzzling to read that God answered them in the pillar of cloud (Exod. 13:21; 33:9, 10; Samuel was not present — to say "it must be due to some legendary tradition" explains nothing). And there seems no obvious purpose in the reference to God's forgiving them and avenging their wrongdoing. Any opinion is tentative; it could be that those who were led by the pillar kept the testimonies (solemn injunctions), were forgiven when penitent and punished when obdurate, were the *people*, represented and ruled by such figures as Moses, Aaron, and Samuel. That is historically true, at any rate.

It *could* then be that, as a part of the annual festival in later years, the names and divine authority of these three were deliberately recalled with reverence, not simply as examples of mediators or as reminders that God is gracious, but because in them the threefold source of authority in the later Jerusalem community was recalled and "recommissioned." By that time after the Exile, the leadership represented by Moses had fallen to the priests, and priesthood was at least nominally Aaronic; besides, these were the prophetic spokesmen who often uttered God's living word within the sanctuaries (as had Jeremiah, 20:1–6; 29:24–28; Amos, 7:10–17; and others, Pss. 81:6–16; 95:8–11). Samuel was the acknowledged founder of the prophetic order (1 Sam. 3:20; 9:11; 10:5; 19:20). The psalmist thus recalls, for another year, the special place in society given to divinely honored leaders like Moses, priests like Aaron, and prophets like Samuel.

All of these called on God's name on behalf of the people, and were answered (v. 6); and *the people* were led, were obedient, were forgiven, and were judged in the perfect righteousness and holiness of their God. And so may it continue in Israel (the psalmist urges) from another festival-time, as the people extol their king, worship at his holy mountain, and remember that the Lord their God is holy.

So another version of the festival themes make its own application of the basic truths to the current situation in another year. If our tentative interpretation is correct, that regular reminder of the true source of all social authority in men chosen and heard by God had a wisdom that modern "Christian" society has by no means outgrown.

New Testament echo: cf. Revelation 15:4.

100 A PERFECT GEM

For heading, see the Introduction, III (ii).

What comment or "explanation" can possibly illumine or underline this utterly simple and beautiful invitation to God's people everywhere (vv. 1, 3; "all men on earth," NEB) to joyous worship?—to form a procession and come (v. 4) "not because you must but because you may." And to come with exulting gladness because of the greatness, the goodness, the shepherd's integrity and care of your God (in v. 3, "not we ourselves" and "and we are his" sound alike in Hebrew).

The psalm's appeal is as universal as its meaning is plain. Tradition linked it with special occasions of thanksgiving (v. 4), but its use among Jews and Christians is unlimited. Its tone of unrestrained joy recalls the eagerness of Psalm 95:1–7.

New Testament echoes: cf. Ephesians 2:10; Colossians 3:16, 17.

101 GUIDELINES FOR GOVERNORS

For heading, see the Introduction, IV (iii).

This somewhat unattractive program of good resolutions, with its rhythmic form and its presence in the hymnbook, may well represent the formal promise to uphold loyalty, steadfast kindness (literally), and justice (v. 1; cf. Isa. 16:5) made by local judges, governors, or (possibly) kings upon taking office. The king's accession was a religious occasion, and that of other officials may have been, though this psalm is not markedly religious, especially if the NEB margin (and others) be right in making "I will follow a course of justice and loyalty" the opening sentence. Promises to hold God in awe and to cleanse the city of God hardly constitute rapturous piety. Verse 8 suggests the speaker is a king and in Jerusalem, unless this be poetic exaggeration; if so, any new official could profess this statement of intent. For lesser governors, the temptation of apostasy (v. 3) to gain advancement was especially strong.

The NEB has "I will" thirteen times and "shall be" three times, indicating the purpose of the poem as a formal response to an installation rite. The RSV's "Oh when wilt thou come to me?" (v. 2) is presumably a prayer for divine help, but the words are too uncertain to argue from; "Trust shall dwell with me" is one version; "Whatever may befall me" is the NEB's version. The vow concerns the new ruler's *guiding principles:* "the way that is blameless" (vv. 2–4), his *personal relationships* (vv. 5–7), and his *daily work* (v. 8).

(i) He will maintain integrity ("purity") in domestic life with "no sordid aim" (NEB), nothing of Belial ("worthlessness," literal Hebrew). He will avoid even the private practices of apostasy (literally "swervings"; the NEB has "disloyalty") and keep his distance from crooked *desires,* from *intentions* "twisted from the right" (literal Hebrew), while remaining innocent of evil *actions*.

(ii) The ruler is especially susceptible to secret slanderers who lay information against their neighbors; these he will "silence." Proud and arrogant pressure-groups who gather round to influence his judgment, fawn upon him, or patronize him — these he will not put up with; the practiced deceiver who lies to him in flattery or who hides truth to further his own purposes he will banish altogether. Only men of good faith will be tolerated in his entourage; only those above reproach shall be among his servants.

(iii) In the daily administration of justice (cf. 2 Sam. 15:2), his purpose will be to rid the land, especially the City of God, of all evildoers.

In our hymnbooks such a poem might perhaps be included "for civic occasions." The expressed intentions are admirable; the anticipations of temptation are shrewd — if only the personal manifesto did not sound so self-assured!

102 IMPERSONAL IMMORTALITY

For theme, complaint, see the Introduction, II (i).

The heading suggests that the poem is written by, or is intended for use by, one in great personal distress, but verses 12–26 have to do with the present distress of Zion. Whether originally two (parts of) psalms, or a poem spoken by a leader representing the harassed community or by an individual beset by sickness and enmity who sees in his trouble a parallel to Zion's condition, the psalm *as pre-*

served presents now a striking contrast between the individual's feeling of mortality and his craving for permanence.

The imagery (some borrowed from other writers) is largely of solitude, wasting, brief life, and certain death. Fever burns his frame; his days drift away like smoke; physical and mental anguish make him wither like grass beneath the hot blast, and cause him even to forget to eat ("cannot find the strength to eat," NEB). His body shrivels, and he is deserted like a vulture ("pelican"? — the word is unknown) in the wilderness, like an owl among ruins, wakeful as a solitary bird fluttering desolately on the housetop.

Yet enemies mock him, using his condition as a curse to wish upon others. He lives, eats, and drinks in perpetual mourning (v. 9). And beneath all else lies a feeling of being distant from God (v. 1), whose face is turned away, who does not listen (v. 2), who once took him up (into favor, v. 10) but now in anger throws him down — a most poignant complaint. God must answer speedily (v. 2), for the psalmist's time is short, like evening shadows passing into night. But he longs not to be taken in the midst of his days.

Inserted into this lament is the comparison with Zion's ruined condition (vv. 12–22; no indication is given of the period intended). God, whose name (literally "memorial" or possibly "throne") endures to all generations, will arise and show pity toward all who so dearly love Jerusalem. When God rebuilds Zion and again appears there in glory, answering the prayers of his afflicted people (cf. Ps. 79:11), then all nations will fear the name of the Lord. The restoration of Zion must be recorded, that people still unborn may come to know and praise God's compassion and power.

In contrast, the poet himself has no personal hope. His strength fails like that of a runner in midcourse (this is more probable than the Greek version: "God's strength withdrawn from him"). So he pleads that the eternal God, whose years endure through all generations, shall not cut him off in the midst of his days.

That thought of God's eternity fills the poet's mind as the poem ends. God is "of old" the creator, and so older than earth and heaven, outlasting all, for years without end. This is the deep source of permanence for man. The lives of the godly do not pass into oblivion, but through their children and successors shall endure and be established, through future years, before the unchanging God.

Though the form of the poem seems broken, the thought is profound and strengthening. The psalmist offers no glimpse of personal immortality; that is what Christian faith can add to this man's vision. But, beset by images and an awareness of mortality, he places a high value on the things that abide: the written record of God's deeds; the city and the cause of God, which will persist after his days; the generations unborn who shall inherit the same vision and serve the same God; and the eternal God himself.

Perhaps we Christians concentrate so much upon the promise of individual eternal life that we do not rejoice as we ought in the other pledges of permanence that are offered us in Christian experience—and which closely resemble those the psalmist treasured.

New Testament echoes: Hebrews 1:10–12 (Greek version); James 1:10; cf. Romans 15:4; 1 Corinthians 10:11; James 1:17; 4:14; 2 Peter 3:10; Revelation 20:11.

103 BLESS THE LORD!

For heading, see the Introduction, IV (iii).

It is difficult to believe that the six marks of returning health in verses 3–5 (forgiveness of the sin which in popular belief caused the sickness; healing; ransom from death; being "surrounded"—NEB—with love and care; returning appetite; renewed youthful vigor mounting like the newly moulted eagle, Isa. 40:31) are mere coincidences or "stylistic" traits. The psalmist has been ill, is convalescing, and in grateful wonder calls upon himself never to forget the experience but to "bless the Lord" henceforth with every physical-emotional organ within him—that is, with his whole personality. Total recovery calls for total praise.

It is also difficult to believe that the psalm does not start from such individual experience of God's lovingkindness, but at once the psalmist recognizes behind his discovery of God's goodness the general experience of the fathers. God has ever acted so, vindicating the oppressed, revealing his modes of action and what he can do (v. 7, NEB). And behind the fathers' experience lies ever the changeless character of God, merciful, gracious, and constant (Exod. 34:6). His steadfast love is as high over those who fear him as the heavens are above the earth, fatherlike in tenderness. He knows, as a father knows, how little, how insignificant, we are, that our "form" (literal Hebrew) is dust (echoing Gen. 2:7) and our life span as brief as the wild flower's before the hot desert wind. Nevertheless, as a faithful God he loves, from everlasting to everlasting, down the generations, all who keep covenant with him and by fulfilling his commands keep themselves within reach of his love.

Behind God's character, again, stands the eternal throne, where his love reigns, while over all mankind there already stands his universal kingdom. The earnest psalmist's thought has carried him, with ever-increasing awe, from his sickroom to the throne of the universe! No wonder that he feels his own praise to be inadequate and calls upon all powers that be to join him: the mighty angel-heroes next to the throne, the subordinate hosts who do God's errands, the innumerable creatures of his hands in all places where his writ runs. The psalm is his way of saying, "Let the whole universe bless the Lord...as I do."

And so will I.

New Testament echoes: cf. Hebrews 1:14; 1 Peter 1:24; James 1:10, 11.

104 THE LIVING GOD IN A TEEMING WORLD

On theme, God and Nature, see the Introduction, II (v).

In this marvelous survey of the natural world, an earth-full of created things (v. 24), there are said to be echoes not only from Genesis but from foreign sources, including an Egyptian hymn to the sun-god, revealing surprisingly wide knowledge. Only a specialist can judge when one ancient writer has borrowed from another, or when he has merely drawn upon common ideas or observed the same world. A few similarities to Psalm 103 have suggested that the poet who there describes God's activity in history has here turned to "God in Nature"; the poem is certainly a glorious celebration of the varied, breathing, moving, endlessly renewed life of the world, the flowing garment of the ever-active God.

The poet's purpose is to declare that God is "very great" (v. 1), to promote his unending glory (v. 31), to sing his praise and offer this meditation upon his handiwork to please him (v. 34). A little perfunctorily, the moralist glances over the poet's shoulder to express the hope that in such a wonderful world sinners will soon "be no more" (v. 35), but the main desire is simply to "bless the Lord" (v. 35; cf. Ps. 103:1, 22).

Jewish reverence limits the description of God himself (vv. 1–4) to his garments — honor, majesty, and light; his dwelling in his "upper rooms" (literal Hebrew) above the stretched tent of the heavens, chambers whose foundation-beams are laid in the waters "above the firmament" (Gen. 1:7); and his using all of Nature's forces (including lightning) as his servants.

The creation of the earth (vv. 5–9) follows the Genesis story in supposing that originally water covered the world (Gen. 1:2), and the creator's initial work was to restrain and channel the "deep," the "abyss" (see the Introduction, II [ii], II [iv]; Pss. 74:12–17; 89:10). Verse 9 recalls the promise following the Flood (Gen. 9:15).

The irrigation of the earth, of extreme importance in Palestine, receives unusual attention (vv. 10–13). "Wild asses" may be zebras; the nesting of birds near water is carefully observed. The idea of a celestial reservoir providing rain lies behind verse 13 — how else to get water to the mountaintops? "Satisfied" (v. 13) means simply "has its fill" from God's provision. No river is mentioned; Palestine's only river was too deep and swift for use.

From the presence of water flows all vegetation (vv. 14–18). The RSV's marginal note for verse 14, "fodder for the animals that serve man," is adopted by the NEB; also possible is "plants as a reward for man's labour," recalling Genesis 3:19. The staple crops of Palestine are named in verse 15: the grape, the olive (for oil), and wheat. The mighty trees of Lebanon only God could have planted— hence, "trees of the Lord." In verse 18 the NEB has "mountain-goat" (literally "climber") and "rock-badger." It is noted how each thing created serves its fellows.

Sun and moon are here merely timekeepers, essential to no-madic peoples. Darkness makes the young lions *pray*; sunrise sees the beasts return and man go forth—an orderly and happy arrange-ment, with no hint of worship of the heavenly bodies (vv. 19–24; the Hebrew for "lie down" implies "stretch themselves"). The great immeasurable sea, "wide on both hands" (Hebrew; as seen from Palestine extending north and south), bearing ships (or sea-monsters), is full of varied creatures. These, like all living things, depend upon God for daily food and continuing life ("breath" equals "spirit"; cf. Eccl. 12:7), and for perpetually new generations (vv. 25–30; the NEB calls Leviathan *God's* plaything; cf. Job 41:5 — probably the whale). Here is clear recognition of God's *ongoing* creation, a continuing marvel.

In the final hymn (vv. 31–35) God's own pleasure in his creation (v. 31) is a remarkable insight (cf. Gen. 1:3). His glance causes earthquakes; his touch triggers eruptions. Such a world, where God is continually active on behalf of his creatures, deserves men who appreciate God's handiwork and bless him all of their lives (vv. 33–35).

This psalm anticipates much of the delight of Jesus in his Father's world. It is a pity that Christianity, with its dualistic dread of things "natural" and "worldly," has not always taken such uninhib-ited joy in the handiwork of God.

New Testament echoes: Hebrews 1:7, 14; cf. Matthew 6:26, 28–30; John 5:17.

105 HISTORY SPEAKS — PART I

For Judaism as for Christianity, truth came through events and not simply by thought. The events had to be interpreted and rightly understood, but the truth so enshrined was presented objectively as historically true, not as ideas to be argued, subjectively "preferred" and accepted or rejected at will. This is the meaning of revelation and the deep motive behind this psalm, the next, and Psalms 78 and 136, all of which hand forward the national religious tradition, in the context of worship, to a new generation. The call to give thanks, addressed appropriately to the seed of Abraham and the sons of Jacob, to proclaim God's deeds, sing his praise, boast in his name, seek his strength ("seek to know" and "seek to grasp," different words), and worship (vv. 1–5), is no mere introduction to remembering his works, his miracles, and the outworking of his judgments. For the purpose of knowing the history is precisely that men may know God. He is present *now*, and for ever remains the same.

Every history reflects the viewpoint of the historian, though it may also be used by others, as verses 1–15 are used in 1 Chronicles 16 and verse 1 itself cites Isaiah 12:4. This summary of the past focuses upon God's faithfulness to his covenant with Abraham, renewed by oath (v. 9) to his descendants (vv. 6–10; cf. Gen. 15:18) and "for ever," for one thousand generations (see Gen. 26:3; 28:13; Exod. 2:24). The only promise here named is the inheritance of Canaan: to that end all the acts of God are designed. "They" (vv. 12, 13) means Israel, in their fewness and nomadic homelessness; verse 14 recalls the story of Sarah (Gen. 12:17) and Rebekah (Gen. 26:8–9). Verse 15 recalls Genesis 26:11; "anointed ones" (literally "messiahs") means "consecrated people"; the expression is only used here.

The sojourn of Israel in Egypt was at every step God's appointing (vv. 16–25). We are told that "staff of bread" in verse 16 signifies not only the support of life but the custom of storing bread impaled on pointed sticks. Verse 18 adds to the story told in Genesis — "bondservant" is perhaps a truer word than "slave." The English Prayer Book Psalter, following the Greek version, has the fanciful "the iron entered into his soul"; this arises from the unusual use of "soul" for "neck," plus inexcusable grammar. Presumably, God's "word" in verse 19 is that given to Joseph in prison, which tested his faith until what he foretold came true (NEB; see Gen. 40, 41). In verse 22, note "bind" for Joseph's authority over the princes, contrasted with his own previously "bound" state; for Ham (cf. v. 24), see the discussion of Psalm 78:51.

Again, the appearance of Moses and the succession of plagues in Egypt, with the resulting exodus of Israel, were wholly God's work (vv. 26–38). Here the number and order of the plagues, differing from the record in Exodus, suggests an independent oral, liturgical tradition (cf. Ps. 78:43–51). In verse 28 the Hebrew has "rebelled not," which may refer to Moses and Aaron or the angels of the plagues (Ps. 78:49), but the Greek version omits "not," as the RSV and the NEB do, assuming the subject is the Egyptians. With verse 36 compare Genesis 49:3 (the NEB translates "firstfruits of their manhood"; v. 37 recalls Exod. 12:35–36; the phrase "no one stumbled" is in Isa. 5:27). The close of the section, verse 38, is most effective.

Yet again, all arrangements for the journey were God's (vv. 39–43). For the cloud, see Exodus 13:21 and 14:19; with verse 41, compare the tradition mentioned in 1 Corinthians 10:4; and with verse 43, compare Exodus 15. Surprisingly, the covenant-making at Sinai is not referred to, but note verse 45. The arrival at Canaan and the expropriation of its existing harvests are still God's *gifts* to Israel —the land and the laws for the land alike. So should men ever praise the Lord (though some think the "Hallelujah—Praise the Lord" belongs to Psalm 106).

Thus, from worshipful beginning to abrupt but praiseful end, from the promise of the land (v. 11) to its possession (v. 44), *all* is of God. The slight impression of the undue prominence of Joseph is due simply to the story ending where it does. The psalmist reads the character of God from his past deeds for present exhortation and experience, as does the Christian creed. Both are saying that fact plus meaning equals gospel. But the past must become the present to every generation if the God of Abraham, Isaac, and Jacob is to be our God. Each generation must make a fresh discovery of God's faithfulness. Yet this is something not started from scratch but based on the experience of the past, told and retold in faith and gratitude.

New Testament echoes: Luke 1:72–73; John 6:31; cf. 1 Corinthians 10:4.

106 HISTORY SPEAKS — PART II

(See the first paragraph on Psalm 105.)

The story begun in Psalm 105 is here continued, but with the viewpoint greatly changed. There the theme was the faithfulness of God; here it is the unfaithfulness of man, as in another retrospective psalm, Psalm 78:8–11, 17–32. For this poet, as for Edward Gibbon, "History...is indeed little more than the register of the crimes, follies, and misfortunes of mankind." It is possible to count over thirty separate accusations against Israel in the forty-three verses, although, with the striking statement of verse 6 before us, the sense of present identification with the sinfulness of the fathers renders the accusations as admissions.

The general likeness to Psalm 105 is plain: it is even possible to see Psalm 106 as a corrective comment on the optimistic review of history in Psalm 105. Certainly all God's acts were faithful, but the burden of this psalm is that the intention so confidently defined in Psalm 105:45 was not fulfilled. Verse 2 could be read as a comment on any such attempt as Psalm 105 to recount all God's "mighty doings"; verse 3 concedes the blessedness of those who do observe God's will, but how few do! Verses 4–5 may be felt to have a touch of irony, as the poet who will recall many and repeated failures prays that when Israel shall at last attain grace, he may live to see and share it.

On the other hand, the latter part of verse 1 is a form of words familiar in the Old Testament, and the call to praise and give thanks is brief but sincere. Some would make verse 4 plural, as do a few ancient versions — "Remember *us*...." Others suggest it was sung by solo voice on behalf of the congregation, introducing the "general confession" of verses 6–43, a spiritual catharsis: "We and our fathers have sinned" (or, as the NEB has it, "we have sinned like our fathers"). The story overlaps that of Psalm 105 by beginning with Israel in Egypt, her insensibility to God's deeds and love, and her rebellious ingratitude at the Sea of Reeds (Exod. 14:11, 12).

In verse 9 (cf. Exod. 14:21–22) "a desert" should be "the wilderness"; on verse 12, consult Exodus 14:31; 15:1; on verses 13–15, consult Numbers 11:4, 13, 31–34 (the Greek and Syriac versions say God gave them "loathing"); verses 16–18 (cf. Num. 16) omit Korah, whose name seems to have been added to this story only in later tradition. Verses 19–23 are equal to Exodus 32:1–6, 11–14. In verse 20 "the glory of God" represents some copies of the Greek version, and so Paul understood the phrase (Rom. 1:23; cf. Jer. 2:11); other versions have "their glory," that which they gloried in — namely, God.

For Ham, see Psalm 78:51. In verse 23 (cf. Exod. 32:9–14), as a hero stands on a breached city-wall between his friends and the foe, so Moses stood between Israel and God in his anger — a daring metaphor (cf. Jer. 18:20). Numbers 13:1–3 lies behind verses 24–27. In verse 25 the NEB translates "they uttered treason..."; verse 27 is thought by some to refer to the Babylonian exile because of the word "descendants." The background of verses 28–31 is Numbers 25:1–13; compare Numbers 23:28. The Greek version of verse 28, "were initiated," may imply obscene rites; verse 28 may refer to offerings made to the departed, but Numbers 25:2 supports the NEB, "lifeless gods." Verse 30 notices Phinehas' perpetual reward of priestly status. For verses 32–33, see Numbers 20:2–11 and the discussion of Psalm 95:8–9. In verse 33 the RSV and the NEB agree against translating "his spirit" as "God's spirit."

Sins in the land of Canaan are rehearsed in verses 34–39 (Exod. 23:23–24, 32–33; Judg. 2:2, 3). "Demons" (v. 37) occurs only here and in Deuteronomy 32:17, in the Hebrew Bible, here meaning foreign demi-gods. (For human sacrifice, cf. Gen. 22; Deut. 12:31; 2 Kgs. 3:27; 16:3; etc.)

Finally, verses 40–46 return to the infinite patience of God, to his anger and discipline, his remembering his covenant and relenting. Verse 40 is repeated often in Judges (2:14, for example), as verse 42 echoes Judges 4:3; 10:8; etc., and verse 43 recalls the sequence of heroes — Othniel, Ehud, Gideon, and the rest. For verse 46, see 1 Kings 8:50. The closing prayer, verse 47, is found in 1 Chronicles 16:35. Here the plural "nations" may imply not rescue from Babylon but the later reconstruction of Israel from the Dispersion among the Gentiles; the NEB translates "that we may...make thy praise our pride."

Verse 48 is not part of the psalm but an editorial note closing Book IV (see the Introduction, IV [v]; Ps. 41:13; 72:18; 89:52).

In the graciousness of God, in spite of all, the psalmist finds hope. As so often is the case, the full truth combines two apparently inconsistent truths. History is, as Psalm 105 says, the record of God's saving initiatives and infinite patience. But it is also, as Psalm 106 says, the record of man's repeated folly and sin. "How often would I...and you would not," said Jesus (Luke 13:34)—that is the story of the church no less than of Israel. Nevertheless, the contention is not between equals, and God's "I will..." shall stand at last.

New Testament echoes: Romans 1:23; 1 Corinthians 10:20, 21; cf. 1 Corinthians 8; 10:6, 9; Hebrews 3:11, 18; Revelation 2:14.

BOOK V
PSALMS 107–150

107 DIVINE INTERVENTIONS

This is one of the neatest of the psalms, its unity of thought matched by its closely patterned structure with a double refrain (vv. 6, 13, 19, and 28, and vv. 8, 15, 21, and 31), showing four examples of God's intervention in answer to prayer. Each example describes an emergency, records a cry to God, declares God's deliverance and its method, and calls for thankful acknowledgment. The first two examples close with reasons, the second two with exhortations. There follows an epilogue, or coda, describing how God reverses situations when he chooses to intervene, whether in Nature or in society. Because of the different content and the absence of the pattern, the refrain, and the call for thanksgiving, some hold that verses 33–43 are a later addition. It can be replied that the poet knew exactly when to drop his pattern and to put the point another way.

The psalmist's purpose is exhortation (in very familiar words) to thanksgiving and testimony. As Psalms 105 and 106 draw lessons from past history, so this poem reads God's hand in men's daily experience and bids them testify, not least because such testimony most effectively silences the boastful denials of the wicked (v. 42). The phrase "gathered in from the lands" (v. 3; "out of every land," NEB), "from the east and from the west, from the north and from the south," suits the time of the Dispersion better than that of the return from exile, the "gathering" being possibly by pilgrimage. Moreover, the Jews became seafarers only later (vv. 23–24), while several quotations in the psalm tend to confirm late composition. In verse 2 in the NEB, "trouble" is personalized as "the enemy."

The several examples have been seen to illustrate some aspects of redemption (v. 2), such as guidance, healing, freedom, and peace, and also aspects of the nation's experience in Babylon as lost, sick, imprisoned, and storm-tossed. Sufficient ingenuity could doubtless find other parallels.

The peril of death by desert-wandering (vv. 4–9) was very real. Praying as never before, the lost are led home by a direct route and fed upon the way. Criminals (vv. 10–16; note v. 11) fettered in dark dungeons find liberation by prayer, for God can break through all barriers (RSV, vv. 10, 14; "gloom" is literally "shadow of death"). "Fools" who by iniquity "afflict themselves" (literally, vv. 17–22), sickening even to death, cry to God, and "his word" (see Isa. 55:11; Ps. 147:15) rescues them from death. They should recite God's deeds with gladness. Seafarers who trade on "the great waters" (vv. 23–32; "make their living," NEB) have especial opportunity to see God's power, first raising the storm (v. 25), and then, when seasickness and helplessness (vv. 26, 27; "their seamanship... all in vain," NEB) drive the sailors to prayer, stilling it again and bringing them safe to the "harbour." They are exhorted to bear witness before the "assembly" and "elders" (v. 32), presumably because happenings at sea would otherwise be unknown. All such experiences witness to the steadfast love and wonderful works of God; they demand due acknowledgment.

But such interventions are consonant with the immense changes God works in Nature (vv. 33–38; Sodom's fate well illustrates v. 34, but such changes in landscape and fertility are common in the Middle East) and in society (vv. 39–42). The NEB resolves a difficulty in verse 39 (which some think is a line out of place, a parenthesis, or a scribal comment) by adding a missing word, "*Ty-rants* lose their strength... in the grip of misfortune and sorrow." This provides a smoother connection with the "princes" in verse 40, the other class whose fortunes God transforms even as he exalts the needy. So God ever intervenes for judgment and salvation; the upright are delighted, the wicked are silenced, and the wise will take note, reflecting much upon the Lord's enduring love.

Even in a book so full of prayer as the Bible, such a testimony to its value and such a call to share our personal knowledge of its power are almost unparalleled. Those of us who deplore the shallowness of modern prayer-experience would do well to remember that while much in Christianity can be *taught*, the life of prayer cannot. It can be made attractive and contagious only by the humble and sincere testimony of those who pray. "Oh that men would..."

New Testament echoes: Luke 1:53, 79; Romans 3:19; Hebrews 13:13; cf. Matthew 8:26; Colossians 3:16, 17.

108 A TREASURED WORD

For heading, see the Introduction, IV (i), IV (iii).

This psalm preserves for a new collection (Book V; see the Introduction, IV [v]) two useful parts of psalms from an earlier collection: verses 1–5 are the equivalent of Psalm 57:7–11; verses 6–13, the equivalent of Psalm 60:5–12. Only the combining of them and a change of spelling of the name of God in verse 3 (equivalent to Ps. 57:9), not usually preserved in English translations, are new. Just why these fragments were brought together can only be conjectured. In a time of defeat, the oracle preserved in verses 6–13 might be appealed to for reassurance, but its original introduction, Psalm 60:1–4, might be felt to be too involved with a particular historic situation. So a new introduction might be chosen for it, the happier Psalm 57:7–11.

Perhaps!

109 WAR OF WORDS

For headings, see the Introduction, IV (i), IV (iii); for theme, vindication, see II (ii).

Several "explanations" are offered for what some see as the exaggerated vindictiveness of this poem. The psalmist was a sick man in dire trouble, not quite himself (vv. 22–25; according to v. 23, frail enough to be shaken off like a locust from a garment). He was a leader, perhaps a king; verse 1 may mean "God who gave me this highly praised position." He is the servant of God (v. 28) and the representative of the people in resisting wrong, so he does not curse opponents (vv. 6–19) for himself. Further, he knows himself to be righteous (vv. 1, 4, 5, 17, 21, 26, 30); thus his enemies are God's enemies —and righteousness must sometimes be indignant. In ancient manuscripts and versions, as in verses 3, 4, 7–8, 28, and 29, the opposition varies between singular and plural, possibly focusing now on a group, now on their ringleader. Like others, this psalm was originally a magical formula, perhaps for exorcising sorcerers. It was never used in Jewish worship, but its recitation was recommended (in medieval times) "as sovereign remedy against the machinations of an enemy." All of this only underlines the psalm's sad need of defense.

It is a prayer for protection and vengeance (not merely vindication). As prayer can rise to gracious blessing of others, so it can sink to cursing. And here the personal note is inescapable, though some expressions may not be as harsh as they sound. Verse 9 *could* mean only "may he die," although the phrasing seems to seek vengeance on the man's wife and children in accord with ideas of solidarity (Exod. 20:5; Deut. 5:9). In verses 14 and 15 the animus is not directed at the parents but at the son who hopes to gain merit from his forebears — may he inherit only their sins! Even so, there is enough here of "bitter prayer" to make us wonder at its preservation.

The underlying conflict is one of words — there are thirteen references to malicious speech. The psalmist's health and position are undermined because of calumnies, false accusation, and curses. His reply is to plead with God to speak (v. 1), to pray for his foes (v. 4), to appeal to the divine justice on his own behalf (vv. 20–21). He pleads God's name and lovingkindness (v. 21), and his own sorry condition (vv. 22–25). He prays that God will vindicate him (vv. 26–29), and he promises that with *his* mouth he will only give thanks and praise to the God who ever "stands at the right hand" of those in need of help before their human judges (so the Hebrew has it).

Understanding of the intervening offending passage, verses 6–19, depends upon the meaning assigned to verses 6 and 7. The RSV supposes the poet to be in court, with "a wicked man" suborned as witness (possibly as judge) and a prosecuting attorney "at his right hand" to accuse. Let the poet be condemned, his plea (to the court) counted as sin, and the dreadful sentence follow—namely, verses 8–19. The cursing is then a speech of the enemy uttered by the court. The poet asks (v. 20) that all this evil may fall upon his accusers instead (see v. 29), while he commits his cause to One who stands at his "right hand" not to accuse but to defend (v. 31). The picture of the court and the prosecutor-adversary ("the Satan" in the Hebrew") closely resembles Job 1:6–7; 2:1–2. This interpretation follows carefully the changes of pronouns; its difficulty arises in verses 16–19, which contradict all the poet claims for himself. This may of course be just the calumny and false witness of which he complains.

The NEB translates: "They say, 'Put up some rascal to denounce him, an accuser....' But when judgement is given, that rascal will be exposed and his follies accounted a sin. May his days be few...." This presumably means that the maledictions following are spoken by the psalmist against this perjured "rascal," the spokesman for all the adversaries. The poet will then be "the friend," and among the downtrodden and the broken-hearted whom the "rascal" is persecuting.

The NEB interpretation is slightly more persuasive: the rascal is cursed as the ringleader, lying for the rest. In verse 8 "goods" is better than "office," "charge" — his responsible civil position (Acts 1:20). In verse 10 "wander about as vagabonds" is meant; in verse 11, "may the money-lender distrain...," as the NEB has it, or "creditor" (*then* "let no one rise to help"). Verse 13 means "May the fundamental Israelite hope of life extending forwards through the generations be denied him"; in verse 17 "blessing" is the opposite of "cursing"; verses 18, 19 vividly express "let his cursing infect his inmost nature, seeping inextricably into his personality."

The pastoral counsel — "If you intend to murder someone, pray about it first" — has something to be said for it, but anyone instructed in Christian prayer to a loving Father would find it extremely bizarre and quite impossible to obey. When Christians "avenge not themselves" upon enemies but give a place to him who said "Vengeance is mine," there is no need to instruct God about what to do—however much better it makes us feel!

New Testament echoes: Matthew 27:39; Acts 1:16, 20 (Greek version); cf. Romans 8:34; 1 John 2:2.

110 PRIEST-KING FOR EVER

For heading, see the Introduction, IV (iii); for "royal" psalms, see II (iv).
Plainly an oracle ("The Lord says...") pronounced by prophet or priest at the enthronement of a king, this beautiful but baffling poem has an importance far beyond its occasion and its length. It almost fulfills the "classic" definition of poetry: "lovely phrases with no clear meaning"! But that it was intended to reassure a new king of divine assistance and dual power—priestly and military—is obvious. Which king, from David to one of the Maccabean rulers, and when —these are the subject of fruitless debate.

The divinely appointed king sits beside God in honor, under God's protection, and as exercising God's authority on earth. "Sit at my right hand, till I make your enemies your footstool" (RSV) suggests the king will no longer share the throne thereafter. Hence the NEB has "You shall sit...when...," with the RSV reading in the margin. Others offer "Sit...so that I may...," which is certainly what the Hebrew intended. For the "footstool" metaphor, compare Joshua 10:24, 25.

The *military* promise continues in verses 2 and 3 (RSV). "Sends forth" means "extends" (over the enemy); the willingness of the people to fight was all-important to a new king; the first royal parade will demonstrate their support. Apparently the king, too, will find his youth renewed like morning dew as he goes forth to fight. The NEB has instruction rather than promise — "When the Lord...hands you the sceptre..., march forth through the ranks of your enemies"—and continues with the customary tribute to a new king's illustrious birth: "At birth you were endowed with princely gifts and resplendent in holiness. You have shone with the dew of youth since your mother bore you" (with footnotes explaining that the Hebrew is uncertain). The esential meaning is that the king was consecrated to sovereignty from birth. It is claimed that the idea was widespread that the morning was "the mother of kings" (cf. Isa. 14:12), and that the dew represented divine power in renewed life. The Greek version has "From the womb, before the day-star, I begat thee" (recall Ps. 2:7). Another suggestion is that "the dew of thy youth" is "Hebrew" for "thy fresh young heroes" (willingly offering to fight).

To military authority is added *priestly* authority in a peculiarly solemn and unalterable manner (v. 4), based upon divine oath, and for ever (that is, throughout the king's life). This is according to a priestly regime older than Aaron's — that of Melchizedek, the Canaanite priest-king of Jerusalem in Abraham's time (Gen. 14:18). That kings on occasion exercised priestly functions is clear (2 Sam. 6:18; 1 Kgs. 3:4, 15; 9:25). The psalmist's declaration would suit David's first assumption of the dual role upon conquering Jerusalem, or function equally well as a defense of the assumption of priestly rule by Maccabean leaders centuries later!

Returning to the subject of military power, the psalmist assures the king of God's presence and assistance in the day of battle. God in judgment will shatter kings, litter the battlefield with corpses, and remove the heads of many nations that refuse the king's authority— so the RSV has it, but the NEB says, "The Lord has broken kings.... So the king...will punish nations," amending the Hebrew considerably. The final promise is that the king will "drink from the torrent beside the path," and thus "[he] will hold his head high" (NEB) or "God will hold his head high." The oracle ends as it began, with the new king exalted, confident, and triumphant.

As with other "royal" psalms, this poem took on messianic meaning when Judah no longer had kings of her own. So it passed into Christian use as a fruitful source of cogent "proof-texts" for the messiahship of Jesus combined with his eternal priesthood. It has not always been remembered how completely Jesus disowned the nationalistic and militaristic sides of the "Son of David" messianic hope and reinterpreted messiahship as service through suffering. But given the Master's own refinement of the concept, the psalm may still stand as an eloquent description of the royal priesthood of Jesus, now and for ever at God's right hand.

> *New Testament echoes:* Matthew 22:44; Mark 12:36; Luke 20:42–43; Acts 2:34–35; Romans 8:34; 1 Corinthians 15:25; Hebrews 1:13 (Greek version); 5:6–7, 10; 6:20; 7:11, 15, 17, 21; 8:1; 10:12, 13; Revelation 3:21; cf. Matthew 26:64; Mark 16:19; Luke 22:69; Ephesians 1:20; Colossians 3:1; Hebrews 1:3, 12:2; 1 Peter 3:22.

111 SIMPLE COMMON SENSE

> *For acrostics, see the Introduction, III (iv) (b); for the "wisdom" school, see II (vi).*

The acrostic form rather than logical connection controls the sequence of thoughts in this neat arrangement of couplets on the works of God. The poet would wholeheartedly praise and give thanks in the company of the godly, perhaps at a festal assembly, by reciting the marks of God's activity. His works are great (v. 2), profound, studied with delight by thoughtful people. His activity manifests the divine qualities of honor, majesty, and righteousness (v. 3)—so different from the squalid activities ascribed to heathen gods. His works are remembered (v. 4) as he willed they should be, leaving an abiding impression of graciousness and mercy shown to the fathers. The allusion here may well be to the divinely ordained Passover "memorial," recalling the outstanding mercy of the Exodus from Egypt; Exodus 12 (vv. 14, 29–36, 42) contains a variant form of the psalmist's word.

God's works in Nature are generous, providing food and keeping covenant with those who look to him (possibly a reference to the covenant with Noah that "seedtime and harvest...shall not cease," Gen. 8:22). His works in history are powerful: "He showed his people what his strength could do, bestowing on them the lands of other nations" (v. 6, NEB), for he is Lord of the destinies of peoples.

God's works are consistent, too (vv. 7, 8)—faithful, trustworthy —again so different from the unpredictable humors and vacillation of other gods. And his work is ever redemptive, rescuing Israel from Egypt, from enemy neighbors, and from exile (v. 9; see Deut. 7:8, 9). It is possible to discover references here to outstanding moments in Israel's historical tradition, not only to the Passover and the Exodus (v. 4) but to the giving of manna (v. 5), the conquest of Canaan (v. 6), the lawgiving at Sinai (vv. 7, 8), and the return from exile (v. 9). But the odd order of these allusions and the difficulty of fitting all of the verses into this scheme suggest that it was not in the poet's mind, though such events do provide further examples of how God works.

The main "lesson" the poet draws is that in a world where God is all the time at work, it is the merest common sense, the very ABC of wisdom, to reverence him. To recognize his reality and activity in the world about us is the beginning, and the chief part, of intelligent living. This was the watchword of the wisdom school (cf. Prov. 1:7; 9:10; etc.), as the observation of the *facts* of Nature and of history, rather than the outpourings of prophets or the rituals of worship, was its characteristic emphasis.

Such "wisdom for living" brings insight, understanding (v. 10); the sentence could run "It is understanding good [profitable] to all who practice it." The final line is usually understood (in the RSV and NEB) as the poem's returning to its opening thought, a little abruptly—but it may be *wisdom's* praise that will endure for ever.

Living, as we all do, in a world where God is ever at work, to keep his activity in mind, to depend upon it, and to cooperate with it is no more than intelligent adaptation to environment! It is hardly an exciting religion or a deeply satisfying one, but it is better than none, and a promising beginning.

112 THE GAIN OF GODLINESS

For acrostics, see the Introduction, III (iv) (b); for the "wisdom" school, see II (vi).

As with Psalm 111, the acrostic form here determines the order of somewhat miscellaneous thoughts, this time (like Psalm 1) on the great advantages of the godly life. In Psalm 111 it is simple common sense to fear the Lord; in Psalm 112 it is also highly profitable. The opening phrases echo Psalm 111:10, and other similarities make common authorship a possibility.

The patterned couplets reflect both the qualities that comprise the ideal of the wisdom school and the manifold blessings that such qualities ensure. Delight in God's commandments, uprightness, graciousness, mercy, righteousness, generosity, probity, steadfast faith in God, and benevolence mark the wise man's character. A little unexpected, yet in keeping with the philosophic approach of the wisdom writers, is the "stoicism" of verses 6–8: the wise man is one unmoved by ill tidings or by fears; he remains upright, staunch, generous—a *good* man.

The blessings assured to such a man include high positions for his children (powerful in society, rather than mighty in war, is intended); wealth (that is, total welfare, comfort; cf. Prov. 3:9, 10; 22:4) and riches, or all-around prosperity (v. 5); security and long-standing repute (v. 6); triumph over his adversaries; and high honor. In verse 9, as in verse 5, "righteousness" means almost respectability, an established character; for the exalted "horn" of verse 9, see the Introduction, III (ii); the NEB has "he carries his head high." The gloating triumph of verse 8 mars the picture but is all too familiar in the consciously righteous. The one verse which remains obscure is verse 4. The RSV makes it part of the blessing of the wise man, presumably a continuing hope in adversity (cf. Ps. 97:11), and adds "the Lord" to the Hebrew text for the second statement, defining the light that rises — namely, "The Lord is gracious. . . ." The NEB has "[the wise man] is gracious, compassionate and good, a beacon in the darkness for honest men," thus making the verse part of the description of the wise man's character. (To say the "light" means "prosperity," citing Isa. 58:10 and Prov. 4:18, 19, is quite unconvincing.)

The closing contrast (vv. 8, 10) with the wicked, condemned to frustration, envy, and futility (their "desire" defeated), only underlines the advantages of life lived "under the great Task-master's eye," as ever does the wise man who fears the Lord. The psalm is slightly smug and over-optimistic. Many find the way of the wise and upright to be less cozy than is described. Christians would place less emphasis upon material prosperity and redefine the "security" and the "stoicism" of the wise and good without doubting the main thesis: that godliness with contentment is great gain.

New Testament echoes: Matthew 8:12; 25:30; 2 Corinthians 9:9; cf. Matthew 6:33; Luke 13:28.

113 THE CONDESCENSION OF GOD

For "Hallel" psalms, see the Introduction, II (iii).

What moved the poet to celebrate God's gracious reversal of human fortunes, we do not know. To raise those who have "sunk low" (and are therefore "poor" also) and those who haunt the dung-and-rubbish heaps for scraps (e.g., outcast beggars, lepers; cf. Job 2:8; Lam. 4:5) to a place among princes may be traditional, "Cinderella-like," rags-to-riches examples, but the unexpected instance—that of the childless wife granted motherhood—may well have had a more personal appeal. The climax of the poem, verses 7–9, is straight out of Hannah's song (1 Sam. 2:8 and 5; for the *reproach* of barrenness, see 1 Sam. 1:6, 7; Gen. 16:4). As the poem was used in public worship, of course, these illustrations of marvelous changes in human circumstances could well be applied to Judah upon her return from Babylon, looking back upon the humiliation and barrenness now left behind (Isa. 61:3; 54:1–5).

Such "providential" transformations are the gracious work of him who dwells in the highest heaven, yet "looks" and "raises up" the most lowly, who "sets his throne so high but deigns to look down so low" (vv. 5, 6, NEB). To introduce and emphasize this divine condescension, the poet begins with the exalted God (vv. 1–5), raised high in the praise not only of Israel but of the world, throughout time (v. 2), throughout the earth (v. 3; "from east to west," not "from morning to night"; see Ps. 50:1; Isa. 59:19; Mal. 1:11), and throughout earth and heaven (v. 4). "The high and lofty One who inhabits eternity, whose name is Holy," dwells "in the high and holy place, and also with him who is of a contrite and humble spirit, to revive the spirit of the humble, and to revive the heart of the contrite" (Isa. 57:15—almost a "text" for this poem).

The final "Praise ye…" probably belongs to Psalm 114. No lesson is drawn; the poet just marvels at the truth and calls men to praise. Christians, with the incarnation, a manger, and a lowly man-for-others before their eyes, cannot but obey.

114 A RIDDLE

For "Hallel" psalms, see the Introduction, II (iii); for part-theme, God and Nature, see II (v).

Verses 5 and 6 have very much the air of a poetic "conceit" in the form of a riddle resembling Samson's (Judg. 14:12–14). Admittedly, the effect is spoiled by the poet's giving at the start so clear a clue to the answer. The final words of Psalm 113 probably belong to this poem — a "grace before poetry." For the rest, this engaging lyric, near-perfect in form, fastens upon the familiar miracles of the story of the Exodus, vigorously condensed into terse phrases. The "going out" from Egypt and the occupation of Canaan by Judah-Israel (either together comprising the one people of God or, later, indicating alternate names for the surviving nation) cover two centuries (since the temple is mentioned) in two verses. The crossing of the Sea of Reeds and the crossing of the Jordan make almost one event. The giving of water from the flinty rock, like the rest, is merely assumed to be familiar (see, respectively, Exod. 12:40–42; Josh. 10:40–43; Exod. 14:19–22; Josh. 3:12–17; Exod. 17:6 with Deut. 8:15; and cf. Ps. 105:23–38).

What truly excited the poet in these events was the awestruck reaction of Nature to the presence of God leading his people forth. The sea fled, Jordan retreated, mountains danced like spring lambs (cf. Judg. 5:5); the earth trembled at God's nearness as the nation and people of God was born. Such ideas, traditional enough, stirred the poet's imagination to lively description—and delighted rhetorical questions! To end with the miracle of water from the rock ("from granite cliffs," NEB; see the discussion of Ps. 95:8) seems at first sight somewhat lame, but the psalm was used at the Passover, the beginning of the dry season, when the assurance that rain would fall again (from the brazen skies) was all-important. It was also used at the Feast of Tabernacles to provide splendid comment on the ritual thanksgiving for water, when priests poured out a libation in the temple courts in memory of the gift of water in the wilderness (cf. John 7:2, 37).

Some ancient versions, thinking the psalm pointless, join it to Psalm 115, but its "point" lies in its sheer delight. The poet's heart leaped up when he recalled what the Lord had done at the founding of Israel; that inner excitement is more than enough excuse for any poem!

115 FAITH'S ANSWER

For "Hallel" psalms, see the Introduction, II (iii).
In the eyes of their neighbors, the Jews (like the early Christians) appeared to be "atheists." The puzzled, challenging demand "Where is their God?" occurs six times in the Old Testament (Pss. 115:2; 42:3, 10; 79:10; Mic. 7:10; Joel 2:17), sometimes with added urgency ("Where is *now* their God?") in view of some crisis, but always with the implication that they who have no visible idols have no deities.

This poetic argument takes up the challenge boldly. It is usually assumed that verse 1 implies some recent defeat (clarifying words having fallen out) from which Israel asks to be delivered for the sake of God's own glory. It seems just as probable that the poet begins with the heart and purpose of all faith and worship, the ascribing of all glory to God, and immediately faces the challenge of the heathen: "But you *have* no God! Where is he?"

The first answer is that God is high over all, working out his sovereign will (v. 3), implying both the spirituality and the superiority of God. The second answer shows, by contrast, the helplessness, the silence, and the powerlessness of the "gods" of the heathen, here regarded as mere images, not embodied spirits, as "things fashioned" or visible but impotent and lifeless. Curiously, verse 7 speaks of no grunt or sigh from their "throat" (vv. 4–8 are mainly reproduced in Ps. 135:15–18). For mockery of idols, compare Isaiah 2:20; 41:21–24; 44:12–20 (especially); and Jeremiah 10; and for the converse of this argument, Psalm 94:9–10. The psalmist's contention is that it is not the god who shows himself visibly who meets man's need, but God, who gets things done.

The third argument is that one grows *like* whatever one worships (v. 8): either (in idolatry) one grows "false" (2 Kgs. 17:15), becomes "nothing" (Isa. 44:9), "worthless" (Jer. 2:5), or (worshiping the true God) one grows "blessed" (vv. 12–15), full of praise (vv. 17–18), responsive to God's steadfast love and faithfulness (v. 1).

The dialogue form of the poem ("antiphonal," with versicles and responses) becomes unmistakable in verses 9–13 (vv. 1–2 may be spoken by a priest, vv. 3–8—note "our"—recited by the congregation). According to the RSV, a spokesman then calls on the nation, the spiritual leaders, and all worshipers (but perhaps especially proselytes, Gentile "God-fearers") to trust in the living, active — though invisible — Lord (vv. 9–11), as though Israel were still tempted by idolatry. He is answered with the confession of faith: "He is their help and their shield." The NEB makes all these lines (vv. 9–11) fit the poem more smoothly as a spokesman's statement of Israel's faith in the light of the heathen challenge.

The congregation (note "us") testifying to their God's goodness in the past and their confidence in him for the future (vv. 12–13), the spokesman expresses the prayer-wish, or benediction, that all will be blessed by him who—so far from needing to be made—himself made heaven and earth (note "you," vv. 14–15). The congregation responds with a good resolution (vv. 16–18). That response covers heaven, earth, and the underworld: heaven is God's dwelling place; the grave is for death and silence; life and praise belong to man's home, the earth, and will do so for all generations. ("Praise the Lord" may belong to Ps. 116.)

While the temptation to idolatry scarcely confronts modern people (except in some extended metaphorical sense), yet the danger of "substitute gods" and the far-reaching truth that we grow like what we worship are valid for all time and all readers.

New Testament echoes: cf. Acts 14:15; Revelation 11:18; 19:5.

116 HOW CAN I REPAY?

For "Hallel" psalms, see the Introduction, II (iii).

Whatever its later, and corporate, use in services of thanksgiving, nothing can hide the intense individual feeling behind this poem, indicated by numerous phrases: "I love the Lord," "my voice," "I will," "as long as I live," "Return, O my soul," "What shall I render?" "*I* will pay my vows...in the presence of all *his people.*" The background experience — of near-fatal illness, distress, anguish (v. 3; note death's entangling cords, net), "being brought low" (v. 6) — is common to many, as is also the thrill of 'answered prayer (vv. 1, 2, God bending to listen; v. 4) and the discovery that God is gracious (v. 5). But intensely personal are the admissions that the poet makes, his "simplicity," his uncomplicated, even foolish reaction (v. 6), his loss of inward peace (v. 7; "Be at rest once more," NEB), his peril of "stumbling" because of the extremity of his fears (v. 8), and his sense of wonder that he should even now be walking before God "in the land of the living" (v. 9). These are private, and heart-wrung, confessions.

The "stumbling" is probably explained in the only obscure verses, verses 10–11 (on account of which the Greek and Latin versions break the poem into two psalms, holding that verses 10–19 have a separate theme). Precise translation is difficult, all versions having to guess something; but the main meaning is clearly that in his panic and "consternation," the poet had to struggle to keep his faith, either in God or in his friends. But he did so, in spite of intense affliction (or, possibly, "humbled" by the recollection of his doubts); his prayer and the vows he then made are evidence of his victory. His deep feeling about his experience does not prevent the poet's borrowing others' words and thoughts — for example, from Psalms 13, 18, 31, 56, 86, 111, and 119.

Several lessons of the poet's experience are drawn in verses 5, 6, 7 ("the Lord showered gifts upon you," NEB), and 15 (that God is deeply concerned with the death of his own, neither trifling with us nor counting our distress trivial but dealing with us faithfully to the end). But the resulting six resolves are what his heart longs to express, to show how deeply he now loves the Lord. The question for the truly grateful is ever "What shall I render? How can I repay?"

Worship, calling always on the Lord (vv. 1, 2), is a natural response. So is offering the appointed sacrifices of thanksgiving (Lev. 22:17), probably with the drink-offering of the thanksgiving meal poured out publicly as a libation of gratitude (v. 17; cf. Num. 28:7; Deut. 32:38). Acknowledgment of the Lord's great and unceasing goodness ("he has given me a hearing whenever I have cried to him," v. 2, NEB), by public testimony and by the prompt and public payment of the promised vows in the appointed place, probably with gifts, is also to be expected of the sincere heart (vv. 14, 18 — though some would omit the repetition as a copyist's mistake—and 19). But all this is done with warmth of feeling and passionate gratitude, as the total self-dedication of verse 16 shows, not least in the insight that such heart-given servitude discovers not the *binding* but the *loosing* of bonds—that God's service is the most perfect freedom (cf. Ps. 86:16).

This is a healthy, mature, admirable individual response to answered prayer. But here, too, is remarkable witness to the *community*—the sharing in common—of private experience. The poem first served the poet's need, then through their hymnbook served his own people's need, and still through the scripture serves our own. For no one who has cried to God in deep distress and been delivered could find anywhere nobler words than these with which to say "Thank you."

New Testament echoes: 2 Corinthians 4:13 (Greek version); 1 Thessalonians 3:9; cf. Romans 3:4.

117 FAR-REACHING FRAGMENT

For "Hallel" psalms, see the Introduction, II (iii).
This is either a "lost" liturgical fragment or a brief "versicle" somewhat like our "grace" before meals, our benediction, or doxology. The two divine qualities named, steadfast love and enduring faithfulness, are central to Israel's mature conception of God, the fruit of her long experience of his ways. The universalist (world-wide) outlook likewise suggests a late and mature point of view. Verse 2 may mean "greater than we deserve" (see the discussion of Ps. 103:11).

New Testament echo: Romans 15:11.

118 PROCESSIONAL

For "Hallel" psalms, see the Introduction, II (iii); on "royal" psalms, see II (iv); on psalms in worship, see II (iii).
Like the verses of Psalm 68, the verses of this psalm are apparently disconnected, but (also like Ps. 68) they gain persuasive coherence when read as the script for a liturgical process. It is well to note first the several things that are clear.
(i) The formal ritual beginning is a very familiar sentence "bidding" the assembled worshippers to give thanks. (ii) Like Psalms 115 and 135, this one uses a familiar "bidding" of the nation, of spiritual

leaders, and of all worshipers (perhaps especially proselytes, Gentile "God-fearers") that resembles Psalm 115:9-11 but substitutes the new response announced in verse 1.

(iii) The repetitions in verses 8 and 9 suggest a united response to the individual testimony of verses 5-7; similarly, verses 15-16 seem a united response to the solo verses 10-14. This does justice to the alternating individual and corporate voices; the alternative appears to be to suppose numerous later insertions into an individualistic poem. (iv) The moment of entry into the temple courts, with a demand voiced by one and answered by the welcoming voices of others (a Levite choir?), is marked in verses 19 and 20 (cf. Ps. 24:17). The assembly (vv. 1-18) had evidently taken place somewhere else, perhaps in the outer court of the temple or at the foot of Zion Hill. A thanksgiving for admission and for the occasion with all it implies (the day of the Lord's acting, vv. 23, 24, or the first day of the feast) is then spoken in reply (vv. 21-22) and answered, probably by the choir (vv. 22/23-25).

(v) Again a welcome is spoken officially (v. 26) — "he who enters" may include all those in the procession, of course, individually welcomed — and instructions are given in verses 26 and 27 for the procession to advance to the altar. The translation "bind the sacrifice with cords to the horns of the altar" (AV/KJV) seriously misunderstands the Hebrew. The "cords" are "twists" of leafy twigs of palm, willow, and myrtle; the word for "sacrifice" occurs in Job 26:10 as "circle," and "bind" also means "arrange," "marshal"; the "horns" of the altar were very small protuberances or edges, and sacrifices could not have been bound to them even if the sacrificial ritual required it—which it never did. The instruction was to let the festival procession (or dance) begin and move to encircle the altar (as the Jewish Mishnah describes). Neither the RSV's "bind the festal procession" nor the NEB's "the ordered line of pilgrims by the horns of the altar" makes much sense.

(vi) The chief figure being welcomed then makes his personal dedication to God (v. 28), and the congregation assents with the same thanksgiving with which the ceremony began (v. 29).

So much is scarcely debatable; the content and the pronouns almost require such an interpretation. But several questions remain, including when the ceremony was held. Verse 27 strongly suggests the Feast of Tabernacles was the occasion; the psalm was sung at all festivals but was an appointed or "proper" psalm for this particular feast. Moreover, thanksgiving was then offered for the gift of light and the pillar of fire that guided the wilderness journeying (v. 27; see Exod. 13:21). Palm branches also figured in this festival, both to make "booths" (or "tents," v. 15; see Lev. 23:42, 43) and to be gaily carried in procession, waved, and beaten upon the ground beside the altar (according to the Mishnah). These branches were later called "hosannas," from constant association with the shout of praise and welcome frequently raised during most festivals. The cry means "Save us," and was used at the Feast of Tabernacles in connection with prayers for rain but also as a general welcome to all pilgrims ("he that cometh"). The seventh festival day was called Hosanna Day (vv. 25, 26; cf. Luke 19:38; Mark 11:10).

The questions — who is the central figure and spokesman in verses 5–19, 21, (22), and 28, and what is the experience through which he has passed—are more difficult. The poet's language is that of conflict, of great danger (vv. 5, 18), of being hard pressed (vv. 10–13), of deliverance (vv. 6, 7, 15–18) and triumph (vv. 7, 15). He is therefore a military figure, but the responses of the assembly (vv. 8, 9, 15–16) show that he is representative of the whole people. He is in all probability the king, already known to be prominent in the ceremonies of the Feast of Tabernacles.

It may be that his kingly authority has been challenged, tested, and proved triumphant by some actual struggle, perhaps with rebels, more probably with neighboring nations. The "stone" saying (v. 22; it is not clear whether foundation-stone or top-stone is meant; see Isa. 28:16; Zech. 4:7, 8) refers to fallible, self-appointed "builders of the state" who attempt to build with their own materials and not God's. The ruler they rejected has become, under God, the capstone of the social structure. He has gained victory with God's help (vv. 10–14, RSV; the varying tenses in the NEB only confuse here). The psalmist's language could certainly convey this meaning; the speech and response in verses 21–25 support it, as does verse 24.

Or, as some think (and as apparently other nations practiced), an annual ritual humiliation of the king was enacted prior to his being newly acclaimed by the people. During this "humiliation" the king called afresh upon God for help, and afterward testified to his renewed loyalty to God henceforth. The psalmist's language would bear this meaning also, but it reduces the conflict, distress, and danger to symbolic make-believe, the prayers and thanksgivings to mere dramatic dialogue. The sympathetic, even dramatic, recalling of an experience long past, as in the Passover, is a familiar religious rite. A "sacramental testing" of the king by a theatrical representation of distress, prayer, and deliverance seems too artificial to justify the earnest language of the psalm. Of course, a deliberate and vivid recalling, at the autumn-New Year's Feast of Tabernacles, of some recent and actual crisis and deliverance with thanksgiving would be altogether natural. Would the psalm be used only in those years when circumstances made it appropriate?

From initial "bidding" to closing praise, the ritual's script promises a most impressive ceremony in which the divine origin and assistance (vv. 5–9) of the throne in Israel, as a dim reflection of the throne of God himself, were solemnly reasserted. Naturally, therefore, the psalm lent itself later to messianic interpretation. But meanwhile, by such a ritual the roots of social order and welfare, deep within religion, were being nourished. The forms and institutions of human authority change, but the fundamental sources of it remain in the eternal rule and grace of God. "The people's will" is a safe foundation for government only when the people themselves recognize a right, a truth, a need for God which discipline that will to righteousness and faith. Without that resource and discipline, "democracy" is only a euphemism for competing and willful self-interest and the tyranny of the mob. This insight Israel's ritual clearly preserved.

New Testament echoes: Matthew 21:9, 42; 23:39; Mark 11:9, 10; 12:10–11; Luke 13:35; 20:17–18; John 12:13; Acts 4:11; Hebrews 13:6 (Greek version); 1 Peter 2:4, 7; cf. Ephesians 2:20; 1 Peter 2:11.

119 "O HOW I LOVE THY LAW"

For acrostics, see the Introduction, III (iv) (b); for "wisdom" school, see II (vi).

When, as here, a poet sets out to say eight things about the "word" of God, each beginning with the letter A, followed by eight things, each beginning with the letter B, eight beginning with the letter C, and so on through the twenty-two letters of the Hebrew alphabet (176 remarks in all!), he must expect certain difficulties to arise.

(i) To avoid tedium, he will need to find as many variants of "word" as he can. Our poet rings changes on "instruction" (law), "admonition" (before witnesses, testimony, almost exhortation), "precept" (command), "statute" (originally as carved, inscribed, laid down), "commandment," "ordinance" (something ordained, an injunction enjoyed), "judgment" (originally a previous decision of the court, a precedent), "word" (the act of speaking) and "saying" (the thing said, an oracle, but sometimes meaning "promise"), and "way" (an acted word, or example). Unfortunately, translators do not attempt to be consistent here. It is striking that the eight main expressions occur together in Psalm 19:7–11, upon which this psalm may fairly be said to be an elaboration.

One or another of these terms is said to appear in every verse of

Psalm 119. The supposed "sole exception," verse 122, may originally have read "Pledge thy *word* as surety...," and in some other verses the terms disappear in modern translations: "according to thy ordinances" becomes "in thy righteousness," for example. Some think each group of eight sayings contains all eight main terms, but this is harder to defend. These varying expressions all mean not simply the written Law but "the divine utterance," God's self-revelation and *self-communication* — since the "word" is here both the embodiment of truth and wisdom and the source of peace, comfort, life, and salvation. The several terms are usually qualified by "thy" (word, judgments, truth, etc.) or "of thy mouth," as if to emphasize that, however the divine communication is given — by commandment, tradition, Nature, or history — it is always essentially a communing with God. God makes known his mind and will *personally* to man; again and again the psalmist declares his love, delight, pleasure, and joy in God's self-revelation because of his love, delight, pleasure, and joy in God himself.

(ii) In a composition so artificial, elaborate, and contrived, more like a crossword puzzle than a great poem, the author cannot expect to construct any very coherent argument, any profound analysis of his subject. The best he can hope for is an anthology of true remarks, epigrams, observations, and proverbs, curiously arranged as a sort of index. It is here that C. S. Lewis speaks of literary "embroidery." Any inner connections between verses will generally be accidental; little is gained by pressing each group of eight to yield some "aspect" or paragraph of the main treatment. Sometimes one thought appears to call up others: "uprightness" may be mainly in mind in verses 1–8, "comfort" in verses 49–56, "persecution" in verses 81–89, and possibly "discipline" in verses 65–72. But no group is consistent: the same themes occur scattered through other verses and no thought is pursued for more than three or possibly four verses. The "discovery" of sustained underlying themes is more ingenious than convincing.

(iii) The author of such an exercise will probably run out of lively, original remarks, and to complete the alphabet he will need to borrow current sayings, epigrams, aphorisms, and proverbs. The psalmist draws upon other psalms, the wisdom literature, the prophets, and additional sources. The resulting compilation is inevitably uneven in insight and in forcefulness, and it contains considerable repetition. But all, whether original or borrowed, is expressed now very personally as the psalmist's own testimony and prayer.

If it is permissible to seek hints as to the author in a collection of sayings from various sources, then we may note some *twenty-four* requests to be taught understanding and wisdom, with verse 66 —

"Teach me good judgment and knowledge"—and verse 99—"I have more understanding than all my teachers"—suggesting a comparatively youthful student. Add the *twenty-seven* pleas to be kept straight, upright, and pure, expressing often a fear of being brought to shame, with verse 133 — "Keep steady my steps...and let no iniquity get dominion over me"—and we feel again behind the psalm a youthful heart engaged still in moral struggles. The writer (or the source he chose to use) remarks, "I understand more than the aged" (v. 100), implying that he does not think of himself as old, while verses 8 and 9 sound like a youthful cry.

One notices also "I will...," "I love...," "I keep...," "my zeal," and similar expressions of confident idealism more natural to the young. The psalmist, in fact, could well be a pupil studying to be a rabbi or a scribe, occasionally thinking of his chosen career and its cost. There are five or six firm rejections of gain, of gold—indeed, of "thousands of gold and silver pieces" (v. 72; note also v. 173: "Let thy hand be ready to help me, for I have chosen thy precepts"; see vv. 36, 57, 127; v. 14 should probably read "more than in all riches"). The writer is not yet an authority in the world ("I am small and despised," v. 141), but he hopes to become one (v. 79: "Let those who fear thee turn to me, that they may know thy testimonies"; the NEB has "...all who cherish thy instruction"). For that end he is working, and will work hard and long (vv. 147, 148). We may even overhear a little self-congratulation as his self-imposed exercise nears its end (v. 159)!

It is of course true that some contrary indications could be collected from these sayings. But perhaps the very attempt at this artificial poetry has the air of youthful energies, the style of an apprentice trying his skill at Hebrew meter and parallelism on a theme very much in the forefront of his mind—a life dedicated to the word of God.

Increased devotion to the revealed word from the past was a product of the Babylonian exile. Then both religious legalism and the scribal profession as custodian of the Law took their rise, though not without opposition. At the beginning of the postexilic period, Ezra and the returned exiles, chastened and stricter, confronted the lax, easy-going "dwellers in the land"; at the end of the period, the Pharisees and scribes confronted the compromising Sadducees. This psalm reflects the beginning of this devotion to the received tradition before legalism was fully developed, for its love and delight are quite spontaneous. At the same time, the psalm betrays considerable anger toward those who are disloyal to God's revealed will (vv. 21–23, 42, 51, 53, 69, 85–87, 109, 113 — "schismatics"? — 126, 136, 150, 154, 157, 158, 161). This too would be appropriate in the years when heathen overlords introduced new ideas into Jewish culture. During such a period the world was increasingly complicated for young minds by the onslaught of Greek civilization in the Middle East. The psalm well expresses the eager, yet inwardly insecure, reaction of a dedicated young mind in such a situation.

Note "Wisdom's" emphasis upon happiness (vv. 1, 2), the admitted need of divine help (v. 8). In verse 9 the NEB has "steer an honest course," but "clean and clear" is the Hebrew meaning; in verse 11 the NEB has "I have laid up thy word in my heart" — by memorizing? — see verse 13 ("I say them over, one by one...," NEB). "Open" in verse 18 means "unveil"; verse 19 means "I am a stranger, and need guidance"; "princes" in verse 23 equals "the powers that be" in the NEB. Note grief unable to stand upright in verse 25, and "When I tell thee of all I have done..." in verse 26; verse 29 may refer to idolatry, the equivalent of harlotry; verse 30 is the opposite of verse 29.

Some think "end" in verse 33 is "reward" (keeping God's law is a reward in itself; the NEB has "in keeping them I shall find my reward"). Note God's work within: "Teach me," "give me," "lead me," "incline my heart," "turn my eyes," "confirm...." In verse 37 "vanities" may again be idols, but the parallel suggests ill-gotten gains. For verse 41 the NEB has "Thy love never fails..."; note verse 45, where "walk at liberty" means "free of restraint." Verse 54 recalls verse 19, but the NEB has "Wherever I make my home." Does verse 55 imply reciting some formula of faith? In verse 57 "the law is my portion" is a possible translation; the NEB has "Thou, Lord, art all I have." For verse 58 the NEB has "With all my heart I have tried to please thee." Note the self-correction by the word in verse 59.

Verse 70 speaks of corresponding physical and spiritual grossness; note how affliction is here *accepted*. The thought in verse 73 seems to be "complete thy work in me." In verse 75 the NEB has "...even in punishing thou keepest faith with me." In verse 78 the Hebrew is said to imply "overthrown me with lies at law." Verse 81 means "I am dying for..."; verse 83 means shriveling in heat, though some ancient versions have "wine skin in hoar frost" to illustrate the same effect. Verse 82 links with verse 84; it is the poet's way of saying, "How many [meaning "few"] are my days—help me in time!" "Pitfalls" becomes "spread tales" in the Greek version (and the NEB).

Note how God's word, which originated Nature, now controls it (vv. 89–91); the first part of verse 91 means "the day [or possibly "day and night"] stands fast according to God's ordinance" or "this day thy decrees stand fast...." "The totality of things serve thee" (v.

91, paraphrase) points toward Romans 8:28. Verse 96 is unfortunately obscure: either the transitoriness of created things or the emptiness of worldly delights may be contrasted with God's word. But in Job 26:11 a very similar word means "horizon," the farthest visible limit of area (see the NEB); such a meaning in verse 96 yields "the horizon bounds my vision of space, but God's commandment is boundless"—that is, applies in all situations?

"Honey" in verse 103 recalls Psalm 19:10. Note the three comparisons in verses 98–100—true because God is teacher (v. 102). In verse 109 the reference to the constant danger of death uses the same metaphor as Judges 12:3. In verse 111, note that when possession of the land was lost, the heritage of the law became all-important. On "end" in verse 112, recall "reward" in verse 33—here (?) "eternal reward." "Double-minded" in verse 113 means "compromisers," not "single-hearted." Verse 120 in the NEB has "...makes my flesh creep." "Just" in verse 121 means "what is ordained"; "act" in verse 126 has a legal flavor, "to administer or execute justice." "Unfolding" in verse 130 is literally "opening" or "*doorway*"—the door, in windowless Eastern houses, admitting the light. "Simple" means "dim," "untaught" in the NEB—a pun in Hebrew: "the door gives light to the dour" (dull). "With open mouth" (v. 131) means expectantly; "thy wont" is literally "as is due by thy decree." The NEB paraphrases verse 139 as "speechless with resentment." "Well tried" (v. 140) is literally "proved," "tested and found genuine, pure."

In verse 148 the NEB has "before the midnight watch." Note "near," "far," and "near" in verses 150–151. The background of the psalm suggests verse 154 means that God should take up the struggle for right (cf. v. 126). For verse 160 the NEB offers "Thy word is founded in truth," but "sum and substance...is truth" seems implied (cf. John 17:17). Verse 161 in the NEB has "the powers that be." One does not "find" spoil (v. 162); perhaps it means "gain from battle," "fight for," "jubilant as a man carrying off much booty." "Seven times a day" may be actual hours of prayer (for pupils?) or a round number. "Peace" (v. 165) has the full Hebrew meaning— "welfare," "well-being," "health"; verse 168 in the NEB has "All my life lies open before thee." "Pour forth" (v. 171) means as a fountain, a spring; verse 172 in the NEB has "let the music of thy promises be on my tongue." Six of the last eight aphorisms are prayers (note the repetition of "Let") in the NEB; the psalm closes with petition, and verse 176 is among the most moving.

It is difficult to imagine any musical or recited use of this psalm in worship or to see it as a code for kings or even a manual of piety for disciples of a teacher—it is too narrow. Possibly it is an exercise in reading and a tool for memorization for young worshipers. Yet the patient labor of assembling and arranging such testimonies is a remarkable tribute to one individual's devotion to the revealed truth of God, one man's insight into its enriching, saving, sustaining, cleansing, comforting, and illuminating power. It is all the more remarkable when one remembers how limited that revelation was before "the Word became flesh, and dwelt among us."

New Testament echoes: Matthew 7:23; John 2:17; 17:17; Romans 6:12; Hebrews 13:15; 1 Peter 1:25; Revelation 6:10; cf. Matthew 5:18; 10:18; 18:12; 24:35; Luke 10:42; 15:4; 21:33; John 1:14; Romans 5:5; 8:28; Hebrews 11:13; 12:10, 11; James 1:8; 4:8; 1 Peter 2:25; 1 John 2:10.

120 SPIRITUAL EXILE

For heading, see the Introduction, II (iii).

The first of the fifteen "Songs of Ascents," all of them "brief, bright, and beautiful" (according to T. Witton Davies), this psalm like some others fits no theory about the meaning of the title. It says nothing about pilgrimage, reveals no "stair-like" movement from word to similar word, and has no discernible relevance to the fifteen steps from "the court of women" to "the court of Israel" within the temple (an "explanation" for which the Mishnah's authority is very precariously claimed). Nor yet has the psalm any connection with the "going up" from Babylon. In fact, Psalm 120 illustrates only our ignorance about the traditional title. If Psalms 121, 122 (especially "go up"), 125:1, 2, and 132:13, 14 be held to support the suggestion that these are "caravan songs" used by pilgrims going to the great Jewish festivals, then Psalm 120, written for another reason, must have been adopted for this purpose only because it suggests the relief which sacred pilgrimage could afford from the constant friction of life in a hostile environment.

The psalmist prays (though the NEB makes v. 1 a testimony to past praying) against the false, slanderous talk that surrounds him. For the seriousness of this peril, see the discussions of Psalms 12 and 64. He asks what God (implied) will do to deceitful talkers ("what more" is part of a formula of oath, or curse: "God do so...and more also..."; 1 Sam. 3:17; 1 Kgs. 2:23). He answers that God will pierce the arrow-tongued (cf. Ps. 64:3) with sharpened (war, not hunting) arrows; he will answer burning words (so evil tongues are described, Prov. 16:27; cf. Jas. 3:5–6) with incendiary weapons of glowing charcoal of broom-wood (still used, as it best retains heat), which set tents on fire. Evil speaking will recoil upon the evil-speaking.

The psalmist also prays against the atmosphere of antagonism in which he constantly dwells, likening his present neighbors to those traditionally held to be most savage and warlike, whose names became a byword for ferocity (cf. "tartar," "vandal"). For Kedar, an Ishmaelite clan among the Arabs, see Genesis 10:2; 25:13; compare also 16:12; Isaiah 21:16, 17. The Meshechites were another reputedly savage people near the Black Sea who seem too remote to be the psalmist's neighbors; in Genesis 25:13, 14 (equal to 1 Chron. 1:29), another Arab tribe is associated with Kedar — it is tempting to suspect some confusion of names. The meaning is unaffected: verse 6 explains verse 5. The poet is tired of living among those who will not even return the friendly, civil "Shalom" ("Peace!"), who respond with only surly, uncivil hostility.

Life amid "falsehood and ferocity" is spiritually wearisome. But the people of God have to live within, and try to love, an antagonistic world. "If the world hates you," said Jesus, "know that it has hated me before it hated you." But there is the escape which the psalmist found through prayer, and sometimes that escape (which he may also have found) by pilgrimage to the sanctuary of like-minded fellowship.

121 ON SETTING OUT

For heading, see the Introduction, II (iii), and the opening paragraph of the discussion of Psalm 120.

The mountains about Jerusalem were both the goal of the pilgrim caravans and the symbol of the divine presence they sought (Ps. 125:2). "Help" was needed because the perils of such a journey were much on the psalmist's mind: bad roads (v. 3); wild beasts and brigands (vv. 3–5; God is six times "guardian"); the dangers of the night (?—including demons—hence v. 4; contrast with Baal, 1 Kgs. 18:27); the dangers of sunstroke (v. 5; "shade" on the south and west as pilgrims journeyed south, for the hottest part of the day; see 2 Kgs. 4:18–20; Isa. 49:10) and of the dreaded "moonstroke," the reputed cause of madness ("lunacy"); and the danger of all forms of "evil," including sudden death (v. 7). All are warded off by the ceaseless guardianship of God, ensuring safe journeying and safe return (v. 8; cf. Deut. 28:6 and 31:2, where age prevents journeying, and 1 Sam. 29:6–7, where the phrase means marching to battle and return).

That verse 2 answers verse 1 and verse 4 answers verse 3 shows that the poem is antiphonal, though whether voices alternated within the sanctuary or pilgrims sang in turn upon the road cannot now be determined (some uncertainty about the pronouns tends to support the latter idea). From Israel's exodus from Egypt to the progress of John Bunyan's Christian, the religious mind has ever conceived of man as a pilgrim journeying through life, moving toward a goal worth reaching. Lacking that goal, secular man is a mere pedestrian. This beautiful psalm offers complete assurance for every journey God requires us to take; we choose our own way at our own peril.

New Testament echo: cf. Revelation 7:16.

122 ON ARRIVING

For headings, see the Introduction, II (iii), and the opening paragraph on Psalm 120; see also IV (iii).

"I was glad when they said to me, 'We will go...' " (the Hebrew and the Greek versions) vividly recaptures the excitement of the neighbors' initial suggestion of pilgrimage, just as "Now we stand within your gates..." (NEB) recaptures in retrospect the wonderful moment of arrival. The first impression of the city as (compared with open towns and villages) an enclosed place, "compact," surrounded by hills, lingers still in the poet's mind, suffused now with the idea that it is the decreed rallying-point (Ps. 81:4; Deut. 16:16, 17) for all the scattered tribes of Israel (including, in later years, the Mediterranean dispersion). We can no longer disentangle his thought: a compact city "symbolic" of a united people ("built to be a city where people come together in unity," NEB).

The pilgrim is thrilled to be at the seat of justice and government (whether v. 5 be what he saw or, as for later users of the psalm, a memory of former days), at the political heart, whence flowed the whole security of the nation (vv. 6, 7) — above all, at the national shrine, where God dwelt (v. 9). It is a tourist's description, equally patriotic and pious (cf. Ps. 84). The prayer for all who love the city and for its privileged citizens, whom the poet is proud to call "my brothers and my friends" (NEB; or, just possibly, he is thinking of other pilgrims still journeying to the festival), is in Hebrew especially beautiful, playing upon the meaning of the name "Shalom"—"Jerushalom." "Peace be within you" is a prayerful farewell; "I will seek your good" is apparently a promise of prayer for the city henceforth.

That same vision of the City of God, center of unity, law, peace, and worship, inherited by Christianity, brings the Bible to a fitting close (Rev. 21), and continues to lend strength and purpose to both Jewish and Christian faith and hope.

New Testament echoes: cf. Galatians 4:26; Revelation 21:2–3.

123 LOOKING UP — AND DOWN

For heading, see the Introduction, II (iii), and the opening paragraph on Psalm 120.

The psalmist looks up for direction, security, and protection because the high and holy God looks down in mercy, whereas earthly "high and mighty ones," to whom men look up with respect and even servility (looking to the "hand" that beckons and feeds), too often only look down in indifference and contempt. Nevertheless, God's favor will compensate for all the proud man's reproach.

This is a poem seemingly without occasion or any connection with pilgrimage. The merely verbal link with Psalm 121:1 is surely accidental. But Jews of the later Dispersion might appreciate a deeper meaning: they would enjoy being able to speak freely, in Jerusalem, of constant contemptuous treatment ("insults," NEB) by the Gentiles among whom they lived. Originally the poem enshrined just a bright idea with self-soothing comfort at its heart: before God, even the most despised on earth may "walk tall."

New Testament echoes: cf. 1 Corinthians 7:22; Colossians 3:22–24.

124 A NARROW ESCAPE

For headings, see the Introduction, II (iii), and the opening paragraph on Psalm 120; see also IV (iii).

In four dramatic metaphors of "miraculous" escape — from the monster that swallows whole; from the sudden raging torrent that races down the dry wadi after the distant storm, carrying all before it (v. 4; "seething waters," NEB; cf. Ps. 69:1–2; Matt. 7:24–27); from the wild beast stalking its prey (v. 6); from the trap unexpectedly broken by the fluttering of the imprisoned bird (v. 7)—the psalmist reiterates the wonderful interventions of God. Only God could have saved Israel: but for the God who made heaven and earth, all would have been lost.

We do not know what crisis evoked this frank acknowledgment, without excuse, qualification, or pretense of valor, though it would seem to be recent, and unexpected. Isaiah uses the flood metaphor of overwhelming invasion (Isa. 8:5–8; cf. Ps. 126:1: "turned the tide"). Jeremiah uses the monster metaphor of the Babylonian exile (Jer. 51:34, 44). Congregations using the psalm might think of the Exodus from Egypt, of the return from exile, or of any recent experience of divine deliverance, as occasion served. If it were used at some festal anniversary of the return from Babylon, its place among the pilgrim songs would be explained, but this is pure speculation.

For the truth illustrated is central, its consequences continuous: God is "on our side," and therein lies salvation.

New Testament echoes: cf. Matthew 1:23; Romans 8:31–32.

125 STEADFAST — AND SURROUNDED

For heading, see the Introduction, II (iii), and the opening paragraph on Psalm 120.

Like a lowlander in the Alps, a visitor to Jerusalem (perhaps a pilgrim from level Esdraelon or Sharon) stands in awe before the height of Zion and the still higher circle of mountaintops that, except to the northwest, encircle the holy city. Of a moralizing turn of mind, he draws two lessons: those who trust in the Lord are as immovable as Mount Zion; and God himself encircles his people like the impregnable guard with which Nature "enfolds" (NEB) Jerusalem.

That in God the immovable are sheltered within the impregnable is a fact of moral experience which the diverse destinies of righteous and wicked will make clear (vv. 3–5). Upon that insight rests the peace of the nation (v. 5). Meanwhile, it is true, alien rule is exercised over "the land allotted to the righteous," threatening corruption of Israel's ways. But God will not let the foreign scepter "rest" there, lest the righteous be tempted to disloyalty (v. 3; still the moralizing approach to situations). The "righteous," the "straight," and the "upright" are the opposite of those who "bend their steps into crooked byways" (v. 5, literal Hebrew; as also in Judg. 5:6). But God will be good to those who are good, and they shall stand fast.

Only some slight similarity to the opening verses of Psalm 121 links this poem with the pilgrim songs. Such an assertion and promise would be valuable in innumerable situations in later Jewish history. The time of the return of the exiles, under the leadership of Nehemiah and Ezra, to the lax and antagonistic "people of the land" led by "the wicked one," Sanballat, governor of Samaria (Neh. 2:10, 19; 5:1–5; Ezra 4:1–2), is but one possible illustration. The poem is a little naive in its black-and-white moralizing, but there is no question that the upright are shielded—even in suffering!

New Testament echo: cf. Galatians 6:16.

126 "DO IT AGAIN, LORD!"

For heading, see the Introduction, II (iii), and the opening paragraph on Psalm 120.

In spite of the misleading word "captivity" in verse 1 (AV/KJV; "those who returned," RSV margin), this poem cannot celebrate a jubilant return from Babylonian exile, for there was none. Haggai (1:6, 11; 2:16–19), Zechariah (7:8–14), and the hardships and disunity under Nehemiah and Ezra make this clear. Moreover, verses 4–6 ask for a repetition. Some therefore find in verses 1–3 a prophecy of the return of the primeval Golden Age, though verse 4 is a prayer and verses 5 and 6 are a general principle, not easy to combine with such a prophecy. The RSV and the NEB are therefore almost certainly right to take verses 1–3 as recalling some dramatic restoration of fortune ("turned the tide of Zion's fortune," NEB; the word must mean this in Job 42:10) which seemed "like a dream" to Israel (the NEB prefers "like men who had found new health," with "like dreamers" in the margin), and appeared miraculous to Gentile onlookers. It is part of the wonder of Israel's history that this could refer to so many actual experiences of divine intervention.

Recalling this occasion and taking up the Gentiles' words, the people ask in some new ill-fortune that God repeat the miracle once more. A metaphor is added, drawn from the waterless southland (Negeb): in high summer there life withers until the rains return to replenish the dried wadis, whose banks swiftly flourish again with green. To the metaphor is added a principle, whether proverb or oracle—namely, that sowing may be a sad, laborious, anxious time, but it leads to joy. There is no need to appeal to the (presumed) ancient rites of mourning over the "burial" of the seed, to explain the weeping of the sower: the casting of precious grain upon the dry soil, in helpless hope of rain, would often seem a desperate choice when wife and children cried for bread. After any poor season and dry summer, sowing cost discipline and tears, demanding deep faith that the seed sack would be exchanged for sheaves.

There may be timely significance in the reference to streams, sad seedtime, and longed-for harvest. The New Year Feast of Tabernacles often included special prayers for rain in the coming weeks to assist preparation for new crops. If the present misfortune (v. 4) was a year of famine and thirst, this psalm would surely find a place among the pilgrim songs. Be that as it may, it is good to be reminded that every calamity may be a *sowing* time if, remembering God's past goodness, we have patience to await his seasons.

New Testament echoes: cf. Luke 1:49; John 12:24–25; 1 Corinthians 15:36; Galatians 6:9.

127 THE MASTER BUILDER

For headings, see the Introduction, II (iii), and the opening paragraph on Psalm 120; see also IV (iii).

In Hebrew, "to build a house" means both "to construct a dwelling" and "to raise a family" (Deut. 25:9; Ruth 4:11; cf. 1 Sam. 2:35; 1 Kgs. 11:38). A city is, first of all, a cluster of such "houses"; Jerusalem was the "home" of the nation. Even in this domestic sphere (the psalmist declares), to attempt to build, to guard, or to provide without God is utterly futile. Not all man's skill, watchfulness, or long, wearisome labor will suffice without God's blessing.

Given that blessing and bounty, all will be well. By God's gift a man will receive the *heritage* (as "enrichment undeserved") and reward (of his faith?) of numerous children, including sons of his youthful strength (see Gen. 49:3). These sons will attain manhood during his lifetime, to be his joy and his pride, perhaps also his defense ("arrows") when he confronts adversaries in the local court (that is, the city gates, as the NEB has it; cf. Josh. 20:4), or discusses with local elders matters of military importance.

The need of God's blessing upon literal house-building would have added meaning for those who still held to the ancient superstition that the "daemon" of the site must be propitiated, often by human sacrifice (see Josh. 6:26), if the building was to stand. The Greek version here makes no reference to Solomon. The psalm is appropriately among pilgrim psalms only to the degree to which the ideas of house (meaning "temple"), city, toil, and fertility were in mind during the autumn festival.

A greater puzzle surrounds the final word of verse 2. The NEB margin says the Hebrew is unintelligible; others claim that it is Aramaic. God does renew strength in sleep, but not by (or instead of) giving food. Nor is "sleep" a metaphor for not being anxious. If amending the text is permitted, then neither "worriers have restless sleep" nor "God gives salvation" nor "God gives prosperity while men sleep" (an appropriate remark in Mark 4:26–27, but scarcely acceptable here as justifying laziness) but "selah" (see the Introduction, IV [ii])—instead of "shenah," meaning "sleep"—is probably right. No suggestion really satisfies.

Only God gives success, even in the most everyday and intimate areas of life; that is a simple and practical lesson which no religious mind can afford to forget.

128 DOMESTIC BLISS

For heading, see the Introduction, II (iii), and the opening paragraph on Psalm 120; on wisdom literature, see II (vi).

In the style of the wisdom literature, and with its emphasis upon the reverent acknowledgment of God, this poem pronounces "happy" (that is, "fortunate," "blessed in circumstances") the man who fears God. It goes on to define that happiness as a happy home, a good wife (monogamy seems assumed), numerous children (like fresh olive shoots around the mature tree; see the discussion of Ps. 127:4–5), and plenty to eat. His "blessing" is also deeper, a well-being of soul (v. 5; a different Hebrew word) emanating from the divine presence in Zion—*wider*, extending now beyond the women's "inner quarters" of the home (v. 3) to the city ("the prosperity of Jerusalem") and to civil life ("Peace be upon Israel!"), and *more permanent*, embracing coming generations ("to see your children's children" is to perpetuate life into the future).

The poem is partly statement (vv. 1–4), partly wish (vv. 5, 6), and thus entirely appropriate as a final blessing upon dispersing pilgrims making their way home at the end of the festival. All its blessing is conceived as flowing from the presence celebrated in the sanctuary out into homes that "fear the Lord." This interdependence of individual, domestic, civic, and social "blessedness" is entirely typical of Hebrew thinking, less typical (unfortunately) of Christian thought, which is so often excessively individualist. Yet whether we realize it or not, whether we like it or not, we are "bound in the bundle of life" with our fellows; "no man is an island"—no woman either, and no generation.

129 "AFFLICTED, BUT NOT CRUSHED"

For heading, see the Introduction, II (iii), and the opening paragraph on Psalm 120.

Accustomed from youth (that is, from Egypt; see Hos. 2:15) to repeated afflictions and frequent invasion, Israel can yet say that her enemies have never prevailed; she survives. She has been like plowed land, gashed by oppressors' scourges (v. 3); she has been like the harnessed and over-driven ox drawing the oppressors' plow — but God, in righteous faithfulness to his promises, has cut the harness (for the word, cf. Job 39:10; Isa. 5:18) and set Israel free. Now she prays that, similarly, all who hate Zion henceforth may be frustrated. To that simple prayer is added a most elaborate metaphor: may the enemy be like the wind-sown, rootless grass on the flat house tops, withered before it flowers, never filling a mower's hand or yielding an armful for the harvester (in the open robe above his waist; so the NEB has it) — and so never the occasion for passersby to offer the customary blessing upon reapers (see Ruth 2:4).

It is curious that this poem imitates Psalm 124, which calls upon Israel to say that, but for the Lord, men would have swallowed her up. It appears to reply that in fact the Lord's deliverance did not always come in time (some suggest v. 2 originally read "and they have prevailed"), since at no date after the Babylonian exile was Israel an independent state. More attractive is the suggestion that the poem reflects the doctrine of Isaiah (in Hezekiah's time) that Jerusalem was inviolate (Isa. 31:4, 5), a doctrine confirmed by the astounding withdrawal of Sennacherib of Assyria from before the city (2 Kgs. 19:32–36). At that time verses 1 and 2 would be true, and verse 3 would be illustrated by Sennacherib's progress to Jerusalem (Isa. 10:28–32). It is significant that Isaiah's reply to Hezekiah about the invasion uses this very metaphor of the rooftop grass, applying it to ravaged Israel (Isa. 37:27; 2 Kgs. 19:26). Isaiah uses also the figure of the ox harness (5:18) and of Israel's back bowed before the enemy (51:23). The psalmist appears to reiterate Isaiah's assurance, and to turn the grass metaphor back upon the enemy; this assurance the nation has preserved among its festival hymns.

The poem mentions neither penitence nor charity toward enemies. They usually stand or fall together. But so do penitence and "inviolability." It was Jeremiah's sad task to contradict Isaiah, declaring that the city *would* fall because the sins of the nation meanwhile had made exile inevitable.

New Testament echo: cf. 2 Corinthians 4:8.

130 "OUT OF THE DEPTHS..."

For heading, see the Introduction, II (iii), and the opening paragraph on Psalm 120.

A remarkable degree of personal feeling pervades this psalm, which yet is linked in some way with the need and experience of Israel. In addition, the psalm shows remarkable insight into the way that divine forgiveness evokes *awe* (v. 4), whereas wrath and judgment evoke only dread. A third remarkable trait is the poet's awareness that instant salvation is not always possible. The penitent soul must often "wait," long and patiently, for the dawn of pardon (v. 6; cf. Ps. 40:1–2), even as the prodigal in the parable of Jesus had to tread his way homeward, *all* the way, alone.

No excuse or plea is offered except God's own "promise" (v. 5) and the argument of how desperate would be man's situation if God "watched" (Hebrew) for sin and "kept account" (NEB) of it, instead of forgiving — who then should "hold up his head"? The "watchmen" simile (v. 6) may refer to the city watch, longing to go off duty, or to the temple watch, waiting for the first gleam of dawn to announce the morning sacrifice. The "depths" (v. 1) may recall the ancient "abyss" of evil, chaotic forces (see the Introduction, II [ii], II [iv]), but the word here seems more probably a simple metaphor for one steeped, and in danger of drowning, in iniquity.

A further remarkable feature of the poem is its extension beyond individual need to Israel's hope in God's mercy and the central faith of Israel concerning her God (vv. 7, 8; cf. Ps. 103:8–14, 17–18). The psalm was undoubtedly used in the corporate worship of the sanctuary. It is often said to be wholly unsuitable for a "pilgrim song," yet if there was any sincerity in the festival search for blessing, confession of sin *must* have had a place in the liturgy. This "penitential poem" would serve that purpose perfectly. Verses 7 and 8 may very well be the response of the presiding priest, conveying the absolution of the divine "love unfailing and great...power...to set men free" (v. 7, NEB).

This is the ultimate truth about God for Jew and Christian alike, but since Jesus died the Christian has the greater assurance of that redeeming love.

New Testament echoes: cf. Luke 1:68; Ephesians 1:7.

131 ''OF SUCH IS THE KINGDOM''

For headings, see the Introduction, II (iii), and the opening paragraph on Psalm 120; see also IV (iii).

Only Christian arrogance need be surprised to find so beautiful a cameo as this, as perfect in its way as Psalm 23, within the Old Testament. The soul at rest at the inmost heart of things is nowhere more acutely or more winsomely described. Even as a practical recipe for contentment it is unparalleled: restless ambition and presumptuous pride are curbed by common sense and a just self-estimate (cf. Rom. 12:3; Sir. 3:17–24 elaborates this). The mind is schooled from abstract, speculative questioning to immediate and practical realities (cf. John 14:1). The mood and emotions are disciplined (literally "leveled" and "silenced") by self-understanding to a childlike, trustful content, like that of a child upon its mother's lap (or "hip"; "a weaned child" — RV, 1881 ed.; cf. 1 Sam. 1:24–27 — from two to five years of age is suggested, old enough to be accustomed to a mother's care and no longer clamoring to be fed).

In public use the poem would become perhaps a preparation for prayer, perhaps a vesper, the closing (?—additional) lines seeking similar quietness of heart for Israel as a whole. Christians who understand Jesus might use the prayer without alteration — and often.

New Testament echoes: cf. Matthew 18:3; 19:14; John 14:1; Romans 12:3; Colossians 3:15.

132 SHRINE, CITY, AND THRONE

For heading, see the Introduction, II (iii), and the opening paragraph on Psalm 120; for "royal" psalms, see II (iv).

This is a patchwork poem: verses 1–5 recall David's resolution to build the temple (2 Sam. 7:2–3; 1 Chron. 22:1–5); verses 6–7 recall his taking the Ark from Kirjath-Jearim to Jerusalem ("Jaar" equals "Jearim"; for a description of the Ark, see the discussion of Ps. 80; for the story, see 1 Sam. 7:1–2; 2 Sam. 6:2–12; 1 Kgs. 8:1–6). The salutation "Arise...go to thy resting place" (vv. 8, 14) is the appointed formula for moving the Ark (Num. 10:35, 36) and was cited at the dedication of Solomon's temple — indeed, verses 8–10 are shared with 2 Chronicles 6:41–42 as the end of Solomon's great prayer on that occasion. The divine "oath" to David's royal line (vv. 11, 12) is taken from the historian's account of the establishment of the Davidic monarchy (2 Sam. 7:11–16); Jerusalem was chosen for the nation's shrine because the temple and the Ark were there (2 Sam. 6:12–18; 24:18–25).

Add to these historically important fragments the various voices in the psalm (solo, vv. 1–5, sung or recited chorus, vv. 6–7, another voice, vv. 8–10, and probably another, vv. 11–18), and the movement implied in verses 7 (summons to form procession) and 8, and it becomes evident that (as with Pss. 24, 68, 118) we have here the script for a dramatic ceremonial. This celebrates (probably at the

New Year Festival — hence "pilgrim song") the origins of the national shrine, the holy city, and the Davidic monarchy. Prayer is offered for their continuance, too (vv. 1–5, 9–10), and a priestly or prophetic response is given in God's name, promising permanence and blessing (vv. 11–18).

Liturgy often preserves otherwise unrecorded history: note here the ancient names in verses 2, 5, and 6, and "ark of thy might" in verse 8. David's efforts in preparing for the temple included an oath (v. 2), and are described as "hardships" ("adversity," NEB). Leviticus 23:27, 29 would justify the translation "self-inflicted denials," defined in verses 3–5. David's "great pains" are mentioned in 1 Chronicles 22:14; "hard work" and "zeal" are also suggested. This becomes the basis for a plea that God will still reward his labor (vv. 1, 10; on pleading the merits of forebears, see Gen. 26:24). New voices imitate the cry of David's helpers (vv. 6, 7; Ephrathah is Bethlehem — Ruth 4:11; Mic. 5:2 — the place where, apparently, rumor of the Ark stirred desire to save it). The resolution to take the Ark to Zion ("let us go" implies "bring") is then re-enacted in the festival. The Ark and Zion need not be *named* if the Ark is actually being borne in procession back to its appointed place, as the formula for carrying it, verses 8 and 14, would suggest. (God's "footstool," v. 7, is probably, here and in Ps. 99:5, the temple; in 1 Chron. 28:2, the Ark.)

As at the temple's dedication, following the re-establishment of the Ark is a prayer for priests, people, and reigning Davidic king (vv. 8–10; the wording of v. 10 suggests this prayer is offered by the king). The assurance concerning monarchy, city, and shrine offered by God's spokesman, reiterating ancient promises (vv. 11–18), answers David's oath with God's (vv. 2, 11; cf. Pss. 89:3, 35, 49; 110:4), though here conditionally (v. 12, echoing 2 Sam. 7:12–16), and stressing the condition much more than Psalm 89:30–37 does. The prayers of the people (vv. 1, 10) are answered in verses 11, 12, 17, and 18; those of verses 8 and 9 by verses 13–16, 16 "improving upon" 9. The permanence and the provision of Zion are guaranteed; the continuance and victory of the monarchy are promised (for "horn," v. 17, see the Introduction, III [ii]). For the king as a "lamp" to his people or as having a lamp burning for him, see 2 Samuel 21:17; 1 Kings 11:36; 15:4; 2 Chronicles 21:7 ("There will I . . . light a lamp for my anointed king," NEB; cf. Ps. 18:28). With the enemies "clothed" with shame, compare Psalms 9 and 16, and with the "glittering" crown (literal Hebrew), compare Psalm 89:39.

The whole psalm, especially verse 10, implies that city and throne shall stand. Later, when the monarchy was past, the psalm stimulated messianic hope. At that time, too, since the Ark no longer existed (note the mention of the Ark in Jer. 3:16 and its absence in

Ezra 1:7–11), the ritual, if maintained dramatically at all, would be imaginative.

The unity of throne and sanctuary, of government and religion, under God—here assumed—is the very heart of the messianic vision. The spiritual reinterpretation of messiahship by Jesus, which offended the Jews, and still offends some Christians, was in direct line with the deep insights of such a psalm as this.

New Testament echoes: Acts 2:30; cf. Luke 1:69; Acts 7:46.

133 REUNION

For heading, see the Introduction, II (iii), and the opening paragraph on Psalm 120.

The family gatherings of the great Jewish festivals of New Testament times doubtless had their forerunners in less formal reunions of the members of scattered families, who for days at a time gathered at the national shrine. It was an enjoyable aspect of pilgrimage, but the psalmist holds that it was much more. Such reunion was "fine, beautiful" (v. 1, Hebrew), like the aromatic anointing oil used at Aaron's consecration, oil that trickled from his head over his beard and collar, fragrant and sanctifying (for "dwell," literally "sit together," the NEB margin paraphrases "worship together"; Hebrew lacks "in unity," though it is implied; Hebrew says "the mouth of the garment," meaning "the neckline"; see Exod. 28:32; 29:7; 30:22–25, 30; Lev. 8:12; Job 30:18).

Reunion was (also) as refreshing and fertilizing as the dew (vital in Palestine), such copious dew as fell, for example, on Mount Hermon, renewing all living things each dawn. To say that Mount Hermon's dew fell upon Zion, which was two hundred miles to the south, may be poetic exaggeration, a free expression for "Hermon-like dew on Zion," or a misspelling (by a mere wriggle in one letter!) for Ijon, a town in the foothills of Hermon (hence the plural "hills"; see 1 Kgs. 15:20; 2 Kgs. 15:29; 2 Chron. 16:4).

There, in Zion, God *constantly* ("evermore") commands his blessing upon the assembled families, renewing family unity, reconstructing family life, and continuing life forward down the generations. If the poem *originated* as a defense of the older custom of the three-generation family unit against the divided one-generation units of later years (brothers leaving the parental home when they married), the presence of the poem among the pilgrim psalms nevertheless gives it this new festal application, fittingly beside Psalms 127 and 128.

This is a fine reminder of the deep unity, and the deeper blessing, enjoyed by the godly family.

New Testament echo: cf. Hebrews 13:1.

134 THROUGH THE NIGHT WATCHES

For heading, see the Introduction, II (iii), and the opening paragraph on Psalm 120.

There are hints in 1 Chronicles 9:33 and Isaiah 30:29, and clearer hints in later Jewish tradition, of nightly vigil-services held before the great festivals. This psalm is often treated as a greeting and response between priests at such nightlong sessions. Yet it seems very slight for such a purpose, or for bidding or invocation. It can be understood as hardly more than a vesper closing the festival day as worshipers leave the shrine for the night. Later, at any rate, twenty-four priests and Levites were appointed to guard-posts around the temple as responsible night-watchmen; this little vesper might bid them stretch hands of praise and prayer toward the holy presence through the night. It is answered by a benediction upon those departing (v. 3), spoken by the priests ("*from* Zion" hardly fits a greeting among priests within the temple). The psalm would thus be a fitting close to a day in the Lord's house, and to the "Songs of Ascents."

New Testament echo: cf. 1 Timothy 2:3.

135 "AS IT WAS IN THE BEGINNING..."

This poem well illustrates how very familiar ideas (God's power in Nature and in history, his superiority above all other gods) and even obviously borrowed verses (v. 1 is equivalent to Ps. 113:1; parts of vv. 6, 15–18, and 19–21 closely follow Ps. 115:3–11; vv. 10–12 resemble Ps. 136:17–22; cf. Num. 21:21–22, 33–34) could be drawn upon to provide worship themes in new settings. That corporate worship is here in view is clear from the repeated call to praise in verses 1–3, embracing ministers and congregation, and in verses 19–21 (which add the house of Levi to Ps. 115:9–11; in v. 3 of the NEB it is "praise" which is good, "honouring his name" which is pleasant).

But the poet's own emphasis is plainly upon the nation's

historic beginnings at the Exodus from Egypt; upon God's choice of Israel (v. 4; see Exod. 19:5; Deut. 7:6); upon his power above that of all other gods, those of Egypt being especially in mind (vv. 5, 8–12; doubtless this is what recalls from Ps. 115 the important affirmation of vv. 15–18); upon his supreme will, evident in the triumph over Egypt (see v. 6, the phrasing of which recalls the second Sinai commandment in Exod. 20:4); and upon his control of Nature (v. 7, borrowed from Jer. 10:13; the NEB puts "lightnings" in the margin, preferring "he opens rifts for the rain"; from Israel's coast, "clouds rise" from the sea as the surrounding "end of the earth"; for God's "storehouses," cf. Ps. 33:9). This emphasis is unmistakable in verses 8–12, with their claim to great victories and to possession of the land as Israel's heritage.

The central lesson of the whole story of Israel's origins, verse 14, is cited from Moses' farewell song. There is little doubt, therefore, that the psalm briefly rehearses the great historic creed of Israel in a form most suitable for the Passover Festival, when the nation's beginnings were deliberately recalled. This the Jewish Mishnah confirms, declaring this to be the morning psalm for Passover day.

The danger of overfamiliarity with elementary truths constantly besets those diligent in worship, whether as leaders or as those led. Yet elementary truths cannot be too often recalled, especially those concerning "the rock from which we were hewn, and the quarry from which we were digged."

New Testament echo: cf. 1 Peter 2:9.

136 RECITING THE STORY

This poem is another fuller, and responsive, version of Psalm 135, likewise appointed for the Passover, elaborating the work of God in Nature and in Israel's history, with much help from Genesis, Exodus, Deuteronomy, Isaiah, Jeremiah, and Proverbs. For the deep significance of such historical reviews, see the opening paragraph on Psalm 105, and compare Psalms 78, 83, and 106. One hopes that priest and congregation recited this poem alternately or that more numerous voices were used to avoid tedium; it is too pedestrian for music. But the effect is a litany of thanksgiving, rehearsing the reasons why Israel above all should be grateful to her God.

For "God of gods," "Lord of lords," compare Deuteronomy 10:17. The "stretching" of the unsupported heavens over man's head requires a special degree of skill also mentioned in Jeremiah 10:12. Whether verse 15 implies the drowning of Pharaoh (only here) is much debated; the name could stand simply for "the Egyptians." The mention of "food to all flesh" in verse 25 is unexpected; unless it is a reminiscence of the manna and quails given on the wilderness journey, it remains unexplained.

Although occasionally intrusive (for example, at vv. 10, 15), the refrain, so often encountered (Pss. 106:1; 107:1; 108:1; and frequently elsewhere), could not be more appropriate. It is the refrain running through Israel's history, central to her faith and experience. "Mercy" is too limited a term for the unique Hebrew "hesed," which is love with loyalty at the heart of it, love that is binding, steadfast, remaining true under all pressures and in all circumstances, "ever faithful, ever sure." That grateful reading of history's meaning is as bracing, and as valid, for Christians as it was and is for Jews.

137   EXILE REMEMBERED

A patriotic folk-song in which God is mentioned incidentally and addressed only by way of cursing, this psalm apparently had no place in Jewish liturgy. Yet it is full of pathos, outraged grief, and homesickness wrung into self-cursing and bitterness toward the enemy. As though the sorrow of exile in Babylon were not enough, when faith was perplexed and songs had turned to sobs, the captors demanded entertainment: "Sing us one of the songs of Zion!" — in other words, "Give us some of your native music, and be merry" (for "mirth," v. 3, NEB, the Greek version has, most improbably, "hymns"; for sitting on the ground to mourn, see Job 2:8; Isa. 3:26). Herodotus describes the encircling river and canals that brought water to the end of most of Babylon's streets (for "willows," the RSV margin, the NEB margin, and others urge "poplars"; see Isa. 44:4).

Such a request for amusement added blasphemy to bitterness; it could not be—and ought not to be—granted. Remembering Zion, the only response that the patriotic heart could make was the oath (a "self-cursing" as in Ps. 7:3–5; Job 31): "If I so far forget Jerusalem as to make her songs mere entertainment, may my right hand wither [literally "fail" to play] and my tongue cease ever to sing again—if I do not prize Jerusalem above all else" (paraphrase). A passionate refusal!

Now, back in Palestine, the poet recalls this experience. He is reminded also of the gloating of his present neighbors, the Edomites, in the day of Jerusalem's disaster (cf. Obadiah; Ezek. 25:12–14; 35:1–15; "Remember against" means "remember to punish," as in Neh. 1:14). For Edom as a pitiless "brother" of Israel, see Amos 1:11; "Raze it" is literally "lay it bare [to its foundations]." The phrase used of Babylon could mean "deserving devastation," but the city was *not* devastated when Persia came to power, as the psalmist would know. The NEB thus translates "Babylon the destroyer" ("daughter" means "city," as it often does—e.g., in Isa. 1:8). The prevalent level of cruelty is often described; see 2 Kings 8:12; Hosea 13:16; Nahum 3:10—"at the head of every street"!

The ironical "bitter beatitudes" of verses 8 and 9, the very reverse of true religion, are among the most repellent words in scripture. But only those who have seen their own babes brutally slaughtered and have not felt insanely wild with anger have any right to be censorious. To emphasize "your" in verse 9, as verse 8 requires us to do, is to feel a little of Jerusalem's agony. Similar retaliation is "promised" in Isaiah 13:16. This reaction to insensate cruelty is entirely natural until grace refines nature.

Israel did learn to sing the Lord's song in strange lands, and she has gone on doing so. Indeed, she brought back from exile her Bible, the synagogue, and these psalms. If she did not return "with songs and everlasting joy," as Isaiah promised, at any rate she learned that every land, however strange, is God's and that her God is everywhere.

New Testament echo: cf. Revelation 18:6.

138 THE DIVINE INTEGRITY

For heading, see the Introduction, IV (i), IV (iii).
A moving utterance of worship (vv. 1–3), followed by a very expansive hope (vv. 4–6) and a strong confession of confidence (vv. 7–8)—this much is obvious about Psalm 138, but for all else about this poem we must rely upon several scanty clues.

(i) Worship offered "before" and "in the presence of" the "gods" and "toward" the holy temple strongly suggests absence in a foreign land (for "gods" as angels, with the Greek version, see the discussion of Pss. 58 and 82, but that meaning is inappropriate here, as would be the suggested, very similar Hebrew word for "kings"; the NEB offers "boldly," without explanation, with "before the gods" in the margin). On prayers of exiles "toward Jerusalem," see 2 Kings 8:48; Daniel 6:10.

(ii) In answer to prayer (v. 3), God has fulfilled his word ("promise") beyond all expectation. The Hebrew (in the RSV margin) implies he has done so beyond even his known reputation for fidelity; the NEB — "made thy promise wide as the heavens" — amends the text to little purpose. The promise is not defined. The answer is unexpected, for the psalmist still walks "in the midst of trouble...the wrath of my enemies...," yet preserved alive (v. 7), and made "bold and valiant-hearted" (v. 3, NEB; the literal Hebrew, "make arrogant in my soul with strength," is variously amended to "encouraged me," "enlarged my soul with strength," "made me exalted, in my soul was glory"). The words plainly imply being lifted above *continuing* "trouble" into strength and freedom. The troubles are not yet past.

(iii) The experience has a wide public and political significance (vv. 4–5), especially as evidence of God's "way" of dealing with men. Though he is high in majesty, yet he "regards the lowly" (exiles) and puts down the haughty, totally reversing men's roles and fortunes (cf. Isa. 57:15; v. 4 should probably read "when they hear," "when they have learned God's deeds they will ponder"—the NEB margin has "walk in the Lord's ways"). The hope so expressed is exceedingly lofty and far-reaching, implying some demonstration of God's fidelity on a universal scale.

(iv) On the other hand, not only do the troubles and the enemies persist, but there is something more of the purposes of God to be fulfilled. The psalmist is confident that it will be, but still prays that God shall not forsake (or "slacken in," literal Hebrew) the work he has begun (v. 8). God has evidently still to complete the answering of prayer with final, perfect release.

It might be possible to imagine one of several kings so praying during some unfinished military struggle, perhaps pleading God's "promise" to David as the "word" given (vv. 2, 4, though "before the gods" would still need explanation). With the four "clues" in mind, it is easier to suppose some poet so praying during the closing years of the Babylonian exile, foreseeing the Return (perhaps hearing already of the edict making return possible). He might well realize the worldwide significance of such a national deliverance, the grace of such divine condescension to deserving captives and slaves, and the conclusions that must be drawn among the heathen about the "ways" of Israel's God.

It is those "ways of the Lord" which here strike us also: his fidelity to his promise, exceeding all expectation; his enlarging with strength and freedom the soul still in the midst of trouble; his amazing condescension from majesty to the lowly in heart, while resisting the proud; the astonishing deliverance yet to be wrought, against all worldly calculation of probabilities; and the certainty that what God has once begun he will surely see through to the end. Such are the gracious "ways" of our glorious God!

New Testament echoes: Luke 1:48; cf. Ephesians 3:20; Philippians 1:6; James 4:6; 1 Peter 5:5.

139 BESET BY GOD

For headings, see the Introduction, IV (i), IV (iii).

One of the greatest passages in scripture, this exquisite poem affirms and analyzes God's perfect knowledge of the individual, describes his constant presence and involvement with each soul he has made, expresses the psalmist's consequent impatience with those who distrust and disobey God, and renews his own submission to God's searching and direction. All is done with keen insight, powerful description, and far-reaching conviction.

God's intimate knowledge of man, for example, is precisely that of a close friend and companion who deeply understands one's emotions and motives (v. 1), the details of one's routine and whereabouts, while reading one's processes of thought (v. 2) and sympathizing with one's eager pursuits, one's rest periods, and all one's habitual ways (v. 3). He anticipates what one is going to say (v. 4), supporting from long-past loyalty yet encouraging one forward, too, laying his hand on one's shoulder to sustain or to check (v. 5). Such companionship is too constant and too deep for superficial comprehension (v. 6). And such a friend is — God. The whole Bible contains no finer exposition of "walking with God" (in v. 3 the NEB has "thou hast traced my journey and my resting places"; in v. 5, "kept close guard before me and behind" where others suggest "encircled me," "besieged me").

And this Friend "sticketh closer than a brother." There is no suggestion of attempted escape; the suppositions are rhetorical, the assurance of God's presence in all extremes—of height and depth (v. 8), of east and west (v. 9), of darkness or light (vv. 11, 12)—is wholly welcome, and wonderful. These ideas of the omnipresent Spirit and of God's presence with his own in Sheol are long strides toward New Testament conceptions. But no pantheism emerges. God is everywhere, but everywhere relationship with him is fully personal. (On God in Sheol, contrast Ps. 88:5, 10–12; Ps. 30:9; cf. Ps. 73:24, and see Job 26:6; Amos 9:2; "ascend" may allude to the passing of Enoch and Elijah, as v. 9 *may* echo poetically the Greek thought of the winged goddess of the dawn; the NEB has "frontiers of the morning," "limit of the western sea"). The psalmist is "beset by God" as others are by problems, circumstances, and enemies, and he rejoices in the fact.

This involvement of God with him is lifelong. It begins at the moment of his conception, and embraces his growing body, opening mind, and quickening spirit; it prepares, and records in anticipation, every day of his coming existence (v. 16). This remarkable paragraph runs more smoothly if verses 13 and 14 are reversed; verse 13 is then a reason that God "knowest me right well." The Greek and Syriac versions, declaring God (not ourselves) to be "fearful and wonderful," make sense of the strange Hebrew (in the RSV margin); the AV/KJV's "I am fearfully and wonderfully made" was another guess at the meaning.

"Inward parts" (v. 13) usually mean "reins, kidneys" as the seat of emotion and thought, the "inner self," around which (it was thought) was "knit together" the outer physical frame. So it is in Job 10:8–11 — note the line "knit me together with bones and sinews." "Intricately wrought" (v. 15) is (literally) "embroidered with threads of various colors," referring (it is said) to the network of sinews and veins visible beneath the skin; but the NEB renders "kneaded into shape." The mother's womb (v. 13) is *described* in verse 15, perhaps euphemistically, as "the depths of the earth," being like Sheol — dark, silent, and remote. Or the human womb is in some way regarded as a *stage* in a birth process which began earlier in "the womb of the Earth Mother," a very ancient idea (see "returning to the earth-womb" in Job 1:21; Sir. 40:1; 2 Esdr. 5:48). The "unformed substance" (v. 16) is an expression used of clay and metal, used for a vessel being made but yet unfinished—here, the embryo.

God's knowledge foresees the whole course of life and forecasts it in his book of "the days that were formed for me" (cf. book of "tears," Ps. 56:8; "book of the living," Ps. 69:28); foreknowledge rather than literal predestination is affirmed. (The NEB construes this quite differently—"in thy book they [my limbs] are all recorded; day by day they were fashioned, not one of them was late in growing" —adding words to the text but achieving little meaning.)

Such depth of divine understanding is beyond comprehension; God's thoughts "of me" are too weighty ("precious") and too many (or profound)—like the sand, uncountable. W. O. E. Oesterley reads verse 18 as "If I were to finish, I should still be counting." The NEB has "to finish the count, my years must equal thine"; the RSV margin, "were I to come to the end I would still be with thee." Neither being very clear, it is tempting to include the phrase with the description of birth and understand it as "as soon as I awake [to life] I am already with thee," but that is a still more speculative translation of very obscure Hebrew.

In spite of God's knowledge and care and his "wonderful works" for men, there are those who mar his world with wickedness. Against such the psalmist expresses utter ("perfect," "wholehearted"; "undying," NEB) hatred, wishing that God would remove them from his creation. Doubtless the psalm would be more comfortable without verses 19–22. So would the world without evil men.

But there is no justification for treating the verses as intrusive. In this instance the psalmist chooses to count God's enemies his own (not vice versa), and he confesses that he himself needs examination. So he returns to God's knowledge of himself, and prays to be set free from any way of wickedness (literally "leading to pain, doom") and to be led in the way leading to continued ("everlasting") life (or "the ancient ways," as in the NEB, the RSV margin, and Jer. 6:16; 18:15).

With only slight adjustments, such a poem might almost stand in the Christian Testament—as it ought to stand in every Christian mind.

New Testament echoes: Matthew 7:13, 14; cf. Romans 8:38, 39; 1 Thessalonians 2:4; 1 John 1:3, 5, 7.

140 RELIGIOUS CONTENTION

For headings, see the Introduction, IV (i), IV (iii); for Selah, see IV (ii); on theme, vindication, see II (ii).

In this psalm, allusions to evil men, violent men planning evil and stirring up daily contention, men serpent-tongued and poisonous, wicked men, treacherous men, and cunning men suggest that there is obviously a party or faction in view against whom the psalmist prays, affirming positively his own total devotion to God. This resembles closely the situation described in the Introduction, II (ii), and noted in the discussions of Psalms 69 and 119, originating in the early days after the Babylonian exile and increasing down to New Testament times. Conservative and zealous devotees of the divine Law confronted, and were persecuted by, the "upper-class" leaders of the subject state. Such leaders of society were anxious to conform with Persian ways, and later with Greek and Roman ways, and so ensure their own survival and prosperity (note that "afflicted" and "needy" — "needy" and "downtrodden" in the NEB — are paralleled by "righteous" and "upright" in vv. 12, 13; in later times Josephus remarks that the compromising Sadducees had their following among the rich; the strict Pharisees, among the poorer multitude).

Religious strife brings out the unscrupulous worst in people, as the repeated references here—to poisoned, malicious talk (probably also implying curses, as v. 9 suggests), to violence and violent hands (when argument fails), to arrogance, and to attempts to ensnare and trip up opponents — all illustrate too plainly ("wars" in v. 2 is inappropriate in the context—hence, "contentions day after day" in the NEB; "viper," v. 3, is "asp" in the Greek version; the NEB's "spiders" amends the Hebrew slightly; the familiar metaphors for

the evil tongue, sharp swords, and poisoned snakes are here mixed!).
The psalmist prays to be delivered from such calumny and peril,
acknowledging that he has already been "strongly delivered" and
"helmeted" in the "day of armour" (v. 7, literally).

But he is anxious also that the cause of the compromisers shall
not succeed in society (v. 8). Its leaders are evidently influential men
(v. 11), and if they "lift up their head" in victory the nation will
suffer. Instead, let their injurious talk recoil upon them like *burning
coals* falling upon them (such as rained upon Sodom?; the meaning
differs from the "incendiary weapons" of Ps. 120:4; cf. instead Ps.
11:6), like *pits* opening before them (of slime or perhaps of asphalt—
pits such as were found near ancient Sodom; the text of vv. 8, 9 is
almost untranslatable, and probably damaged; the NEB offers without explanation, "If any of those at my table rise against me...").

Verse 11 may be taken with verses 12 and 13 as a splendid
affirmation of faith: "slander" (evil teaching, propaganda) shall not
be established, violence shall itself be hounded, the Lord will maintain the cause of the afflicted, the righteous will surely give thanks,
the upright (in the end) shall dwell in the presence of God (continue
in the land and the temple).

The deepest longing of the godly in an ungodly time must be
to see godliness triumphant. But if in praying for the defeat of evil
the spirit is to be kept pure from vengefulness and self-righteousness,
the prayer must always focus upon the psalmist's declaration: "I
know that the Lord maintains the cause of the afflicted." In that
conviction lies confidence for every religious struggle—and humility,
too.

New Testament echoes: Romans 3:13; cf. Romans 12:20; James 3:8.

141 "LORD, SAVE ME — FROM MYSELF!"

For heading, see the Introduction, IV (i), IV (iii).

With great earnestness, even urgency, the poet pleads to be heard,
presenting his petition with all the seriousness of the evening ritual
sacrifice. The terms used recall Numbers 28:1–8 and Leviticus 2:1–2
and 6:14, 15; the reference to evening sacrifice made this psalm the
accompaniment for the lighting of lamps in early Christian churches.
The implied equation of prayer with sacrifice and incense may be
related to the movement away from animal sacrifices toward wholly
spiritual worship (see Pss. 40, 50, 51, 69; note the RSV margin for
Hos. 14:2—"we shall render as bullocks the offerings of our lips"—

and the later synagogue prayers corresponding to the temple sacrifices; also Jer. 7:22; Amos 5:25). For "spreading hands" in prayer, see Isaiah 1:15. The occasion for the urgency is not named, but the psalmist is evidently under pressure.

His danger is to speak ill (v. 3), to desire and become involved in evil deeds (v. 4; "incline," "bend," or "lean not my heart" amounts to "Keep me straight," "Do not allow evil inclinations to develop within me," "Lead me not into temptation"). Even more, apparently, the poet desires to be preserved from evil company (vv. 4, 5; "not for me the delights of their table," NEB). He is wise enough to prefer the rebuke, even the blows of a faithful friend to the flattering hospitality of men with evil intent (v. 5; so the RSV has it; the reference is to oil provided for guests by hospitable hosts, as in Ps. 23:5; Eccl. 9:8; and Luke 7:46; the NEB has "My head shall not be anointed with the oil of wicked men, for that would make me a party to their crimes"). Less plausible is "Let the righteous . . . smite me, it shall be a kindness; and let him reprove me, it shall be as oil upon the head; let not my head refuse it" (RV, 1881 ed.). Instead of courting evil company, he will persevere in prayer against their wicked practices.

The RSV margin warns three times that the Hebrew of verses 5–7 is obscure, and the NEB also amends verse 4. Innumerable attempts at repairing the text yield no agreed-upon translation. The NEB takes "those who condemn" (who administer justice) as "justice," the "true" or "acceptable" word as that of the psalmist (so the Hebrew has it, though he may speak for the Lord), and it assumes that while "rock" is "shattered," to "cleave" implies "wood." The NEB thus translates, "They shall founder on the rock of justice and shall learn how acceptable my words are. Their bones shall be scattered at the mouth of Sheol, like splinters of wood or stone on the ground." This adjudication between conjectures is probably near to the intended meaning: evil men will surely get their deserved punishment, and the psalmist wants no part in that.

So he asks again for refuge and protection; the closing phrase of verse 8 is literally "pour not out my soul," meaning "do not let me die" (see Isa. 53:12). And he prays that the wicked shall fall into the pitfalls they prepared, while he "altogether escapes" ("whilst I pass in safety, all alone," NEB).

So many need to pray at all times to be kept out of temptation's way that the psalm could serve any man, even David. But numerous touches—the snares and nets, the evil speaking, possibly the "dainties" if they are understood as foreign foods forbidden by Jewish dietary laws, and the prayers to be kept from the blandishments of an evil group — recall the struggle of the stricter Jews against the compromisers under alien rule (see the discussion of Ps. 140).

Not all who pray earnestly against the insidious temptations of the surrounding world recognize so frankly that the real power of these "alien" influences lies in the inclinations and desires already within the soul, willing to be enticed. Nor do they realize that the real cure rests not in flight from the evil environment but in inward purity, in prayer, in the strong support of good friends, and in taking constant refuge in God.

New Testament echoes: cf. Luke 1:10; 1 Corinthians 15:33; Hebrews 13:159 Revelation 5:8; 8:3, 4.

142 "I BELIEVE; HELP MY UNBELIEF"

For headings, see the Introduction, IV (ii), IV (iii), IV (iv); on theme, complaint, see II (i) (with "Prayer of David," contrast Ps. 72:20).

Someone in great distress—troubled, faint, baited, unhelped, without escape (one Hebrew word for "refuge") or friend—someone "very low," persecuted, "in prison," cries volubly to God (makes vocal his plea, vv. 1, 2). He does so with insistence and earnestness, for God is his security (another Hebrew word for "refuge") and his "portion" (see the discussion of Ps. 16:5). God knows all his "way," including the trap set for him on the path (v. 3). He promises thanksgiving, and knows that the righteous will again be his companions (?) when God shall deal generously with him, as God surely will. The tone is personal and plaintive, the outpouring of an overcharged heart; only the last line is relieved by clear faith (v. 5 appears to have been ineffective, since it is followed by v. 6). It is not surprising that though the poem is present in the Jewish hymnbook, it had no fixed liturgical usage.

So vague and general are the poem's terms that almost anything can be made of them. (i) Whoever supplied the heading (cf. Ps. 57) thought that David might have written it "in the cave," probably at En-gedi (1 Sam. 24, though a cave is not a prison, which is mentioned in v. 7; in the so-celled "cave" or stronghold of Adullam —1 Sam. 22:1–2; 2 Sam. 23:14—David was not alone, nor was he later joined by "the righteous"). Nothing in the psalm is illumined by this heading, while the several echoes of other psalms, together with its general style, suggest a late poem. (ii) It has been suggested that an individual has been wrongly imprisoned by means of slander(?). There, forsaken, in close confinement, he clings desperately to God and to the hope that, in due time, the righteous will "crowd around him." But when he looked to his right hand, where God should stand as his defender (Pss. 16:8; 73:23; 109:31), he found God absent (v. 4).

(iii) The NEB leaves the impression that the poet is pouring out his complaint while the crisis continues. He is faint, confronted with a trap skillfully laid for him, with no one to aid him, no friend at his side, no way of escape open to him, and no rescuer in sight, only "pursuers" behind him. So he cries to God alone—"all I have in the land of the living" (NEB) — for liberty from this "prison" (or dilemma). Then he will praise and be "crowned with garlands" by the righteous when God gives him his due reward.

(iv) Still others think that all the poem's terms are certainly metaphorical. The trouble, the trap, the loneliness ("there is none who takes notice of me," v. 4, an echo of Isa. 63:16), the persecution, and especially the "prison" (cf. Ps. 107:10–11) are all in the mind and mood of the downcast poet. But *God's* "righteousness" will encompass ("encircle" or "crown") him, and his bounty deliver him. (v) Saint Francis of Assisi found comfort in applying the language of the psalm to his approaching death, and died reciting it.

Plainly the circumstances and the original application of the psalm are now lost to us; the meaning is generalized by time and by obscurity. Only the frank complaint made directly to God, the clinging to him in candid disappointment while waiting for his favor to return remain to give words to our own distress, in whatever dark hour life may bring.

New Testament echoes: cf. Matthew 27:46; Mark 9:24.

143 UNEASILY LONGING FOR GOD

For heading, see the Introduction, IV (iii); for Selah, see IV (ii).

This is a strangely mixed poem, expressing apparently genuine thirst for God and containing perceptive prayers to be taken into favor, to be taught God's will and led by God's Spirit, together with strong complaint of treatment received and an unusually "vindictive" prayer for the destruction of the poet's enemies (translations vary from the NEB's "reduce to silence...bring destruction..." to "annihilate...destroy..."; see the Introduction, II [ii]). The explanation probably lies in the strained and tumultuous emotions that accompany hard-won penitence. The psalmist asks that God show justice

(vv. 1, 11; "be true to thyself," "as thou art just," NEB) to one who is certainly "a servant of God" (vv. 2, 11; in view of the "enemies," possibly the king). Yet he is aware that before God's justice no man can stand acquitted; to plead in God's court requires clean hands (v. 2). He knows that God might well hide his face (v. 7), and he nowhere protests innocence. If the implied confession seems a little formal, almost suggesting "I am no worse than all flesh," the repeated prayers for help in self-reform (v. 8—"to thee I offer all my heart," NEB — and v. 10) acknowledge a real spiritual need for instruction and upholding.

And the poet needs still more. In accordance with traditional training, he has turned back in his spiritual distress to ponder past mercies and recall God's actions in history, his works in Nature (v. 5; cf. Ps. 77:5, 11, 12). But he remains unsatisfied. He thirsts for *present* blessing (v. 6; for "outstretched hands," see Ps. 141:2; Isa. 1:15), *immediate* favor (v. 7), quick reassurance of God's unvarying love (v. 8; see Ps. 90:14— "quickly," "soon"). Those who have trodden the penitent's way will be familiar with all these vacillations of thought and feeling, of trust and fear, of longing for God yet dreading his reproach.

This is especially true when penitence is mixed with immediate fears, perhaps awakened by them. Verses 3 and 4 dramatically suggest this (the NEB has "An enemy has hunted me down...ground my living body under foot...[I am] dazed with despair..."; cf. Ps. 7:5). "In darkness" suggests the shadow of death, Sheol, and "those long dead" probably means "and forgotten," as in Psalm 88:5, 6, though the words may convey a sense of "receding further from life" as the body disintegrates (cf. Ezek. 37). The repeated, urgent prayer for deliverance from his foes and the strength of his plea for their destruction confirm this fear. Only such deliverance, and soon, will make God's pardon and favor realities to his troubled heart.

It is not surprising that the supplied title to the psalm associates this experience with David, the Greek version adding a reference to Absalom's "persecution" of his father (2 Sam. 15). Both the intensity of David's suffering and his guilty awareness of its being self-caused (by the sin with Bathsheba) justify such an allusion. But this in no way illumines the psalm, while the constant quotation of phrases from other psalms makes a Davidic origin unlikely.

The poet's insight and true feeling concerning the experience of the frightened penitent win Christian assent and admiration. The absence of self-justification and of any appeal to ritual absolution is significant. But also absent is any firm basis for such hope in God's unvarying love, in spite of sin; for that hope the Christian can only be deeply grateful for the fuller revelation in the life and death of Jesus.

New Testament echoes: Romans 3:20; cf. Galatians 2:16.

144 HAPPY THAT PEOPLE!

For heading, see the Introduction, IV (iii).

The opening "praise" (the word for "blessed" in v. 1) and prayer (vv. 1–7) in this psalm rely heavily on a number of verses in Psalm 18 (in this order: vv. 2, 46, 34, [39], 47, 9, 14, 16, 44), forming a brief summary of much of that psalm (see the discussion of that psalm). The king (to judge from the use of similar phrases elsewhere, especially "my steadfast love"—v. 2, Hebrew—and from the end of v. 2, where the NEB adopts the RSV margin, "under me"; cf. Ps. 18:47) gives thanks in traditional, perhaps liturgical, language for some recent victory, addressing God as his tutor in battle (see Ps. 24:8). He elaborates David's humble exclamation of unworthiness in similar circumstances (2 Sam. 7:18) in a fuller version of Psalm 8:4, adding too that man is but "a puff of wind," "a passing shadow." He then adapts statements of Psalm 18:9–15 in a prayer that God will come still, in power, to rescue and deliver him. Without explanation the NEB changes this to "If thou, Lord, but tilt the heavens, down they come; touch the mountains, and they smoke," statements which add little light in this context. "Many waters" appears to be a general metaphor for peril. Whether the reference to alien liars that occurs in verse 11 should be added to verses 7–8 is very doubtful—the NEB omits it.

In gratitude the king offers further praise (vv. 9–10), "new" perhaps in comparison with the numerous traditional phrases so far quoted, but still praise for victory. Remarkable here is the use of "David" as though it meant the monarchy generally, parallel to "kings"; verse 10 echoes Psalm 18:50. The prayer for rescue is resumed, with special concern expressed about aliens whose mouths and right hands are false. The false right hand could refer to deceitful deeds, but from the raising of the right hand (toward God) in making an oath, the aliens' foresworn treachery is probably in mind.

Verses 12–15 provide a charming description of the happy prosperity of the people "whose God is the Lord." Their sons are like saplings, early full-grown ("tall towers," NEB), their daughters like gracefully carved corners of buildings (or cornices in houses; Greek female "caryatids" come to mind, but that would argue a very late Greek influence on the poet). Abundant provision (literally "of every kind"), with no calamity to raise lament in the city's squares, will demonstrate the great contentment of people whom God blesses.

The NEB makes this description a statement of fact unrelated to the foregoing praise and prayer. The RSV makes it a prayer, as though the blessing being sought by the king is to flow outward also upon his people. This illustrates the main perplexity of the psalm. To some it appears as three fragments (praise, prayer for deliverance, promise); to others it appears as two poems, with perhaps intrusive comments at verses 3 and 4, and repetition (vv. 7–8 are equivalent to v. 11; v. 12 begins very abruptly in Hebrew). The attempt has been made to show the psalm to be a unity within the ritual framework of Psalm 18, a "sacramental" humiliation of the king with promises of blessing on his proving worthy by calling God to his aid. The reference to the "many waters" (v. 7) would then echo Psalm 18:15–16, and the struggle of God and his servants against the primeval forces of chaos (see the Introduction, II [iv]).

In such confusion of suggestions the true source of the composition seems beyond recall. But as it has been preserved for us, the poem offers very forcefully this single argument: that whether in war and danger or in peace and plenty, happy are those people — and those alone — whose God, defender, and provider is the Lord.

New Testament echo: cf. Hebrews 2:6.

145 THE KINGDOM, THE POWER, AND THE GLORY

For heading, see the Introduction, IV (i), IV (iii); on acrostics, see III (iv) (b).

A "bracelet" of praise, each link a testimony, this beautiful poem is also an acrostic which despite its mechanical, alphabetic structure attains spontaneous gladness and heartfelt thanksgiving, demonstrating the many evidences and facets of God's goodness. Curiously, one letter of the alphabet is omitted (or has dropped out), which the RSV "restores" before verse 14 with marginal explanation, and the NEB adopts without remark (possibly because the words are now found in a copy from the Qumran).

Though closely connected thought is not to be expected, the poem moves, in general, from God's unsearchable greatness and power (vv. 1–7), to his graciousness, mercy, and long-suffering (vv. 8–13), and on to his care of his own, who stumble and are bowed down in want. Especially noticeable are the emphasis on God's wide and timeless dominion, his "everlasting" rule (vv. 1, 11–13), and the emphasis on the way future generations are kept within hail (vv. 4, 13, 21). The tone of praise makes this psalm a fitting preface to the final "Hallel" group of psalms (see the Introduction, II [iii]). The variation between "*his* greatness," "*thy* terrible acts," "*the Lord* is faithful," and "*Thou* openest *thy* hand" shows how the thought moves from praise offered to God to testimony offered to others, though poetic license and numerous quotations from earlier psalms may also explain this variety of address.

The manifold nature of this "testimony" is striking: men extol, bless, praise, laud, declare, proclaim, pour forth, sing, speak, tell, and make known the goodness and glory of the Lord. The themes of testimony are also manifold: God is to be praised for his greatness, works, mighty acts, majesty, terrible deeds, abundant goodness, righteousness, mercy, steadfast love, compassion, glory, power, kingdom, faithfulness, and upholding; he raises the bowed down and is bountiful, just, kind, and near; he hears, saves, and preserves those who love him, and destroys the wicked. That is the theology of experience.

Jewish tradition says this psalm was recited thrice daily in the synagogues (v. 2), adding "he who takes to himself this psalm is already a son of the world to come." It is possible that each verse was then followed by a congregational refrain, either "for ever and ever" (see vv. 1, 2, 21) or, as in some manuscripts, the words of Psalm 115:18. One Qumran copy has after every verse, "Blessed be the Lord and blessed be his name, for ever and ever" (cf. Ps. 136).

There is something infectious, and kindling, about the smooth repetitions of verses 1–3; verse 6 includes judgments on wickedness (cf. v. 20); verse 13 recurs in Daniel 3:33 and 4:31; in verse 14 in the NEB, "who stumble" is a refreshingly individual touch. "Bowed down" is often associated with the cringing of the habitual beggar, which would make verse 16 appropriate, but the NEB has "straightens backs which are bent," presumably with toil. "Near" (v. 18) is another refreshing touch.

The poet's awareness of the age-long, unchanging divine dominion, hidden so often yet ever present and sovereign, anticipates Christ's conception of the heavenly kingdom, ever present and ever coming. The Psalmist's noble conception of the king—his power and majesty, faithfulness and truth, lovingkindness and individual compassion—anticipates likewise Christ's teaching on the character of the kingly Father. Inevitably, therefore, the psalm has become as widely used in Christianity as it was in Judaism.

New Testament echoes: Revelation 11:33; cf. Matthew 6:13 (AV/KJV); John 4:24.

146 PRAISE THE LORD
— FOR WHAT HE IS

On "Hallel" psalms, see the Introduction, II (iii).

The personal tone of the resolve and vow (vv. 1, 2) persists through this poem despite its echoes of other writers, and suggests that the warning of verses 3 and 4 arises from personal disappointment over something undertaken and not fulfilled (cf. Ps. 118:9). There seems no need to think of "faithless heathen rulers" (as T. Witton Davies does). The failure of "help" ("no power to save," NEB) is said to stem from the princes' *mortality,* which cancels "on that very day" all men's plans (the NEB has "thinking," while others offer "purposes"; note the quotation of this verse in 1 Macc. 2:62–63 concerning Antiochus IV: "Do not fear the words of a sinner, for his splendour will turn into dung and worms. Today he will be exalted, but tomorrow he will not be found because he has returned to the dust and his plans will perish"). In contrast with man's impermanence the psalmist deliberately sets God's keeping "faith for ever" (v. 6) and his continuing "to all generations" (v. 10; "breath," v. 4, means "spirit"; for "his earth," cf. Ps. 104:29; Gen. 3:19).

"Happy," therefore, is he whose help and hope are not in men, however exalted, but in God (v. 5, the twenty-fifth and last occurrence of the Hebrew "blessed" in the Psalter). God is then introduced as the God of history ("Jacob") and of the individual ("his" God). He created all things, and unlike men "keeps faith for ever," guaranteeing justice in social relations and provision for individual need — a wide-ranging welfare (vv. 6–7; the NEB's "who serves wrongdoers as he has sworn" limits God's keeping faith to evildoers, presumably to improve the antithetical parallelism). Giving "food to the hungry" is the creator's continuing task through seed, soil, and harvest.

The six lines beginning with "The Lord..." impressively list God's gracious activities: liberating prisoners and giving sight to the blind, which typify his assistance to all the helpless (see, on both classes, Isa. 42:7; 61:1–2); lifting the "bowed down" (see the discussion of Ps. 145:14); loving (cherishing, defending) the righteous; watching over strangers (resident aliens; the use of the word for "proselytes" comes later); upholding ("gives heart to," NEB) widows and orphans (literally not "fatherless"; for strangers and orphans, see Deut. 10:18, 19); frustrating evildoers (literally "making crooked," misdirecting, their aim; the NEB paraphrases it as "turns the course of the wicked to their ruin"). Finally, and significantly, God endures; *he* never disappoints.

Such is the gracious quality of God's kingship, championing the defenseless and the lowly, continuing for ever (v. 10). And this is the deepest personal reason for men's "Hallelujah" (vv. 1, 10). The poet has perceived the sharp contrast between the pretensions of human rulers and the divine activities of the eternal King. The words of Jesus about "them that rule among the gentiles, called Benefactors," and his own ministry among the neediest amply vindicate the psalmist's judgment. Jesus, too—sixteen times—declared "blessed" those who live under the gracious divine rule; theirs is the kingdom.

New Testament echoes: Acts 14:15; cf. Luke 4:16-23; 13:11–13; 1 Corinthians 2:6.

147 PRAISE THE LORD — FOR ALL HE DOES

On "Hallel" psalms, see the Introduction, II (iii); for part-theme, God and Nature, see II (v).

This poem is sometimes treated as three, with new beginnings at verses 7 and 12, or as two poems (the Greek version and ancient commentators start afresh at v. 12, although the word "praise" there is not "hallel"). But the Jerusalem theme links verses 2, 12–14, and 20, and the Nature theme unites verses 8–9 with verses 16–19, while the three calls to praise are not unlike congregational responses to a singer's splendid declarations. The psalm comes down to us as one, and the nuances of the NEB suggest that what God has done and is still doing, in the better years following the initial hardships of the return from exile (see the discussion of Ps. 126), is the original occasion of this call to praise.

The value and pleasantness of the exercise to the singer are unusual reasons for praising God. But the deeper reason is God's "graciousness" (v. 1), as evidenced by the restoration of Jerusalem, the regathering of the exiles, and the healing of the nation's sore wounds (vv. 2–3). Moreover, God has demonstrated his *mastery* of the stars by his abundant power and unsearchable wisdom, as the great prophet of the Return had promised he would (vv. 4, 5; so it is in Isa. 40:26, 28, where also the superiority of God over the gods and astral powers worshiped in Babylon is the theme; mastery is indicated by God's *determining* their number and *marshaling* them by name, as in Isaiah, not "giving" their names). Thus God controls the forces that were thought to control history. In fine, God has uplifted downtrodden Israel and brought wicked Babylon to the ground (v. 6). No wonder the worshipers happily respond (v. 7).

Now, at last (contrast Hag. 1, 2), the neglected land is becoming fertile—even the mountains that men cannot cultivate (v. 8)—and food becomes abundant. God shows favor ("takes pleasure") not to the military might of cavalry or foot soldiers (v. 10) but to his own people (v. 11; at end of v. 8 the NEB restores a line only the Greek version has—"and green plants for the use of man"; see Ps. 104:14). "Young ravens," literally "sons of ravens," are said to be early deserted by their parents; their raucous cry is taken as prayer to God in the Greek translation, as in Job 38:4. For the war-horse, see Job 39:19–25. (It is said, too, that Assyrian sculptures emphasize the strong legs of runners and foot soldiers.) Again, perhaps, the congregation calls for praise, this time especially from renewed Jerusalem (v. 12).

For God "has put new bars in your gates" (v. 13, NEB), blessing the growing young within the city, giving peace to the border territory, and restoring the city's provisions (v. 14; for the bars, cf. Neh. 3:3, 6, 13, 15; for "fat wheat" (fully ripened?), see Ps. 81:16; Deut. 32:14). All this fulfills God's swift and powerful word, which again echoes the great prophet of the Return (Isa. 55:10–11), the word which Nature obeys in its changing seasons ("hoar frost" and "ashes" sound alike in Hebrew, a kind of pun; "ice like crumbs" is hail). The odd question "who can stand before his cold?" almost certainly should be "water stands frozen" before his cold, as the NEB has it, but God's new word and warming wind melt it—another miracle to ancient thought. But then, God has ever "declared his word" to Israel from Jacob's time; no other nation so knows him (Deut. 4:7–8). For all this present experience of God's graciousness, unique among the nations, God surely should be praised.

Tentative though this interpretation of the present form of the poem must be, it avoids the incoherence of which some complain, and is surely not far from the message the poet had in mind. Israel's God has ever been and is still an active, dynamic God, unlike the static, passive idols of the heathen, the abstract "divine principle" of the philosophers, and the absent (retired?) God of some Christians. This truth of the living, active intervening God, unique to Israel among ancient peoples, is underlined and fulfilled in the incarnation of God in Christ, and in the continuing presence and activity of the Spirit. He is still the Spirit of reconstruction, of new beginnings.

New Testament echoes: Matthew 6:26; cf. Luke 12:24; Romans 3:2.

148 PRAISE THE LORD
— ALL THAT HE MADE

On "Hallel" psalms, see the Introduction, II (iii).

The Psalter's "Saint Francis" gathers the whole universe, heaven (vv. 1–6) and earth (vv. 7–14), into one vast choir to worship God, not for his acts or for the experience of healing and salvation, but for the very existence of life and beauty and Nature's pulsing world. All that *is* calls for adoration in a lyrical "bidding" joyous with the feeling of Nature itself, glad to be alive, and praising God for being its maker. Amid that universal chorus, let Israel especially take full part as the people in closest relation to the maker of all. The whole psalm elaborates Psalm 103:21–22. For "hosts" as angels, compare 1 Kings 22:19 and Nehemiah 9:6; the Jewish Talmud speaks of seven concentric heavens, with God at the unapproachable center. For waters above the firmament, see Genesis 1:6, 7.

The emphasis on God's command (Gen. 1: "And God said...") —on his continually sustaining creation (v. 6; Sir. 43:26; Col. 1:17), establishing the "natural law" ("statute" in Hebrew, "decree" in the Greek version) which governs the being and function of every creature, and on Nature's "fulfilling his command" (v. 8), while his glory "is above earth and heaven" (v. 13) — is all directed against the prevalent Nature-worship. It seems prosaic to argue how far the poet's personification of natural objects implies animistic or mythical overtones. His insistence upon God's supremacy over all he made could hardly be clearer. The sea monsters ("dragons," AV/KJV; "extensive things," Hebrew; "water spouts," NEB; but see Ps. 104:26; Sir. 43:24–25: "Those who sail the sea tell of its dangers and we marvel at what we hear. For in it are strange and marvellous works, all kinds of living things and huge creatures of the sea") are not here enemies but creatures praising God; on "deeps," see Job 38:8–11, and on both, Psalm 74:13–14. "Fire" (v. 8) may mean lightning (less probably, in this context, volcanic lava, as in Ps. 18:12); for "frost" the NEB has "ice," following the Greek version.

The classification of creatures continues upward to man: animals, wild and domesticated (v. 10); the more mysterious flying and crawling creatures; then men in their varied classes ("rulers" means "judges"). "Earth and heaven" (v. 13) sums up the psalm. But at the crown of all is Israel, "his people" (for "horn," see the Introduction, III [ii]; the NEB has "he has exalted his people in the pride of power and crowned with praise his loyal servants"). These are "near" him, which may mean "friends," "those acceptable," or "those privileged to draw near to him," as in Psalm 65:4 and Jeremiah 30:21; see also Psalm 149.

This divine joy in all things bright and beautiful marked Greek thought even more than Jewish, and has been sadly overlaid in Christianity by a deep suspicion of "Nature" and a negative rejection of created loveliness as "of the flesh" — or the devil. A healthier, more Christlike spirit breathes in this happy psalm, which says to all, "This is God's world, all of it praising him; but they who know him best should praise him most" (v. 14).

New Testament echo: cf. Ephesians 2:17.

149 PRAISE THE LORD — ESPECIALLY HIS OWN

On "Hallel" psalms, see the Introduction, II (iii).

This psalm takes up the closing thought of Psalm 148, the special privilege of Israel. But singing (v. 1), dancing (v. 3) while lying on couches (v. 5) with a sword in one hand (v. 6) and a timbrel or lyre in the other, ready to fetter the foe (v. 8) while glorying in victory (vv. 4, 9), makes a very confused picture. Some explain it as "eschatological," postponing illumination to the distant future. Others explain it as liturgical, the couches being meal divans or prayer mats (v. 5; "let them shout...as they kneel before him," NEB), and the dances and swords theatrical and symbolic. Yet others explain it as realistic, as the reaction of still-armed warriors to some recent victory in a thanksgiving along traditional lines. The couches then represent the relaxation of peace after battle (?); the vengeance and the judgment (vv. 7, 9) mark determination to put an end to war. If such a victory of God's own was large, the psalm must be an early one, but its language and parallels in the Maccabean writings suggest it is a late production.

This "historical" interpretation, implying some formal thanksgiving with songs and dance, seems the most probable. Three references (vv. 1, 5, 9) to "the faithful" (so the RSV and the NEB have it; others have "pious ones," "saints"; the Hebrew gives "Hasidim"; note also "sons of Zion," suggesting "God's own" in some meritorious sense) link the poem with the term increasingly used in later years for the orthodox "conservative" resisters of foreign influence. These were also called the "humble," or "meek" (v. 4), because they were of little political and social account under foreign rule; see the Introduction, II (ii), and further, the discussion of Psalm 140.

"Then there united with [the Maccabean family] a company of Hasideans, mighty warriors of Israel, every one who offered himself willingly for the law.... Those of the Jews who are called Hasideans, whose leader is Judas Maccabeus, are keeping up war and stirring up sedition, and will not let the kingdom attain tranquillity.... Judas and his men met the enemy in battle with invocation to God and prayers. So, fighting with their hands and praying to God in their hearts, they laid low no less than thirty-five thousand men, and were greatly gladdened by God's manifestation" (1 Macc. 2:42; 2 Macc. 14:6; 15:26, 27). To link Psalm 149 directly with any Maccabean victory would be speculative. But the Hasidean-Maccabean dedication to waging a "holy war" for the Law of God against the corruption arising from heathen occupation, with their mingled religious and military zeal and their rejoicing in God's help, is precisely what confronts us throughout the psalm (note v. 6).

For religious dancing, see Exodus 15:20 and Judges 11:34; "timbrels" are hand-drums, what the NEB calls "tambourines"; compare Psalm 68:24. In verse 4 the RSV's "the Lord takes pleasure" ("is favourable" or "gracious" toward, "the Lord deals with in grace") and the NEB's "the Lord accepts the service of his people" are variant translations of the same Hebrew expression. "Adorns with victory" may indicate special "military parade" garments. To amend "on their couches" to "in endless joy" is pure guesswork. A two-edged sword is mentioned as unusual in Judges 3:16; the Hebrew has "sword of two mouths," "all devouring." "Vengeance," "chastisement," and "judgment" express the conviction that the battle was the Lord's, not man's, and victory is God's "favor" to Israel. "Written" (v. 9) may mean "as destined," as "judgement decreed" (NEB), or "as foretold" (Isa. 45:14–17; 49:7, 23). For God's written record and warnings, see the discussion of Psalm 139:16; see also Isaiah 65:6 and Job 13:26. The "glory" of God's faithful champions must ever be to taste victory for God (v. 9).

This is truly a "new" song (v. 1), that of religious-military triumph, a basis for praise very different from that in the other "Hallel" psalms. It is scarcely relevant to talk about "soldiers of Christ," "weapons of spiritual warfare," and "the sword of the Spirit" as Christian parallels to Hasidean resistance "unto blood" against the moral corruption of a generation. Christians very often have had to be, quite literally, faithful unto death, and may need to be so again. Yet Christ's kingdom is not of this world. Force, even in the hands of God's own, can at best only *keep the way open* for the victory of truth and the Spirit, which has still to be won by other means when force is ended, and by a struggle no less heroic, no less costly. But come what may, the victory *will* be God's.

150 PRAISE THE LORD — EVERY WAY YOU CAN

on "Hallel" psalms, see the Introduction, II (iii).

It demands considerable poetic skill and zeal to turn an orchestral catalogue into a jubilant "Hallelujah Chorus," and one entirely adequate to close not only Book V but the whole golden treasury of praise. This psalm may well have been written by the psalm collector for this place and purpose, though we may imagine it was used with great enthusiasm and appropriate sound effects at certain festivals.

The "precentor" first calls upon heavenly beings in the divine sanctuary to lead the praise for God's acts of power and for his excelling greatness. For the address to angel-hosts, compare Psalms 29:1; 148:1, 2 (note "sanctuary," here parallel to "firmament," RSV, and "vault of heaven," NEB — on this, see the discussion of Ps. 104:3; the phrase "strong" or "mighty" firmament recalls primitive wonder at the unsupported arch of the sky). With a resounding "Hallelu" ("Praise ye") at each step, the leader then demands "fanfares on the trumpet" (NEB, literally the "ram's horn"), the ancient stirring summons to attend to God. As the strong blast swells, it is joined by the sweet and evocative melody of the plucked strings of lute and harp. At the next "Hallelu" their rhythm is taken up by the percussion instrument, a tambourine-like hand-drum, which sets the dancers' feet tapping (the Hebrew suggests a "whirling" dance; see the discussion of Ps. 149:3).

As the pace quickens, other strings "and pipe" are called in (the "pipe" is probably a flute; the strange introduction here of "strings" again could be a misspelling for "seven-toned" flute). Then the lighter "dancing-stick" cymbals — thin copper blades with wooden handles that beat out the rhythm with a metallic, "Eastern" ring—are bidden to commence; and finally, in a grand crescendo of orchestral joy, the "loud clashing cymbals" (described by Josephus as large metal plates struck together) reach a maximum volume and peak excitement at the same moment. At last the patient congregation get their call ("Let everything that breathes praise the Lord!"), and all present—angels, instrumentalists, choir, and congregation—unite in a final, resounding Hallelujah!

All the complaint and the pain, the struggle and the doubt of the Psalter is now left behind. Music has the last word in a glorious outburst of joy in God. The only adequate comment is that of the Son of Sirach:

Though we speak much we cannot reach the end,
  And the sum of our words is: 'He is the all'.
Where shall we find strength to praise him?
  For he is greater than all his works.
Terrible is the Lord and very great,
  And marvellous is his power.
When you praise the Lord, exalt him as much as you can;
  For he will surpass even that.
When you exalt him, put forth all your strength
  And do not grow weary, for you cannot praise him enough.

                                        (43:27–30)